AN AUTOBIOGRAPHY

ANTHONY TROLLOPE, the fourth of six surviving children, was born on 24 April 1815 in London. As he describes in his *Autobiography*, poverty and debt made his childhood acutely unhappy and disrupted his education: his school fees at Harrow and Winchester were frequently unpaid. His family attempted to restore their fortunes by going to America, leaving the young Anthony alone in England, but it was not until his mother, Frances, began to write that there was any improvement in the family's finances. Her success came too late for her husband, who died in exile in Belgium in 1835. Trollope was unable to afford a university education, and in 1834 he became a junior clerk in the Post Office. He achieved little until he was appointed Surveyor's Clerk in Ireland in 1841. There he worked hard, travelled widely, took up hunting and still found time for his literary career. He married Rose Heseltine, the daughter of a bank manager, in 1844; they had two sons, one of whom emigrated to Australia. Trollope frequently went abroad for the Post Office and did not settle in England again until 1859. He is still remembered as the inventor of the letter-box. In 1867 he resigned from the Post Office and became the editor of *St Paul's Magazine* for the next three years. He failed in his attempt to enter Parliament as a Liberal in 1868. Trollope took his place among London literary society and counted William Thackeray, George Eliot and G. H. Lewes among his friends. He died on 6 December 1882 as the result of a stroke.

Anthony Trollope wrote forty-seven novels and five volumes of short stories as well as travel books, biographies and collections of sketches. The Barsetshire series and the six Palliser or 'political' books were the first novel-sequences to be written in English. His works offer an unsurpassed portrait of the professional and landed classes of Victorian England. In his *Autobiography* (published posthumously in 1883) Trollope describes the self-discipline that enabled his prolific output: he would produce a given number of words per hour in the early morning, before work; he always wrote while travelling by rail or sea, and as soon as he finished one novel he began another. His efforts resulted in his becoming one of England's most successful and popular writers.

An Autobiography (1883) was completed six years before Trollope died. In 1878 he told his son that he had written it and left him a letter, to be opened after his death, that contained his instructions for publication. His son saw the book through the press, making no additions or alterations as his father had requested, although he did 'suppress some few passages, but not more than would amount to two printed pages'. The *Autobiography* was received with some consternation by contemporary critics who felt that Trollope revealed too much of a workaday attitude to the business and profits of writing. His reputation suffered for some time but the *Autobiography* is now recognized as a testament to the character, methods and beliefs of one of Britain's best-loved novelists.

AN AUTOBIOGRAPHY

ANTHONY TROLLOPE

PENGUIN BOOKS

PENGUIN BOOKS

Published by the Penguin Group
Penguin Books Ltd, 27 Wrights Lane, London W8 5TZ, England
Penguin Books USA Inc., 375 Hudson Street, New York, New York 10014, USA
Penguin Books Australia Ltd, Ringwood, Victoria, Australia
Penguin Books Canada Ltd, 10 Alcorn Avenue, Toronto, Ontario, Canada M4V 3B2
Penguin Books (NZ) Ltd, 182–190 Wairau Road, Auckland 10, New Zealand

Penguin Books Ltd, Registered Offices: Harmondsworth, Middlesex, England

First published 1883
Published in Penguin Books 1993
1 3 5 7 9 10 8 6 4 2

Printed in England by Clays Ltd, St Ives plc

CONTENTS

PREFACE (1883)

It may be well that I should put a short preface to this book. In the summer of 1878 my father told me that he had written a memoir of his own life. He did not speak about it at length, but said that he had written me a letter, not to be opened until after his death, containing instructions for publication.

This letter was dated 30th April 1876. I will give here as much of it as concerns the public : 'I wish you to accept as a gift from me, given you now, the accompanying pages which contain a memoir of my life. My intention is that they shall be published after my death, and be edited by you. But I leave it altogether to your discretion whether to publish or to suppress the work ;— and also to your discretion whether any part or what part shall be omitted. But I would not wish that anything should be added to the memoir. If you wish to say any word as from yourself, let it be done in the shape of a preface or introductory chapter.' At the end there is a postscript : 'The publication, if made at all, should be effected as soon as possible after my death.' My father died on the 6th of December 1882.

It will be seen, therefore, that my duty has been merely to pass the book through the press conformably to the above instructions. I have placed headings to the right-hand pages throughout the book, and I do not conceive that I was precluded from so doing. Additions of any other sort there have been none; the few footnotes are my father's own additions or corrections. And I have made no alterations. I have suppressed some few passages, but not more than would amount to two printed pages has been omitted. My father has not given any of his own letters, nor was it his wish that any should be published.

I see from my father's manuscript, and from his papers, that the first two chapters of this memoir were written in the latter part of 1875, that he began the third chapter early in January 1876, and that he finished the record before the middle of April in that year. I state this, though there are indications in the book by which it might be seen at what time the memoir was being written.

So much I would say by way of preface. And I think I may also give in a few words the main incidents in my father's life after he completed his autobiography.

He has said that he had given up hunting; but

he still kept two horses for such riding as may be had in or about the immediate neighbourhood of London. He continued to ride to the end of his life : he liked the exercise, and I think it would have distressed him not to have had a horse in his stable. But he never spoke willingly on hunting matters. He had at last resolved to give up his favourite amusement, and that as far as he was concerned there should be an end of it. In the spring of 1877 he went to South Africa, and returned early in the following year with a book on the colony already written. In the summer of 1878, he was one of a party of ladies and gentlemen who made an expedition to Iceland in the *Mastiff*, one of Mr. John Burns' steam-ships. The journey lasted altogether sixteen days, and during that time Mr. and Mrs. Burns were the hospitable entertainers. When my father returned, he wrote a short account of *How the 'Mastiffs' went to Iceland*. The book was printed, but was intended only for private circulation.

Every day, until his last illness, my father continued his work. He would not otherwise have been happy. He demanded from himself less than he had done ten years previously, but his daily task was always done. I will mention now the titles of his books that were published after the last included in the list which he

himself has given at the end of the second
volume :

At the time of his death he had written four-
fifths of an Irish story, called *The Landleaguers*,
shortly about to be published ; and he left in
manuscript a completed novel, called *An Old
Man's Love*, which will be published by Messrs.
Blackwood & Sons in 1884.

In the summer of 1880 my father left London,
and went to live at Harting, a village in Sussex,
but on the confines of Hampshire. I think he
chose that spot because he found there a house
that suited him, and because of the prettiness of
the neighbourhood. His last long journey was
a trip to Italy in the late winter and spring of 1881 ;
but he went to Ireland twice in 1882. He went
there in May of that year, and was then absent

nearly a month. This journey did him much good, for he found that the softer atmosphere relieved his asthma, from which he had been suffering for nearly eighteen months. In August following he made another trip to Ireland, but from this journey he derived less benefit. He was much interested in, and was very much distressed by, the unhappy condition of the country. Few men knew Ireland better than he did. He had lived there for sixteen years, and his Post Office work had taken him into every part of the island. In the summer of 1882 he began his last novel, *The Landleaguers*, which, as stated above, was unfinished when he died. This book was a cause of anxiety to him. He could not rid his mind of the fact that he had a story already in the course of publication, but which he had not yet completed. In no other case, except *Framley Parsonage*, did my father publish even the first number of any novel before he had fully completed the whole tale.

On the evening of the 3rd of November 1882 he was seized with paralysis on the right side, accompanied by loss of speech. His mind also had failed, though at intervals his thoughts would return to him. After the first three weeks these lucid intervals became rarer, but it was always very difficult to tell how far his mind was sound or how far astray. He died on the evening of the

6th of December following, nearly five weeks from the night of his attack.

I have been led to say these few words, not at all from a desire to supplement my father's biography of himself, but to mention the main incidents in his life after he had finished his own record. In what I have here said I do not think I have exceeded his instructions.

HENRY M. TROLLOPE.

September 1883.

AUTOBIOGRAPHY

OF

ANTHONY TROLLOPE

CHAPTER I

MY EDUCATION

1815–1834

In writing these pages, which, for the want of a better name, I shall be fain to call the autobiography of so insignificant a person as myself, it will not be so much my intention to speak of the little details of my private life, as of what I, and perhaps others round me, have done in literature; of my failures and successes such as they have been, and their causes; and of the opening which a literary career offers to men and women for the earning of their bread. And yet the garrulity of old age, and the aptitude of a man's mind to recur to the passages of his own life, will, I know, tempt me to say something of myself;—nor, without doing so, should I know how to throw my matter into any recognised and intelligible form. That I, or any man, should tell everything of himself, I hold to be impossible. Who could endure to own the doing of a mean thing? Who is there that has

B

done none ?   But this I protest ;—that nothing
that I say shall be untrue. I will set down naught
in malice ; nor will I give to myself, or others,
honour which I do not believe to have been fairly
won.

My boyhood was, I think, as unhappy as that
of a young gentleman could well be, my misfortunes arising from a mixture of poverty and
gentle standing on the part of my father, and from
an utter want on my own part of that juvenile
manhood which enables some boys to hold up their
heads even among the distresses which such a
position is sure to produce.

I was born in 1815, in Keppel Street, Russell
Square ; and while a baby, was carried down to
Harrow, where my father had built a house on
a large farm which, in an evil hour, he took on
a long lease from Lord Northwick. That farm
was the grave of all my father's hopes, ambition,
and prosperity, the cause of my mother's sufferings,
and of those of her children, and perhaps the
director of her destiny and of ours. My father
had been a Wykamist and a fellow of New College,
and Winchester was the destination of my brothers
and myself ; but as he had friends among the
masters at Harrow, and as the school offered an
education almost gratuitous to children living in
the parish, he, with a certain aptitude to do things
differently from others, which accompanied him
throughout his life, determined to use that august
seminary as a ' t'other school ' for Winchester, and
sent three of us there, one after the other, at the
age of seven. My father at this time was a Chancery
barrister practising in London, occupying dingy,
almost suicidal chambers, at No. 23 Old Square,

Lincoln's Inn,—chambers which on one melancholy occasion did become absolutely suicidal.[1] He was, as I have been informed by those quite competent to know, an excellent and most conscientious lawyer, but plagued with so bad a temper, that he drove the attorneys from him. In his early days he was a man of some small fortune and of higher hopes. These stood so high at the time of my birth, that he was felt to be entitled to a country house, as well as to that in Keppel Street; and in order that he might build such a residence, he took the farm. This place he called Julians, and the land runs up to the foot of the hill on which the school and church stand,—on the side towards London. Things there went much against him; the farm was ruinous, and I remember that we all regarded the Lord Northwick of those days as a cormorant who was eating us up. My father's clients deserted him. He purchased various dark gloomy chambers in and about Chancery Lane, and his purchases always went wrong. Then, as a final crushing blow, an old uncle, whose heir he was to have been, married and had a family! The house in London was let; and also the house he built at Harrow, from which he descended to a farmhouse on the land, which I have endeavoured to make known to some readers under the name of Orley Farm. This place, just as it was when we lived there, is to be seen in the frontispiece to the first edition of that novel, having had the good fortune to be delineated by no less a pencil than that of John Millais.

My two elder brothers had been sent as day-boarders to Harrow School from the bigger house,

[1] A pupil of his destroyed himself in the rooms.

and may probably have been received among the aristocratic crowd,—not on equal terms, because a day-boarder at Harrow in those days was never so received,—but at any rate as other day-boarders. I do not suppose that they were well treated, but I doubt whether they were subjected to the ignominy which I endured. I was only seven, and I think that boys at seven are now spared among their more considerate seniors. I was never spared; and was not even allowed to run to and fro between our house and the school without a daily purgatory. No doubt my appearance was against me. I remember well, when I was still the junior boy in the school, Dr. Butler, the head-master, stopping me in the street, and asking me, with all the clouds of Jove upon his brow and all the thunder in his voice, whether it was possible that Harrow School was disgraced by so disre-putably dirty a little boy as I! Oh, what I felt at that moment! But I could not look my feelings. I do not doubt that I was dirty;—but I think that he was cruel. He must have known me had he seen me as he was wont to see me, for he was in the habit of flogging me constantly. Perhaps he did not recognise me by my face.

At this time I was three years at Harrow; and, as far as I can remember, I was the junior boy in the school when I left it.

Then I was sent to a private school at Sunbury, kept by Arthur Drury. This, I think, must have been done in accordance with the advice of Henry Drury, who was my tutor at Harrow School, and my father's friend, and who may probably have expressed an opinion that my juvenile career was not proceeding in a satisfactory manner at Harrow.

To Sunbury I went, and during the two years I was there, though I never had any pocket-money, and seldom had much in the way of clothes, I lived more nearly on terms of equality with other boys than at any other period during my very prolonged school-days. Even here, I was always in disgrace. I remember well how, on one occasion, four boys were selected as having been the perpetrators of some nameless horror. What it was, to this day I cannot even guess; but I was one of the four, innocent as a babe, but adjudged to have been the guiltiest of the guilty. We each had to write out a sermon, and my sermon was the longest of the four. During the whole of one term-time we were helped last at every meal. We were not allowed to visit the playground till the sermon was finished. Mine was only done a day or two before the holidays. Mrs. Drury, when she saw us, shook her head with pitying horror. There were ever so many other punishments accumulated on our heads. It broke my heart, knowing myself to be innocent, and suffering also under the almost equally painful feeling that the other three—no doubt wicked boys—were the curled darlings of the school, who would never have selected me to share their wickedness with them. I contrived to learn, from words that fell from Mr. Drury, that he condemned me because I, having come from a public school, might be supposed to be the leader of wickedness! On the first day of the next term he whispered to me half a word that perhaps he had been wrong. With all a stupid boy's slowness, I said nothing; and he had not the courage to carry reparation further. All that was fifty years ago, and it burns me now as though it were yesterday. What lily-livered curs those boys must have been not to have told the truth !—at any rate as far as I was concerned. I remember their names well, and almost wish to write them here.

When I was twelve there came the vacancy at Winchester College which I was destined to fill. My two elder brothers had gone there, and the younger had been taken away, being already supposed to have lost his chance of New College. It had been one of the great ambitions of my father's life that his three sons, who lived to go to Winchester, should all become fellows of New College. But that suffering man was never destined to have an ambition gratified. We all lost the prize which he struggled with infinite labour to put within our reach. My eldest brother all but achieved it, and afterwards went to Oxford, taking three exhibitions from the school, though he lost the great glory of a Wykamist. He has since made himself well known to the public as a writer in connection with all Italian subjects. He is still living as I now write. But my other brother died early.

While I was at Winchester my father's affairs went from bad to worse. He gave up his practice at the bar, and, unfortunate that he was, took another farm. It is odd that a man should conceive,—and in this case a highly educated and a very clever man,—that farming should be a business in which he might make money without any special education or apprenticeship. Perhaps of all trades it is the one in which an accurate knowledge of what things should be done, and the best manner of doing them, is most necessary. And it is one also for success in which a sufficient capital is indispensable. He had no knowledge, and, when he took this second farm, no capital. This was the last step preparatory to his final ruin.

Soon after I had been sent to Winchester, my mother went to America, taking with her my brother Henry and my two sisters, who were then no more than children. This was, I think, in 1827. I have no clear knowledge of her object, or of my father's; but I believe that he had an idea that money might be made by sending goods,—little goods, such as pin-cushions, pepper-boxes, and pocket-knives,—out to the still unfurnished States; and that she conceived that an opening might be made for my brother Henry by erecting some bazaar or extended shop in one of the Western cities. Whence the money came I do not know, but the pocket-knives and the pepper-boxes were bought, and the bazaar built. I have seen it since in the town of Cincinnati,—a sorry building! But I have been told that in those days it was an imposing edifice. My mother went first, with my sisters and second brother. Then my father followed them, taking my elder brother before he went to Oxford. But there was an interval of some year and a half during which he and I were at Winchester together.

Over a period of forty years, since I began my manhood at a desk in the Post Office, I and my brother, Thomas Adolphus, have been fast friends. There have been hot words between us, for perfect friendship bears and allows hot words. Few brothers have had more of brotherhood. But in those school-days he was, of all my foes, the worst. In accordance with the practice of the college, which submits, or did then submit, much of the tuition of the younger boys from the elder, he was

my tutor; and in his capacity of teacher and
ruler, he had studied the theories of Draco. I
remember well how he used to exact obedience after
the manner of that lawgiver. Hang a little boy
for stealing apples, he used to say, and other little
boys will not steal apples. The doctrine was
already exploded elsewhere, but he stuck to it with
conservative energy. The result was that, as a
part of his daily exercise, he thrashed me with a
big stick. That such thrashings should have been
possible at a school as a continual part of one's
daily life, seems to me to argue a very ill condition
of school discipline.

At this period I remember to have passed one
set of holidays—the midsummer holidays—in my
father's chambers in Lincoln's Inn. There was often
a difficulty about the holidays,—as to what should
be done with me. On this occasion my amusement
consisted in wandering about among those old
deserted buildings, and in reading Shakespeare
out of a bi-columned edition, which is still among
my books. It was not that I had chosen Shakespeare, but that there was nothing else to read.

After a while my brother left Winchester and
accompanied my father to America. Then another
and a different horror fell to my fate. My college
bills had not been paid, and the school tradesmen
who administered to the wants of the boys were
told not to extend their credit to me. Boots,
waistcoats, and pocket-handkerchiefs, which,
with some slight superveillance, were at the
command of other scholars, were closed luxuries
to me. My schoolfellows of course knew that it
was so, and I became a Pariah. It is the nature of
boys to be cruel. I have sometimes doubted

whether among each other they do usually suffer much, one from the other's cruelty ; but I suffered horribly ! I could make no stand against it. I had no friend to whom I could pour out my sorrows. I was big, and awkward, and ugly, and, I have no doubt, skulked about in a most unattractive manner. Of course I was ill-dressed and dirty. But, ah ! how well I remember all the agonies of my young heart ; how I considered whether I should always be alone ; whether I could not find my way up to the top of that college tower, and from thence put an end to everything ? And a worse thing came than the stoppage of the supplies from the shopkeepers. Every boy had a shilling a week pocket-money, which we called battels, and which was advanced to us out of the pocket of the second master. On one awful day the second master announced to me that my battels would be stopped. He told me the reason,—the battels for the last half-year had not been repaid ; and he urged his own unwillingness to advance the money. The loss of a shilling a week would not have been much,—even though pocket-money from other sources never reached me,—but that the other boys all knew it ! Every now and again, perhaps three or four times in a half-year, these weekly shillings were given to certain servants of the college, in payment, it may be presumed, for some extra services. And now, when it came to the turn of any servant, he received sixty-nine shillings instead of seventy, and the cause of the defalcation was explained to him. I never saw one of those servants without feeling that I had picked his pocket.

When I had been at Winchester something over

three years, my father returned to England and took me away. Whether this was done because of the expense, or because my chance of New College was supposed to have passed away, I do not know. As a fact, I should, I believe, have gained the prize, as there occurred in my year an exceptional number of vacancies. But it would have served me nothing, as there would have been no funds for my maintenance at the University till I should have entered in upon the fruition of the founder's endowment, and my career at Oxford must have been unfortunate.

When I left Winchester, I had three more years of school before me, having as yet endured nine. My father at this time having left my mother and sisters with my younger brother in America, took himself to live at a wretched tumble-down farmhouse on the second farm he had hired! And I was taken there with him. It was nearly three miles from Harrow, at Harrow Weald, but in the parish; and from this house I was again sent to that school as a day-boarder. Let those who know what is the usual appearance and what the usual appurtenances of a boy at such a school, consider what must have been my condition among them, with a daily walk of twelve miles through the lanes, added to the other little troubles and labours of a school life!

Perhaps the eighteen months which I passed in this condition, walking to and fro on those miserably dirty lanes, was the worst period of my life. I was now over fifteen, and had come to an age at which I could appreciate at its full the misery of expulsion from all social intercourse. I had not only no friends, but was despised by all my com-

panions. The farmhouse was not only no more
than a farmhouse, but was one of those farmhouses
which seem always to be in danger of falling into
the neighbouring horse-pond. As it crept downwards from house to stables, from stables to
barns, from barns to cowsheds, and from cowsheds
to dung-heaps, one could hardly tell where one
began and the other ended ! There was a parlour
in which my father lived, shut up among big books ;
but I passed my most jocund hours in the kitchen,
making innocent love to the bailiff's daughter. The
farm kitchen might be very well through the
evening, when the horrors of the school were over ;
but it all added to the cruelty of the days. A sizar
at a Cambridge college, or a Bible-clerk at Oxford,
has not pleasant days, or used not to have them
half a century ago ; but his position was recognised and the misery was measured. I was a sizar
at a fashionable school, a condition never pre-
meditated. What right had a wretched farmer's
boy, reeking from a dunghill, to sit next to the sons
of peers,—or much worse still, next to the sons of
big tradesmen who had made their ten thousand
a-year ? The indignities I endured are not to be
described. As I look back it seems to me that all
hands were turned against me,—those of masters
as well as boys. I was allowed to join in no plays.
Nor did I learn anything,—for I was taught nothing. The only expense, except that of books, to
which a house-boarder was then subject, was the
fee to a tutor, amounting, I think, to ten guineas.
My tutor took me without the fee ; but when I
heard him declare the fact in the pupil-room before
the boys, I hardly felt grateful for the charity.
I was never a coward, and cared for a thrashing as

little as any boy, but one cannot make a stand against the acerbities of three hundred tyrants without a moral courage of which at that time I possessed none. I know that I skulked, and was odious to the eyes of those I admired and envied. At last I was driven to rebellion, and there came a great fight,—at the end of which my opponent had to be taken home for a while. If these words be ever printed, I trust that some schoolfellow of those days may still be left alive who will be able to say that, in claiming this solitary glory of my school-days, I am not making a false boast.

I wish I could give some adequate picture of the gloom of that farmhouse. My elder brother — Tom as I must call him in my narrative, though the world, I think, knows him best as Adolphus— was at Oxford. My father and I lived together, he having no means of living except what came from the farm. My memory tells me that he was always in debt to his landlord and to the tradesmen he employed. Of self-indulgence no one could accuse him. Our table was poorer, I think, than that of the bailiff who still hung on to our shattered fortunes. The furniture was mean and scanty. There was a large rambling kitchen-garden, but no gardener ; and many times verbal incentives were made to me,—generally, I fear, in vain,—to get me to lend a hand at digging and planting. Into the hay-field on holidays I was often compelled to go, —not, I fear, with much profit. My father's health was very bad. During the last ten years of his life, he spent nearly the half of his time in bed, suffering agony from sick headaches. But he was never idle unless when suffering. He had at this time commenced a work,—an Encyclopædia

Ecclesiastica, as he called it,—on which he laboured to the moment of his death. It was his ambition to describe all ecclesiastical terms, including the denominations of every fraternity of monks and every convent of nuns, with all their orders and subdivisions. Under crushing disadvantages, with few or no books of reference, with immediate access to no library, he worked at his most ungrateful task with unflagging industry. When he died, three numbers out of eight had been published by subscription; and are now, I fear, unknown, and buried in the midst of that huge pile of futile literature, the building up of which has broken so many hearts.

And my father, though he would try, as it were by a side wind, to get a useful spurt of work out of me, either in the garden or in the hay-field, had constantly an eye to my scholastic improvement. From my very babyhood, before those first days at Harrow, I had to take my place alongside of him as he shaved at six o'clock in the morning, and say my early rules from the Latin Grammar, or repeat the Greek alphabet; and was obliged at these early lessons to hold my head inclined towards him, so that in the event of guilty fault, he might be able to pull my hair without stopping his razor or dropping his shaving-brush. No father was ever more anxious for the education of his children, though I think none ever knew less how to go about the work. Of amusement, as far as I can remember, he never recognised the need. He allowed himself no distraction, and did not seem to think it was necessary to a child. I cannot bethink me of aught that he ever did for my gratification; but for my welfare,—for the welfare

of us all,—he was willing to make any sacrifice. At
this time, in the farmhouse at Harrow Weald, he
could not give his time to teach me, for every hour
that he was not in the fields was devoted to his
monks and nuns ; but he would require me to sit
at a table with Lexicon and Gradus before me. As
I look back on my resolute idleness and fixed
determination to make no use whatever of the
books thus thrust upon me, or of the hours, and as
I bear in mind the consciousness of great energy
in after-life, I am in doubt whether my nature is
wholly altered, or whether his plan was wholly
bad. In those days he never punished me, though
I think I grieved him much by my idleness ; but
in passion he knew not what he did, and he has
knocked me down with the great folio Bible which
he always used. In the old house were the two
first volumes of Cooper's novel, called *The Prairie*,
a relic—probably a dishonest relic—of some subscription to Hookham's library. Other books of
the kind there was none. I wonder how many
dozen times I read those two first volumes.

It was the horror of those dreadful walks backwards and forwards which made my life so bad.
What so pleasant, what so sweet, as a walk along
an English lane, when the air is sweet and the
weather fine, and when there is a charm in walking ?
But here were the same lanes four times a-day, in
wet and dry, in heat and summer, with all the
accompanying mud and dust, and with disordered
clothes. I might have been known among all the
boys at a hundred yards' distance by my boots
and trousers,—and was conscious at all times that
I was so known. I remembered constantly that
address from Dr. Butler when I was a little boy.

Dr. Longley might with equal justice have said the same thing any day,—only that Dr. Longley never in his life was able to say an ill-natured word. Dr. Butler only became Dean of Peterborough, but his successor lived to be Archbishop of Canterbury.

I think it was in the autumn of 1831 that my mother, with the rest of the family, returned from America. She lived at first at the farmhouse, but it was only for a short time. She came back with a book written about the United States, and the immediate pecuniary success which that work obtained enable her to take us all back to the house at Harrow,—not to the first house, which would still have been beyond her means, but to that which has since been called Orley Farm, and which was an Eden as compared to our abode at Harrow Weald. Here my schooling went on under somewhat improved circumstances. The three miles became half a mile, and probably some salutary changes were made in my wardrobe. My mother and my sisters, too, were there. And a great element of happiness was added to us all in the affectionate and life-enduring friendship of the family of our close neighbour, Colonel Grant. But I was never able to overcome—or even to attempt to overcome—the absolute isolation of my school position. Of the cricket-ground or racket-court I was allowed to know nothing. And yet I longed for these things with an exceeding longing. I coveted popularity with a covetousness that was almost mean. It seemed to me that there would be an Elysium in the intimacy of those very boys whom I was bound to hate because they hated me. Something of the disgrace of my school-days has

clung to me all through life. Not that I have ever
shunned to speak of them as openly as I am writing
now, but that when I have been claimed as schoolfellow by some of those many hundreds who were
with me either at Harrow or at Winchester, I have
felt that I had no right to talk of things from most
of which I was kept in estrangement.

Through all my father's troubles he still desired
to send me either to Oxford or Cambridge. My
elder brother went to Oxford, and Henry to
Cambridge. It all depended on my ability to get
some scholarship that would help me to live at the
University. I had many chances. There were
exhibitions from Harrow—which I never got.
Twice I tried for a sizarship at Clare Hall,—but in
vain. Once I made a futile attempt for a scholarship at Trinity, Oxford,—but failed again. Then
the idea of a university career was abandoned.
And very fortunate it was that I did not succeed,
for my career with such assistance only as a
scholarship would have given me, would have
ended in debt and ignominy.

When I left Harrow I was all but nineteen, and
I had at first gone there at seven. During the
whole of those twelve years no attempt had been
made to teach me anything but Latin and Greek,
and very little attempt to teach me those languages.
I do not remember any lessons either in writing or
arithmetic. French and German I certainly was
not taught. The assertion will scarcely be credited,
but I do assert that I have no recollection of other
tuition except that in the dead languages. At the
school at Sunbury there was certainly a writing
master and a French master. The latter was an
extra, and I never had extras. I suppose I must

have been in the writing master's class, but though
I can call to mind the man, I cannot call to mind
his ferule. It was by their ferules that I always
knew them, and they me. I feel convinced in my
mind that I have been flogged oftener than any
human being alive. It was just possible to obtain
five scourgings in one day at Winchester, and I
have often boasted that I obtained them all.
Looking back over half a century, I am not quite
sure whether the boast is true ; but if I did not,
nobody ever did.

And yet when I think how little I knew of Latin
or Greek on leaving Harrow at nineteen, I am
astonished at the possibility of such waste of time.
I am now a fair Latin scholar,—that is to say, I
read and enjoy the Latin classics, and could
probably make myself understood in Latin prose.
But the knowledge which I have, I have acquired
since I left school,—no doubt aided much by that
groundwork of the language which will in the process of years make its way slowly, even through the
skin. There were twelve years of tuition in which
I do not remember that I ever knew a lesson !
When I left Harrow I was nearly at the top of the
school, being a monitor, and, I think, the seventh
boy. This position I achieved by gravitation
upwards. I bear in mind well with how prodigal
a hand prizes used to be showered about ; but I
never got a prize. From the first to the last there
was nothing satisfactory in my school career,—
except the way in which I licked the boy who had
to be taken home to be cured.

CHAPTER II

MY MOTHER

THOUGH I do not wish in these pages to go back to the origin of all the Trollopes, I must say a few words of my mother,—partly because filial duty will not allow me to be silent as to a parent who made for herself a considerable name in the literature of her day, and partly because there were circumstances in her career well worthy of notice. She was the daughter of the Rev. William Milton, vicar of Heckfield, who, as well as my father, had been a fellow of New College. She was nearly thirty when, in 1809, she married my father. Six or seven years ago a bundle of love-letters from her to him fell into my hand in a very singular way, having been found in the house of a stranger, who, with much courtesy, sent them to me. They were then about sixty years old, and had been written some before and some after her marriage, over the space of perhaps a year. In no novel of Richardson's or Miss Burney's have I seen a correspondence at the same time so sweet, so graceful, and so well expressed. But the marvel of these letters was in the strange difference they bore to the love-letters of the present day. They are, all of them, on square paper, folded and sealed, and addressed to my father on circuit; but the language in each, though it almost borders on the romantic, is beautifully chosen, and fit, without change of a syllable, for the most critical eye. What girl now studies the words with which she shall address her lover, or seeks to charm him with grace of diction? She dearly likes a little slang, and revels in the luxury of entire familiarity with a new and strange being. There is something in that, too, pleasant to our thoughts, but I fear that this phase of life does not conduce to a taste for poetry among our girls. Though my mother was a writer of prose, and revelled in satire, the poetic feeling clung to her to the last.

In the first ten years of her married life she became the mother of six children, four of whom died of consumption at different ages. My elder sister married, and had children, of whom one still lives; but she was one of the four who followed each other at intervals during my mother's lifetime. Then my brother Tom and I were left to her, —with the destiny before us three of writing more books than were probably ever before produced by a single family.[1] My married sister added to the number by one little anonymous high church story, called *Chollerton*.

From the date of their marriage up to 1827, when my mother went to America, my father's affairs had always been going down in the world. She had loved society, affecting a somewhat liberal *rôle*, and professing an emotional dislike to tyrants, which sprung from the wrongs of would-be

---

[1] The family of Estienne, the great French printers of the fifteenth and sixteenth centuries, of whom there were at least nine or ten, did more perhaps for the production of literature than any other family. But they, though they edited, and not unfrequently translated the works which they published, were not authors in the ordinary sense.

regicides and the poverty of patriot exiles. An
Italian marquis who had escaped with only a second
shirt from the clutches of some archduke whom he
had wished to exterminate, or a French *prolétaire*
with distant ideas of sacrificing himself to the
cause of liberty, were always welcome to the
modest hospitality of her house. In after years,
when marquises of another caste had been gracious
to her, she became a strong Tory, and thought that
archduchesses were sweet. But with her politics
were always an affair of the heart,—as, indeed, were
all her convictions. Of reasoning from causes,
I think that she knew nothing. Her heart was
in every way so perfect, her desire to do good to
all around her so thorough, and her power of self-
sacrifice so complete, that she generally got herself
right in spite of her want of logic ; but it must be
acknowledged that she was emotional. I can
remember now her books, and can see her at her
pursuits. The poets she loved best were Dante
and Spenser. But she raved also of him of whom
all such ladies were raving then, and rejoiced in the
popularity and wept over the persecution of Lord
Byron. She was among those who seized with
avidity on the novels, as they came out, of the
then unknown Scott, and who could still talk of the
triumphs of Miss Edgeworth. With the literature
of the day she was familiar, and with the poets of
the past. Of other reading I do not think she had
mastered much. Her life, I take it, though latterly
clouded by many troubles, was easy, luxurious, and
idle, till my father's affairs and her own aspirations
sent her to America. She had dear friends among
literary people, of whom I remember Mathias,
Henry Milman, and Miss Landon ; but till long

after middle life she never herself wrote a line for publication.

In 1827 she went to America, having been partly instigated by the social and communistic ideas of a lady whom I well remember,—a certain Miss Wright,—who was, I think, the first of the American female lecturers. Her chief desire, however, was to establish my brother Henry; and perhaps joined with that was the additional object of breaking up her English home without pleading broken fortunes to all the world. At Cincinnati, in the State of Ohio, she built a bazaar, and I fancy lost all the money which may have been embarked in that speculation. It could not have been much, and I think that others also must have suffered. But she looked about her, at her American cousins, and resolved to write a book about them. This book she brought back with her in 1831, and published it early in 1832. When she did this she was already fifty. When doing this she was aware that unless she could so succeed in making money, there was no money for any of the family. She had never before earned a shilling. She almost immediately received a considerable sum from the publishers,—if I remember rightly, amounting to two sums of £400 each within a few months; and from that moment till nearly the time of her death, at any rate for more than twenty years, she was in the receipt of a considerable income from her writings. It was a late age at which to begin such a career.

The Domestic Manners of the Americans was the first of a series of books of travels, of which it was probably the best, and was certainly the best known. It will not be too much to say of it that it

had a material effect upon the manners of the
Americans of the day, and that that effect has been
fully appreciated by them. No observer was
certainly ever less qualified to judge of the prospects
or even of the happiness of a young people. No
one could have been worse adapted by nature
for the task of learning whether a nation was in
a way to thrive. Whatever she saw she judged, as
most women do, from her own standing-point.
If a thing were ugly to her eyes, it ought to be
ugly to all eyes,—and if ugly, it must be bad. What
though people had plenty to eat and clothes to
wear, if they put their feet upon the tables and did
not reverence their betters? The Americans
were to her rough, uncouth, and vulgar,—and
she told them so. Those communistic and social
ideas, which had been so pretty in a drawing-room,
were scattered to the winds. Her volumes were
very bitter; but they were very clever, and they
saved the family from ruin.

Book followed book immediately,—first two
novels, and then a book on Belgium and Western
Germany. She refurnished the house which I have
called Orley Farm, and surrounded us again with
moderate comforts. Of the mixture of joviality
and industry which formed her character, it is
almost impossible to speak with exaggeration.
The industry was a thing apart, kept to herself.
It was not necessary that any one who lived with
her should see it. She was at her table at four
in the morning, and had finished her work before
the world had begun to be aroused. But the
joviality was all for others. She could dance with
other people's legs, eat and drink with other
people's palates, be proud with the lustre of other

people's finery. Every mother can do that for her
own daughters; but she could do it for any girl
whose look, and voice, and manners pleased her.
Even when she was at work, the laughter of those
she loved was a pleasure to her. She had much,
very much, to suffer. Work sometimes came hard
to her, so much being required,—for she was
extravagant, and liked to have money to spend;
but of all people I have known she was the most
joyous, or, at any rate, the most capable of joy.

We continued this renewed life at Harrow for
nearly two years, during which I was still at the
school, and at the end of which I was nearly nineteen. Then there came a great catastrophe. My
father, who, when he was well, lived a sad life
among his monks and nuns, still kept a horse and
gig. One day in March 1834, just as it had been
decided that I should leave the school then, instead
of remaining, as had been intended, till midsummer, I was summoned very early in the morning, to drive him up to London. He had been ill,
and must still have been very ill indeed when he
submitted to be driven by any one. It was not
till we had started that he told me that I was to
put him on board the Ostend boat. This I did,
driving through the city down to the docks. It
was not within his nature to be communicative,
and to the last he never told me why he was going
to Ostend. Something of a general flitting abroad
I had heard before, but why he should have flown
the first, and flown so suddenly, I did not in the
least know till I returned. When I got back with
the gig, the house and furniture were all in the
charge of the sheriff's officers.

The gardener who had been with us in former

days stopped me as I drove up the road, and with gestures, signs, and whispered words, gave me to understand that the whole affair—horse, gig, and harness—would be made prize of if I went but a few yards farther. Why they should not have been made prize of I do not know. The little piece of dishonest business which I at once took in hand and carried through successfully was of no special service to any of us. I drove the gig into the village, and sold the entire equipage to the ironmonger for £17, the exact sum which he claimed as being due to himself. I was much complimented by the gardener, who seemed to think that so much had been rescued out of the fire. I fancy that the ironmonger was the only gainer by my smart-ness.

When I got back to the house a scene of devasta-tion was in progress, which still was not without its amusement. My mother, through her various troubles, had contrived to keep a certain number of pretty-pretties which were dear to her heart. They were not much, for in those days the ornamenta-tion of houses was not lavish as it is now ; but there was some china, and a little glass, a few books, and a very moderate supply of household silver. These things, and things like them, were being carried down surreptitiously, through a gap between the two gardens, on to the premises of our friend Colonel Grant. My two sisters, then sixteen and seventeen, and the Grant girls, who were just younger, were the chief marauders. To such forces I was happy to add myself for any enterprise, and between us we cheated the creditors to the extent of our powers, amidst the anathemas, but good-humoured abstinence from personal

violence, of the men in charge of the property.
I still own a few books that were thus purloined.

For a few days the whole family bivouacked
under the Colonel's hospitable roof, cared for
and comforted by that dearest of all women, his
wife. Then we followed my father to Belgium,
and established ourselves in a large house just
outside the walls of Bruges. At this time, and till
my father's death, everything was done with
money earned by my mother. She now again
furnished the house,—this being the third that she
had put in order since she came back from America
two years and a half ago.

There were six of us went into this new banishment. My brother Henry had left Cambridge and
was ill. My younger sister was ill. And though
as yet we hardly told each other that it was so, we
began to feel that that desolating fiend, consumption, was among us. My father was broken-
hearted as well as ill, but whenever he could sit at
his table he still worked at his ecclesiastical records.
My elder sister and I were in good health, but
I was an idle, desolate hanger-on, that most
hopeless of human beings, a hobbledehoy of nineteen, without any idea of a career, or a profession,
or a trade. As well as I can remember I was fairly
happy, for there were pretty girls at Bruges with
whom I could fancy that I was in love; and I had
been removed from the real misery of school. But
as to my future life I had not even an aspiration.
Now and again there would arise a feeling that it
was hard upon my mother that she should have to
do so much for us, that we should be idle while she
was forced to work so constantly; but we should
probably have thought more of that had she not

taken to work as though it were the recognised condition of life for an old lady of fifty-five.

Then, by degrees, an established sorrow was at home among us. My brother was an invalid, and the horrid word, which of all words was for some years after the most dreadful to us, had been pronounced. It was no longer a delicate chest, and some temporary necessity for peculiar care,—but consumption! The Bruges doctor had said so, and we knew that he was right. From that time forth my mother's most visible occupation was that of nursing. There were two sick men in the house, and hers were the hands that tended them. The novels went on, of course. We had already learned to know that they would be forthcoming at stated intervals,—and they always were forthcoming. The doctor's vials and the ink-bottle held equal places in my mother's rooms. I have written many novels under many circumstances; but I doubt much whether I could write one when my whole heart was by the bedside of a dying son. Her power of dividing herself into two parts, and keeping her intellect by itself clear from the troubles of the world, and fit for the duty it had to do, I never saw equalled. I do not think that the writing of a novel is the most difficult task which a man may be called upon to do; but it is a task that may be supposed to demand a spirit fairly at ease. The work of doing it with a troubled spirit killed Sir Walter Scott. My mother went through it unscathed in strength, though she performed all the work of day-nurse and night-nurse to a sick household;—for there were soon three of them dying.

At this time there came from some quarter an

offer to me of a commission in an Austrian cavalry
regiment ; and so it was apparently my destiny to
be a soldier. But I must first learn German and
French, of which languages I knew almost nothing.
For this a year was allowed me, and in order that it
might be accomplished without expense, I under-
took the duties of a classical usher to a school then
kept by William Drury at Brussels. Mr. Drury
had been one of the masters at Harrow when I
went there at seven years old, and is now, after an
interval of fifty-three years, even yet officiating as
clergyman at that place.[1] To Brussels I went,
and my heart still sinks within me as I reflect that
any one should have intrusted to me the tuition of
thirty boys. I can only hope that those boys
went there to learn French, and that their parents
were not particular as to their classical acquirements. I remember that on two occasions I was
sent to take the school out for a walk ; but that
after the second attempt Mrs. Drury declared that
the boys' clothes would not stand any further
experiments of that kind. I cannot call to mind
any learning by me of other languages ; but as
I only remained in that position for six weeks,
perhaps the return lessons had not been as yet
commenced. At the end of the six weeks a letter
reached me, offering me a clerkship in the General
Post Office, and I accepted it. Among my mother's
dearest friends she reckoned Mrs. Freeling, the
wife of Clayton Freeling, whose father, Sir Francis
Freeling, then ruled the Post Office. She had
heard of my desolate position, and had begged
from her father-in-law the offer of a berth in his
own office.

[1] He died two years after these words were written.

I hurried back from Brussels to Bruges on my way to London, and found that the number of invalids had been increased. My younger sister, Emily, who, when I had left the house, was trembling on the balance,—who had been pronounced to be delicate, but with that false-tongued hope which knows the truth, but will lie lest the heart should faint, had been called delicate, but only delicate,—was now ill. Of course she was doomed. I knew it of both of them, though I had never heard the word spoken, or had spoken it to any one. And my father was very ill,—ill to dying, though I did not know it. And my mother had decreed to send my elder sister away to England, thinking that the vicinity of so much sickness might be injurious to her. All this happened late in the autumn of 1834, in the spring of which year we had come to Bruges ; and then my mother was left alone in a big house outside the town, with two Belgian women-servants, to nurse these dying patients—the patients being her husband and children—and to write novels for the sustenance of the family ! It was about this period of her career that her best novels were written.

To my own initiation at the Post Office I will return in the next chapter. Just before Christmas my brother died, and was buried at Bruges. In the following February my father died, and was buried alongside of him,—and with him died that tedious task of his, which I can only hope may have solaced many of his latter hours. I sometimes look back, meditating for hours together, on his adverse fate. He was a man, finely educated, of great parts, with immense capacity for work, physically strong very much beyond the average

of men, addicted to no vices, carried off by no
pleasures, affectionate by nature, most anxious for
the welfare of his children, born to fair fortunes,—
who, when he started in the world, may be said to
have had everything at his feet. But everything
went wrong with him. The touch of his hand
seemed to create failure. He embarked in one
hopeless enterprise after another, spending on each
all the money he could at the time command. But
the worse curse to him of all was a temper so
irritable that even those whom he loved the best
could not endure it. We were all estranged from
him, and yet I believe that he would have given
his heart's blood for any of us. His life as I knew
it was one long tragedy.

After his death my mother moved to England,
and took and furnished a small house at Hadley,
near Barnet. I was then a clerk in the London
Post Office, and I remember well how gay she
made the place with little dinners, little dances,
and little picnics, while she herself was at work
every morning long before others had left their
beds. But she did not stay at Hadley much above
a year. She went up to London, where she again
took and furnished a house, from which my
remaining sister was married and carried away
into Cumberland. My mother soon followed her,
and on this occasion did more than take a house.
She bought a bit of land,—a field of three acres near
the town,—and built a residence for herself. This,
I think, was in 1841, and she had thus established
and re-established herself six times in ten years.
But in Cumberland she found the climate too
severe, and in 1844 she moved herself to Florence,
where she remained till her death in 1863. She

continued writing up to 1856, when she was seventy-six years old,—and had at that time produced 114 volumes, of which the first was not written till she was fifty. Her career offers great encouragement to those who have not begun early in life, but are still ambitious to do something before they depart hence.

She was an unselfish, affectionate, and most industrious woman, with great capacity for enjoyment and high physical gifts. She was endowed, too, with much creative power, with considerable humour, and a genuine feeling for romance. But she was neither clear-sighted nor accurate ; and in her attempts to describe morals, manners, and even facts, was unable to avoid the pitfalls of exaggeration.

CHAPTER III

THE GENERAL POST OFFICE

1834–1841

WHILE I was still learning my duty as an usher at Mr. Drury's school at Brussels, I was summoned to my clerkship in the London Post Office, and on my way passed through Bruges. I then saw my father and my brother Henry for the last time. A sadder household never was held together. They were all dying; except my mother, who would sit up night after night nursing the dying ones and writing novels the while,—so that there might be a decent roof for them to die under. Had she failed to write the novels, I do not know where the roof would have been found. It is now more than forty years ago, and looking back over so long a lapse of time I can tell the story, though it be the story of my own father and mother, of my own brother and sister, almost as coldly as I have often done some scene of intended pathos in fiction; but that scene was indeed full of pathos. I was then becoming alive to the blighted ambition of my father's life, and becoming alive also to the violence of the strain which my mother was enduring. But I could do nothing but go and leave them. There was something that comforted me in the idea that I need no longer be a burden,—a fallacious idea, as it soon proved. My salary was to be £90 a year, and on that I was to live in London.

keep up my character as a gentleman, and be
happy. That I should have thought this possible
at the age of nineteen, and should have been
delighted at being able to make the attempt, does
not surprise me now ; but that others should have
thought it possible, friends who knew something
of the world, does astonish me. A lad might have
done so, no doubt, or might do so even in these
days, who was properly looked after and kept under
control,—on whose behalf some law of life had been
laid down. Let him pay so much a week for his
board and lodging, so much for his clothes, so
much for his washing, and let him understand that
he has—shall we say ?—sixpence a day left for
pocket money and omnibuses, Any one making
the calculation will find the sixpence far too much.
No such calculation was made for me or by me.
It was supposed that a sufficient income had been
secured to me, and that I should live upon it as
other clerks lived.

But as yet the £90 a year was not secured to
me. On reaching London I went to my friend
Clayton Freeling, who was then secretary at the
Stamp Office, and was taken by him to the scene
of my future labours in St. Martin's le Grand.
Sir Francis Freeling was the secretary, but he was
greatly too high an official to be seen at first by a
new junior clerk. I was taken, therefore, to his
eldest son, Henry Freeling, who was the assistant
secretary, and by him I was examined as to my
fitness. The story of that examination is given
accurately in one of the opening chapters of a
novel written by me, called *The Three Clerks*. If
any reader of this memoir would refer to that
chapter and see how Charley Tudor was supposed

to have been admitted into the Internal Naviga-
tion Office, that reader will learn how Anthony
Trollope was actually admitted into the Secretary's
office of the General Post Office in 1834. I was
asked to copy some lines from the *Times* newspaper
with an old quill pen, and at once made a series of
blots and false spellings. ' That won't do, you
know,' said Henry Freeling to his brother Clayton.
Clayton, who was my friend, urged that I was ner-
vous, and asked that I might be allowed to do a bit
of writing at home and bring it as a sample on the
next day. I was then asked whether I was a pro-
ficient in arithmetic. What could I say ? I had
never learned the multiplication table, and had no
more idea of the rule of three than of conic sections.
' I know a little of it,' I said humbly, whereupon
I was sternly assured that on the morrow, should
I succeed in showing that my handwriting was
all that it ought to be, I should be examined as to
that little of arithmetic. If that little should not be
found to comprise a thorough knowledge of all the
ordinary rules, together with practised and quick
skill, my career in life could not be made at the
Post Office. Going down the main stairs of the
building,—stairs which have I believe been now
pulled down to make room for sorters and stampers,
—Clayton Freeling told me not to be too down-
hearted. I was myself inclined to think that I
had better go back to the school in Brussels. But
nevertheless I went to work, and under the
surveillance of my elder brother made a beautiful
transcript of four or five pages of Gibbon. With
a faltering heart I took these on the next day to
the office. With my caligraphy I was contented,
but was certain that I should come to the ground

C

among the figures.   But when I got to 'The Grand,' as we used to call our office in those days, from its site in St. Martin's le Grand, I was seated at a desk without any further reference to my competency.   No one condescended even to look at my beautiful penmanship.

That was the way in which candidates for the Civil Service were examined in my young days. It was at any rate the way in which I was examined. Since that time there has been a very great change indeed ;—and in some respects a great improvement.   But in regard to the absolute fitness of the young men selected for the public service, I doubt whether more harm has not been done than good.   And I think that good might have been done without the harm.   The rule of the present day is, that every place shall be open to public competition, and that it shall be given to the best among the comers.   I object to this, that at present there exists no known mode of learning who is best, and that the method employed has no tendency to elicit the best.   That method pretends only to decide who among a certain number of lads will best answer a string of questions, for the answering of which they are prepared by tutors, who have sprung up for the purpose since this fashion of election has been adopted. When it is decided in a family that a boy shall ' try the Civil Service ', he is made to undergo a certain amount of cramming.   But such treatment has, I maintain, no connection whatever with education.   The lad is no better fitted after it than he was before for the future work of his life. But his very success fills him with false ideas of his own educational standing, and so far unfits him.

And, by the plan now in vogue, it has come to
pass that no one is in truth responsible either for
the conduct, the manners, or even for the character
of the youth. The responsibility was perhaps
slight before ; but existed, and was on the increase.

There might have been,—in some future time of
still increased wisdom, there yet may be,—a
department established to test the fitness of
acolytes without recourse to the dangerous
optimism of competitive choice. I will not say
but that there should have been some one to
reject me,—though I will have the hardihood to
say that, had I been so rejected, the Civil Service
would have lost a valuable public servant. This
is a statement that will not, I think, be denied by
those who, after I am gone, may remember anything of my work. Lads, no doubt, should not be
admitted who have none of the small acquirements
that are wanted. Our offices should not be schools
in which writing and early lessons in geography,
arithmetic, or French should be learned. But all
that could be ascertained without the perils of
competitive examination.

The desire to insure the efficiency of the young
men selected, has not been the only object—
perhaps not the chief object—of those who have
yielded in this matter to the arguments of the
reformers. There had arisen in England a system
of patronage, under which it had become gradually
necessary for politicians to use their influence for
the purchase of political support. A member of
the House of Commons, holding office, who might
chance to have five clerkships to give away in a
year, found himself compelled to distribute them
among those who sent him to the House. In this

there was nothing pleasant to the distributer of patronage. Do away with the system altogether, and he would have as much chance of support as another. He bartered his patronage only because another did so also. The beggings, the refusings, the jealousies, the correspondence, were simply troublesome. Gentlemen in office were not therefore indisposed to rid themselves of the care of patronage. I have no doubt their hands are the cleaner and their hearts are the lighter ; but I do doubt whether the offices are on the whole better manned.

As what I now write will certainly never be read till I am dead, I may dare to say what no one now does dare to say in print,—though some of us whisper it occasionally into our friends' ears. There are places in life which can hardly be well filled except by ' Gentlemen '. The word is one the use of which almost subjects one to ignominy. If I say that a judge should be a gentleman, or a bishop, I am met with a scornful allusion to ' Nature's Gentlemen '. Were I to make such an assertion with reference to the House of Commons, nothing that I ever said again would receive the slightest attention. A man in public life could not do himself a greater injury than by saying in public that the commissions in the army or navy, or berths in the Civil Service, should be given exclusively to gentlemen. He would be defied to define the term,—and would fail should he attempt to do so. But he would know what he meant, and so very probably would they who defied him. It may be that the son of the butcher of the village shall become as well fitted for employments requiring gentle culture as the son of the parson.

Such is often the case. When such is the case, no one has been more prone to give the butcher's son all the welcome he has merited than I myself; but the chances are greatly in favour of the parson's son. The gates of the one class should be open to the other; but neither to the one class nor to the other can good be done by declaring that there are no gates, no barrier, no difference. The system of competitive examination is, I think, based on a supposition that there is no difference.

I got into my place without any examining. Looking back now, I think I can see with accuracy what was then the condition of my own mind and intelligence. Of things to be learned by lessons I knew almost less than could be supposed possible after the amount of schooling I had received. I could read neither French, Latin, nor Greek. I could speak no foreign language,—and I may as well say here as elsewhere that I never acquired the power of really talking French. I have been able to order my dinner and take a railway ticket, but never got much beyond that. Of the merest rudiments of the sciences I was completely ignorant. My handwriting was in truth wretched. My spelling was imperfect. There was no subject as to which examination would have been possible on which I could have gone through an examination otherwise than disgracefully. And yet I think I knew more than the average of young men of the same rank who began life at nineteen. I could have given a fuller list of the names of the poets of all countries, with their subjects and periods,—and probably of historians,—than many others; and had, perhaps, a more accurate idea of the manner in which my own country was governed.

I knew the names of all the Bishops, all the Judges, all the Heads of Colleges, and all the Cabinet Ministers,—not a very useful knowledge indeed, but one that had not been acquired without other matter which was more useful. I had read Shakespeare and Byron and Scott, and could talk about them. The music of the Miltonic line was familiar to me. I had already made up my mind that *Pride and Prejudice* was the best novel in the English language,—a palm which I only partially withdrew after a second reading of *Ivanhoe*, and did not completely bestow elsewhere till *Esmond* was written. And though I would occasionally break down in my spelling, I could write a letter. If I had a thing to say, I could so say it in written words that the readers should know what I meant, —a power which is by no means at the command of all those who come out from these competitive examinations with triumph. Early in life, at the age of fifteen, I had commenced the dangerous habit of keeping a journal, and this I maintained for ten years. The volumes remained in my possession unregarded—never looked at—till 1870, when I examined them, and, with many blushes, destroyed them. They convicted me of folly, ignorance, indiscretion, idleness, extravagance, and conceit. But they had habituated me to the rapid use of pen and ink, and taught me how to express myself with facility.

I will mention here another habit which had grown upon me from still earlier years,—which I myself often regarded with dismay when I thought of the hours devoted to it, but which, I suppose, must have tended to make me what I have been. As a boy, even as a child, I was thrown much upon myself. I have explained, when speaking of my school-days, how it came to pass that other boys would not play with me. I was therefore alone, and had to form my plays within myself. Play of some kind was necessary to me then, as it has always been. Study was not my bent, and I could not please myself by being all idle. Thus it came to pass that I was always going about with some castle in the air firmly built within my mind. Nor were these efforts in architecture spasmodic, or subject to constant change from day to day. For weeks, for months, if I remember rightly, from year to year, I would carry on the same tale, binding myself down to certain laws, to certain proportions, and proprieties, and unities. Nothing impossible was ever introduced,—nor even anything which, from outward circumstances, would seem to be violently improbable. I myself was of course my own hero. Such is a necessity of castle-building. But I never became a king, or a duke,—much less when my height and personal appearance were fixed could I be an Antinous, or six feet high. I never was a learned man, nor even a philosopher. But I was a very clever person, and beautiful young women used to be fond of me. And I strove to be kind of heart, and open of hand, and noble in thought, despising mean things ; and altogether I was a very much better fellow than I have ever succeeded in being since. This had been the occupation of my life for six or seven years before I went to the Post Office, and was by no means abandoned when I commenced my work. There can, I imagine, hardly be a more dangerous mental practice ; but I have often doubted whether, had it not been my

practice, I should ever have written a novel.
I learned in this way to maintain an interest in a
fictitious story, to dwell on a work created by my
own imagination, and to live in a world altogether
outside the world of my own material life.   In
after years I have done the same,—with this
difference, that I have discarded the hero of my
early dreams, and have been able to lay my own
identity aside.

I must certainly acknowlege that the first seven
years of my official life were neither creditable to
myself nor useful to the public service.   These
seven years were passed in London, and during
this period of my life it was my duty to be present
every morning at the office punctually at 10 a.m.
I think I commenced my quarrels with the
authorities there by having in my possession a
watch which was always ten minutes late.   I
know that I very soon achieved a character for
irregularity, and came to be regarded as a black
sheep by men around me who were not themselves,
I think, very good public servants.   From time
to time rumours reached me that if I did not take
care I should be dismissed ; especially one rumour
in my early days, through my dearly beloved
friend Mrs. Clayton Freeling,—who, as I write
this, is still living, and who, with tears in her eyes,
besought me to think of my mother.   That was
during the life of Sir Francis Freeling, who died,—
still in harness,—a little more than twelve months
after I joined the office.   And yet the old man
showed me signs of almost affectionate kindness,
writing to me with his own hand more than once
from his death-bed.

Sir Francis Freeling was followed at the Post

Office by Colonel Maberly, who certainly was not
my friend. I do not know that I deserved to find a
friend in my new master, but I think that a man with
better judgment would not have formed so low
an opinion of me as he did. Years have gone by,
and I can write now, and almost feel, without
anger ; but I can remember well the keenness of
my anguish when I was treated as though I were
unfit for any useful work. I did struggle—not to
do the work, for there was nothing which was not
easy without any struggling—but to show that
I was willing to do it. My bad character nevertheless stuck to me, and was not to be got rid of by
any efforts within my power. I do admit that I
was irregular. It was not considered to be much
in my favour that I could write letters—which was
mainly the work of our office—rapidly, correctly,
and to the purpose. The man who came at ten,
and who was always still at his desk at half-past
four, was preferred before me, though when at his
desk he might be less efficient. Such preference
was no doubt proper ; but, with a little encouragement, I also would have been punctual. I got
credit for nothing, and was reckless.

As it was, the conduct of some of us was very
bad. There was a comfortable sitting-room up-
stairs, devoted to the use of some one of our
number who in turn was required to remain in the
place all night. Hither one or two of us would
adjourn after lunch, and play *écarté* for an hour or
two. I do not know whether such ways are
possible now in our public offices. And here we
used to have suppers and card-parties at night—
great symposiums, with much smoking of tobacco ;
for in our part of the building there lived a whole

bevy of clerks. These were gentlemen whose duty it then was to make up and receive the foreign mails. I do not remember that they worked later or earlier than the other sorting-clerks ; but there was supposed to be something special in foreign letters, which required that the men who handled them should have minds undistracted by the outer world. Their salaries, too, were higher than those of their more homely brethren ; and they paid nothing for their lodgings. Consequently there was a somewhat fast set in those apartments, given to cards and to tobacco, who drank spirits and water in preference to tea. I was not one of them, but was a good deal with them.

I do not know that I should interest my readers by saying much of my Post Office experiences in those days. I was always on the eve of being dismissed, and yet was always striving to show how good a public servant I could become, if only a chance were given me. But the chance went the wrong way. On one occasion, in the performance of my duty, I had to put a private letter containing bank-notes on the secretary's table,—which letter I had duly opened, as it was not marked private. The letter was seen by the Colonel, but had not been moved by him when he left the room. On his return it was gone. In the meantime I had returned to the room, again in the performance of some duty. When the letter was missed I was sent for, and there I found the Colonel much moved about his letter, and a certain chief clerk, who, with a long face, was making suggestions as to the probable fate of the money. ' The letter has been taken,' said the Colonel, turning to me angrily, ' and, by G——! there has been nobody in the

room but you and I.'   As he spoke, he thundered
his fist down upon the table. 'Then,' said I, ' by
G——— ! you have taken it.' And I also thundered
my fist down ;—but, accidentally, not upon the
table. There was there a standing movable desk,
at which, I presume, it was the Colonel's habit to
write, and on this movable desk was a large bottle
full of ink. My fist unfortunately came on the
desk, and the ink at once flew up, covering the
Colonel's face and shirt-front. Then it was a sight
to see that senior clerk, as he seized a quire of
blotting-paper, and rushed to the aid of his
superior officer, striving to mop up the ink ; and
a sight also to see the Colonel, in his agony, hit
right out through the blotting-paper at that senior
clerk's unoffending stomach. At that moment
there came in the Colonel's private secretary, with
the letter and the money, and I was desired to go
back to my own room. This was an incident not
much in my favour, though I do not know that it
did me special harm.

I was always in trouble. A young woman down
in the country had taken it into her head that she
would like to marry me,—and a very foolish young
woman she must have been to entertain such a
wish. I need not tell that part of the story more at
length, otherwise than by protesting that no
young man in such a position was ever much less
to blame than I had been in this. The invitation
had come from her, and I had lacked the pluck to
give it a decided negative ; but I had left the house
within half an hour, going away without my dinner,
and had never returned to it. Then there was a
correspondence,—if that can be called a correspondence in which all the letters came from one

side.   At last the mother appeared at the Post
Office. My hair almost stands on my head now as
I remember the figure of the woman walking into
the big room in which I sat with six or seven other
clerks, having a large basket on her arm and an
immense bonnet on her head. The messenger had
vainly endeavoured to persuade her to remain in
the ante-room. She followed the man in, and
walking up the centre of the room, addressed me
in a loud voice : ' Anthony Trollope, when are you
going to marry my daughter ? ' We have all had
our worst moments, and that was one of my worst.
I lived through it, however, and did not marry
the young lady. These little incidents were all
against me in the office.

And then a certain other phase of my private
life crept into official view, and did me a damage.
As I shall explain just now, I rarely at this time
had any money wherewith to pay my bills.   In
this state of things a certain tailor had taken from
me an acceptance for, I think £12, which found
its way into the hands of a money-lender. With
that man, who lived in a little street near Mecklenburgh Square, I formed a most heart-rending but
a most intimate acquaintance. In cash I once
received from him £4. For that and for the original
amount of the tailor's bill, which grew monstrously
under repeated renewals, I paid ultimately something over £200. That is so common a story as to
be hardly worth the telling ; but the peculiarity
of this man was that he became so attached to
me as to visit me every day at my office. For a
long period he found it to be worth his while to
walk up those stone steps daily, and come and
stand behind my chair, whispering to me always

the same words : ' Now I wish you would be
punctual. If you only would be punctual,
I should like you to have anything you want.'
He was a little, clean, old man, who always wore
a high starched white cravat, inside which he
had a habit of twisting his chin as he uttered
his caution. When I remember the constant
persistency of his visits, I cannot but feel that he
was paid very badly for his time and trouble.
Those visits were very terrible, and can have hardly
been of service to me in the office.

Of one other misfortune which happened to me
in those days I must tell the tale. A junior clerk
in the secretary's office was always told off to
sleep upon the premises, and he was supposed to
be the presiding genius of the establishment when
the other members of the Secretary's department
had left the building. On an occasion when I was
still little more than a lad,—perhaps one-and-
twenty years old,—I was filling this responsible
position. At about seven in the evening word was
brought to me that the Queen of,—I think Saxony,
but I am sure it was a Queen,—wanted to see the
night mails sent out. At this time, when there
were many mail-coaches, this was a show, and
august visitors would sometimes come to see it.
But preparation was generally made beforehand,
and some pundit of the office would be at hand to
do the honours. On this occasion we were taken
by surprise, and there was no pundit. I therefore
gave the orders, and accompanied her Majesty
around the building, walking backwards, as I
conceived to be proper, and often in great peril
as I did so, up and down the stairs. I was, however, quite satisfied with my own manner of per-

forming an unaccustomed and most important duty. There were two old gentlemen with her Majesty, who, no doubt, were German barons, and an ancient baroness also. They had come and, when they had seen the sights, took their departure in two glass coaches. As they were preparing to go, I saw the two barons consulting together in deep whispers, and then as the result of that conversation one of them handed me half-a-crown ! That also was a bad moment.

I came up to town, as I said before, purporting to live a jolly life upon £90 per annum. I remained seven years in the General Post Office, and when I left it my income was £140. During the whole of this time I was hopelessly in debt. There were two intervals, amounting together to nearly two years, in which I lived with my mother, and therefore lived in comfort,—but even then I was overwhelmed with debt. She paid much for me,— paid all that I asked her to pay, and all that she could find out that I owed. But who in such a condition ever tells all and makes a clean breast of it ? The debts, of course, were not large, but I cannot think now how I could have lived, and sometimes have enjoyed life, with such a burden of duns as I endured. Sheriff's officers with uncanny documents, of which I never understood anything, were common attendants on me. And yet I do not remember that I was ever locked up, though I think I was twice a prisoner. In such emergencies some one paid for me. And now, looking back at it, I have to ask myself whether my youth was very wicked. I did no good in it ; but was there fair ground for expecting good from me ? When I reached London no mode of life was prepared for me,—no advice even given to me. I went into lodgings, and then had to dispose of my time. I belonged to no club, and knew very few friends who would receive me into their houses. In such a condition of life a young man should no doubt go home after his work, and spend the long hours of the evening in reading good books and drinking tea. A lad brought up by strict parents, and without having had even a view of gayer things, might perhaps do so. I had passed all my life at public schools, where I had seen gay things, but had never enjoyed them. Towards the good books and tea no training had been given me. There was no house in which I could habitually see a lady's face and hear a lady's voice. No allurement to decent respectability came in my way. It seems to me that in such circumstances the temptations of loose life will almost certainly prevail with a young man. Of course if the mind be strong enough, and the general stuff knitted together of sufficiently stern material, the temptations will not prevail. But such minds and such material are, I think, uncommon. The temptation at any rate prevailed with me.

I wonder how many young men fall utterly to pieces from being turned loose into London after the same fashion. Mine was, I think, of all phases of such life the most dangerous. The lad who is sent to mechanical work has longer hours, during which he is kept from danger, and has not generally been taught in his boyhood to anticipate pleasure. He looks for hard work and grinding circumstances. I certainly had enjoyed but little pleasure, but I had been among those who did enjoy it and were taught to expect it. And I had filled my mind with the ideas of such joys. And now, except during official hours, I was entirely without control,—without the influences of any decent household around me. I have said something of the comedy of such life, but it certainly had its tragic aspect. Turning it all over in my own mind, as I have constantly done in after years, the tragedy has always been uppermost. And so it was as the time was passing. Could there be any escape from such dirt ? I would ask myself ; and I always answered that there was no escape. The mode of life was itself wretched. I hated the office. I hated my work. More than all I hated my idleness. I had often told myself since I left school that the only career in life within my reach was that of an author, and the only mode of authorship open to me that of a writer of novels. In the journal which I read and destroyed a few years since, I found the matter argued out before I had been in the Post Office two years. Parliament was out of the question. I had not means to go to the Bar. In official life, such as that to which I had been introduced, there did not seem to be any opening for real success. Pens and paper I could command. Poetry I did not believe to be within my grasp. The drama, too, which I would fain have chosen, I believed to be above me. For history, biography, or essay writing I had not sufficient erudition. But I thought it possible that I might write a novel. I had resolved very early that in that shape must the attempt be made. But the months and years ran on, and no attempt was made. And yet no day was passed without thoughts of attempting, and a mental acknowledgment of the disgrace of postponing it. What reader will not understand the agony of remorse produced by such a condition of mind ? The gentleman from Mecklenburgh Square was always with me in the morning,—always angering me by his hateful presence,—but when the evening came I could make no struggle towards getting rid of him.

In those days I read a little, and did learn to read French and Latin. I made myself familiar with Horace, and became acquainted with the works of our own greatest poets. I had my strong enthusiasms, and remember throwing out of the window in Northumberland Street, where I lived, a volume of Johnson's *Lives of the Poets*, because he spoke sneeringly of *Lycidas*. That was Northumberland Street by the Marylebone Workhouse, on to the back-door of which establishment my room looked out—a most dreary abode, at which I fancy I must have almost ruined the good-natured lodging-house keeper by my constant inability to pay her what I owed.

How I got my daily bread I can hardly remember. But I do remember that I was often unable to get myself a dinner. Young men generally now have their meals provided for them. I kept house, as it were. Every day I had to find myself with the day's food. For my breakfast I could get some credit at the lodgings, though that credit would frequently come to an end. But for all that I had often breakfast to pay day by day ; and at your eating-house credit is not given. I had no friends on whom I could sponge regularly. Out on the Fulham Road I had an uncle, but his house was four miles from the Post Office, and almost as far from my own lodgings. Then came borrowings of money, sometimes absolute want, and almost constant misery.

Before I tell how it came about that I left this wretched life, I must say a word or two of the friendships which lessened its misfortunes. My earliest friend in life was John Merivale, with whom I had been at school at Sunbury and Harrow, and who was a nephew of my tutor, Harry Drury. Herman Merivale, who afterwards became my friend, was his brother, as is also Charles Merivale, the historian and Dean of Ely. I knew John when I was ten years old, and am happy to be able to say that he is going to dine with me one day this week. I hope I may not injure his character by stating that in those days I lived very much with him. He, too, was impecunious, but he had a home in London, and knew but little of the sort of penury which I endured. For more than fifty years he and I have been close friends. And then there was one W—— A——, whose misfortunes in life will not permit me to give his full name, but whom I dearly loved. He had been at Winchester and at Oxford, and at both places had fallen into trouble. He then became a schoolmaster,—or perhaps I had better say usher,—and finally he took orders. But he was unfortunate in all things, and died some years ago in poverty. He was most perverse; bashful to very fear of a lady's dress; unable to restrain himself in anything, but yet with a conscience that was always stinging him; a loving friend, though very quarrelsome; and, perhaps, of all men I have known, the most humorous. And he was entirely unconscious of his own humour. He did not know that he could so handle all matters as to create infinite amusement out of them. Poor W—— A——! To him there came no happy turning-point at which life loomed seriously on him, and then became prosperous.

W—— A——, Merivale, and I formed a little club, which we called the Tramp Society, and subjected to certain rules, in obedience to which we wandered on foot about the counties adjacent to London. Southampton was the furthest point we ever reached; but Buckinghamshire and Hertfordshire were more dear to us. These were the happiest hours of my then life—and perhaps not the least innocent, although we were frequently in peril from the village authorities whom we outraged. Not to pay for any conveyance, never to spend above five shillings a day, to obey all orders from the elected ruler of the hour (this enforced under heavy fines), were among our statutes. I would fain tell here some of our adventures:—how A—— enacted an escaped madman and we his pursuing keepers, and so got ourselves a lift in a cart, from which we ran away as we approached the lunatic asylum; how we were turned out of a little town at night, the townsfolk frightened by the loudness of our mirth; and how we once crept into a hayloft and were wakened in the dark morning by a pitchfork,—and how the juvenile owner of that pitchfork fled through the window when he heard the complaints of the wounded man! But the fun was the fun of W—— A——, and would cease to be fun as told by me.

It was during these years that John Tilley, who has now been for many years the permanent senior officer of the Post Office, married my sister,

whom he took with him into Cumberland, where
he was stationed as one of our surveyors. He has
been my friend for more than forty years; as has
also Peregrine Birch, a clerk in the House of Lords,
who married one of those daughters of Colonel
Grant who assisted us in the raid we made on the
goods which had been seized by the Sheriff's
officer at Harrow. These have been the oldest
and dearest friends of my life; and I can thank
God that three of them are still alive.

When I had been nearly seven years in the
Secretary's office of the Post Office, always hating
my position there, and yet always fearing that I
should be dismissed from it, there came a way of
escape. There had latterly been created in the service a new body of officers called surveyors' clerks.
There were at that time seven surveyors in England,
two in Scotland, and three in Ireland. To each of
these officers a clerk had been lately attached,
whose duty it was to travel about the country
under the surveyor's orders. There had been
much doubt among the young men in the office
whether they should or should not apply for these
places. The emoluments were good and the work
alluring; but there was at first supposed to be
something derogatory in the position. There was
a rumour that the first surveyor who got a clerk
sent the clerk out to fetch his beer; and that
another had called upon his clerk to send the linen
to the wash. There was, however, a conviction
that nothing could be worse than the berth of a
surveyor's clerk in Ireland. The clerks were all
appointed, however. To me it had not occurred
to ask for anything, nor would anything have
been given me. But after a while there came a

report from the far west of Ireland that the man sent there was absurdly incapable. It was probably thought then that none but a man absurdly incapable would go on such a mission to the west of Ireland. When the report reached the London office I was the first to read it. I was at that time in dire trouble, having debts on my head and quarrels with our Secretary-Colonel, and a full conviction that my life was taking me downwards to the lowest pits. So I went to the Colonel boldly, and volunteered for Ireland if he would send me. He was glad to be so rid of me, and I went. This happened in August 1841, when I was twenty-six years old. My salary in Ireland was to be but £100 a year; but I was to receive fifteen shillings a day for every day that I was away from home, and sixpence for every mile that I travelled. The same allowances were made in England; but at that time travelling in Ireland was done at half the English prices. My income in Ireland, after paying my expenses, became at once £400. This was the first good fortune of my life.

CHAPTER IV

IRELAND—MY FIRST TWO NOVELS

1841-1848

In the preceding pages I have given a short record of the first twenty-six years of my life, —years of suffering, disgrace, and inward remorse. I fear that my mode of telling will have left an idea simply of their absurdities; but in truth I was wretched,—sometimes almost unto death, and have often cursed the hour in which I was born. There had clung to me a feeling that I had been looked upon always as an evil, an encumbrance, a useless thing,—as a creature of whom those connected with him had to be ashamed. And I feel certain now that in my young days I was so regarded. Even my few friends who had found with me a certain capacity for enjoyment were half afraid of me. I acknowledge the weakness of a great desire to be loved,—of a strong wish to be popular with my associates. No child, no boy, no lad, no young man, had ever been less so. And I had been so poor; and so little able to bear poverty. But from the day on which I set my foot in Ireland all these evils went away from me. Since that time who has had a happier life than mine? Looking round upon all those I know, I cannot put my hand upon one. But all is not over yet. And, mindful of that, remembering how great is the agony of adversity, how crushing

the despondency of degradation, how susceptible
I am myself to the misery coming from contempt,—remembering also how quickly good things
may go and evil things come,—I am often again
tempted to hope, almost to pray, that the end
may be near. Things may be going well now—

'Sin aliquem infandum casum, Fortuna, minaris ;
Nunc, o nunc liceat crudelem abrumpere vitam.'

There is unhappiness so great that the very fear
of it is an alloy to happiness. I had then lost
my father, and sister, and brother,—have since
lost another sister and my mother ;—but I have
never as yet lost a wife or a child.

When I told my friends that I was going on
this mission to Ireland they shook their heads,
but said nothing to dissuade me. I think it must
have been evident to all who were my friends
that my life in London was not a success. My
mother and elder brother were at this time abroad,
and were not consulted ;—did not even know my
intention in time to protest against it. Indeed, I
consulted no one, except a dear old cousin, our
family lawyer, from whom I borrowed £200 to
help me out of England. He lent me the money,
and looked upon me with pitying eyes,—shaking
his head. 'After all you were right to go,' he
said to me when I paid him the money a few years
afterwards.

But nobody then thought I was right to go.
To become clerk to an Irish surveyor, in Connaught, with a salary of £100 a year, at twenty-six
years of age ! I did not think it right even myself,—
except that anything was right which would take
me away from the General Post Office and from
London.

My ideas of the duties I was to perform were
very vague, as were also my ideas of Ireland
generally. Hitherto I had passed my time, seated
at a desk, either writing letters myself, or copying
into books those which others had written. I had
never been called upon to do anything I was
unable or unfitted to do. I now understood that
in Ireland I was to be a deputy-inspector of country
post offices, and that among other things to be
inspected would be the postmasters' accounts !
But as no other person asked a question as to my
fitness for this work, it seemed unnecessary for me
to do so.

On the 15th of September 1841, I landed in
Dublin, without an acquaintance in the country,
and with only two or three letters of introduction
from a brother clerk in the Post Office. I had
learned to think that Ireland was a land flowing
with fun and whisky, in which irregularity was
the rule of life, and where broken heads were
looked upon as honourable badges. I was to live
at a place called Banagher, on the Shannon, which
I had heard of because of its having once been
conquered, though it had heretofore conquered
everything, including the devil. And from
Banagher my inspecting tours were to be made,
chiefly into Connaught, but also over a strip of
country eastwards, which would enable me occasionally to run up to Dublin. I went to a hotel
which was very dirty, and after dinner I ordered
some whisky punch. There was an excitement in
this, but when the punch was gone I was very
dull. It seemed so strange to be in a country in
which there was not a single individual whom
I had ever spoken to or ever seen. And it was to

be my destiny to go down into Connaught and adjust accounts,—the destiny of me who had never learned the multiplication table, or done a sum in long division !

On the next morning I called on the Secretary of the Irish Post Office, and learned from him that Colonel Maberly had sent a very bad character with me. He could not have sent a very good one ; but I felt a little hurt when I was informed by this new master that he had been informed that I was worthless, and must in all probability be dismissed. ' But,' said the new master, ' I shall judge you by your own merits.' From that time to the day on which I left the service, I never heard a word of censure, nor had many months passed before I found that my services were valued. Before a year was over, I had acquired the character of a thoroughly good public servant.

The time went very pleasantly. Some adventures I had ;—two of which I told in the *Tales of All Countries*, under the names of *The O'Conors of Castle Conor*, and *Father Giles of Ballymoy*. I will not swear to every detail in these stories, but the main purport of each is true. I could tell many others of the same nature, were this the place for them. I found that the surveyor to whom I had been sent kept a pack of hounds, and therefore I bought a hunter. I do not think he liked it, but he could not well complain. He never rode to hounds himself, but I did ; and then and thus began one of the great joys of my life. I have ever since been constant to the sport, having learned to love it with an affection which I cannot myself fathom or understand. Surely no man has laboured at it as I have done, or hunted under such drawbacks as to distances, money, and natural disadvantages. I am very heavy, very blind, have been—in reference to hunting—a poor man, and am now an old man. I have often had to travel all night outside a mail-coach, in order that I might hunt the next day. Nor have I ever been in truth a good horseman. And I have passed the greater part of my hunting life under the discipline of the Civil Service. But it has been for more than thirty years a duty to me to ride to hounds ; and I have performed that duty with a persistent energy. Nothing has ever been allowed to stand in the way of hunting,—neither the writing of books, nor the work of the Post Office, nor other pleasures. As regarded the Post Office, it soon seemed to be understood that I was to hunt, and when my services were re-transferred to England, no word of difficulty ever reached me about it. I have written on very many subjects, and on most of them with pleasure ; but on no subject with such delight as that on hunting. I have dragged it into many novels,—into too many no doubt,—but I have always felt myself deprived of a legitimate joy when the nature of the tale has not allowed me a hunting chapter. Perhaps that which gave me the greatest delight was the description of a run on a horse accidentally taken from another sportsman,—a circumstance which occurred to my dear friend Charles Buxton, who will be remembered as one of the members for Surrey.

It was altogether a very jolly life that I led in Ireland. I was always moving about, and soon found myself to be in pecuniary circumstances which were opulent in comparison with those of my past life. The Irish people did not murder me, nor did they even break my head. I soon found them to be good-humoured, clever—the working classes very much more intelligent than those of England—economical, and hospitable. We hear much of their spendthrift nature ; but extravagance is not the nature of an Irishman. He will count the shillings in a pound much more accurately than an Englishman, and will with much more certainty get twelve pennyworth from each. But they are perverse, irrational, and but little bound by the love of truth. I lived for many years among them—not finally leaving the country until 1859, and I had the means of studying their character.

I had not been a fortnight in Ireland before I was sent down to a little town in the far west of county Galway, to balance a defaulting postmaster's accounts, find out how much he owed, and report upon his capacity to pay. In these days such accounts are very simple. They adjust themselves from day to day, and a Post Office surveyor has nothing to do with them. At that time, though the sums dealt with were small, the forms of dealing with them were very intricate. I went to work, however, and made that defaulting postmaster teach me the use of those forms. I then succeeded in balancing the account, and had no difficulty whatever in reporting that he was altogether unable to pay his debt. Of course he was dismissed ;—but he had been a very useful man to me. I never had any further difficulty in the matter.

But my chief work was the investigating of complaints made by the public as to postal matters. The practice of the office was and is

to send one of its servants to the spot to see the
complainant and to inquire into the facts, when
the complainant is sufficiently energetic or sufficiently big to make himself well heard. A great
expense is often incurred for a very small object;
but the system works well on the whole as confidence is engendered, and a feeling is produced in
the country that the department has eyes of its
own and does keep them open. This employment
was very pleasant, and to me always easy, as it
required at its close no more than the writing of
a report. There were no accounts in this business,
no keeping of books, no necessary manipulation of
multitudinous forms. I must tell of one such
complaint and inquiry, because in its result I think
it was emblematic of many.

A gentleman in county Cavan had complained
most bitterly of the injury done to him by some
arrangement of the Post Office. The nature of
his grievance has no present significance; but it
was so unendurable that he had written many
letters, couched in the strongest language. He was
most irate, and indulged himself in that scorn
which is so easy to an angry mind. The place was
not in my district, but I was borrowed, being
young and strong, that I might remember the
edge of his personal wrath. It was mid-winter,
and I drove up to his house, a squire's country
seat, in the middle of a snow-storm, just as it was
becoming dark. I was on an open jaunting-car,
and was on my way from one little town to another,
the cause of his complaint having reference to
some mail conveyance between the two. I was
certainly very cold, and very wet, and very un-
comfortable when I entered his house. I was

admitted by a butler, but the gentleman himself
hurried into the hall. I at once began to explain
my business. ' God bless me ! ' he said, ' you are
wet through. John, get Mr. Trollope some brandy
and water,—very hot.' I was beginning my story
about the post again when he himself took off my
greatcoat, and suggested that I should go up to
my bedroom before I troubled myself with business.
' Bedroom ! ' I exclaimed. Then he assured me
that he would not turn a dog out on such a night
as that, and into a bedroom I was shown, having
first drank the brandy and water standing at
the drawing-room fire. When I came down I was
introduced to his daughter, and the three of us
went into dinner. I shall never forget his righteous
indignation when I again brought up the postal
question on the departure of the young lady.
Was I such a Goth as to contaminate wine with
business ? So I drank my wine, and then heard
the young lady sing while her father slept in his
armchair. I spent a very pleasant evening, but
my host was too sleepy to hear anything about
the Post Office that night. It was absolutely
necessary that I should go away the next morning
after breakfast, and I explained that the matter
must be discussed then. He shook his head and
wrung his hands in unmistakable disgust,—almost
in despair. ' But what am I to say in my report ? '
I asked. ' Anything you please,' he said. ' Don't
spare me, if you want an excuse for yourself.
Here I sit all the day,—with nothing to do ; and
I like writing letters.' I did report that Mr. ——
was now quite satisfied with the postal arrangement
of his district ; and I felt a soft regret that I should
have robbed my friend of his occupation. Perhaps

he was able to take up the Poor Law Board, or to attack the Excise. At the Post Office nothing more was heard from him.

I went on with the hunting surveyor at Banagher for three years, during which, at Kingstown, the watering-place near Dublin, I met Rose Heseltine, the lady who has since become my wife. The engagement took place when I had been just one year in Ireland; but there was still a delay of two years before we could be married. She had no fortune, nor had I any income beyond that which came from the Post Office; and there were still a few debts, which would have been paid off no doubt sooner, but for that purchase of the horse. When I had been nearly three years in Ireland we were married on the 11th of June 1844;—and perhaps I ought to name that happy day as the commencement of my better life, rather than the day on which I first landed in Ireland.

For though during these three years I had been jolly enough, I had not been altogether happy. The hunting, the whisky punch, the rattling Irish life,—of which I could write a volume of stories were this the place to tell them,—were continually driving from my mind the still cherished determination to become a writer of novels. When I reached Ireland I had never put pen to paper; nor had I done so when I became engaged. And when I was married, being then twenty-nine, I had only written the first volume of my first work. This constant putting off of the day of work was a great sorrow to me. I certainly had not been idle in my new berth. I had learned my work, so that every one concerned knew that it was safe in my hands; and I held a position altogether the reverse of that in which I was always trembling while I remained in London. But that did not suffice,—did not nearly suffice. I still felt that there might be a career before me, if I could only bring myself to begin the work. I do not think I much doubted my own intellectual sufficiency for the writing of a readable novel. What I did doubt was my own industry, and the chances of the market.

The vigour necessary to prosecute two professions at the same time is not given to every one, and it was only lately that I had found the vigour necessary for one. There must be early hours, and I had not as yet learned to love early hours. I was still, indeed, a young man; but hardly young enough to trust myself to find the power to alter the habits of my life. And I had heard of the difficulties of publishing,—a subject of which I shall have to say much should I ever bring this memoir to a close. I had dealt already with publishers on my mother's behalf, and knew that many a tyro who could fill a manuscript lacked the power to put his matter before the public;— and I knew, too, that when the matter was printed, how little had then been done towards the winning of the battle! I had already learned that many a book—many a good book—

> ' is born to blush unseen,
> And waste its sweetness on the desert air.'

But still the purpose was strong within me, and the first effort was made after the following fashion. I was located at a little town called Drumsna, or rather village, in the county Leitrim.

where the postmaster had come to some sorrow
about his money; and my friend John Merivale
was staying with me for a day or two. As we
were taking a walk in that most uninteresting
country, we turned up through a deserted gate-
way, along a weedy, grass-grown avenue, till we
came to the modern ruins of a country house. It
was one of the most melancholy spots I ever
visited. I will not describe it here, because I have
done so in the first chapter of my first novel.
We wandered about the place, suggesting to each
other causes for the misery we saw there, and while
I was still among the ruined walls and decayed
beams I fabricated the plot of *The Macdermots of
Ballycloran,* As to the plot itself, I do not know
that I ever made one so good,—or, at any rate, one
so susceptible of pathos. I am aware that I broke
down in the telling, not having yet studied the
art. Nevertheless, *The Macdermots* is a good novel,
and worth reading by any one who wishes to
understand what Irish life was before the potato
disease, the famine, and the Encumbered Estates
Bill.

When my friend left me, I set to work and
wrote the first chapter or two. Up to this time
I had continued that practice of castle-building
of which I have spoken; but now the castle I
built was among the ruins of that old house. The
book, however, hung with me. It was only now
and then that I found either time or energy for
a few pages. I commenced the book in September
1843, and had only written a volume when I was
married in June 1844.

My marriage was like the marriage of other
people, and of no special interest to any one

except my wife and me. It took place at Rotherham in Yorkshire, where her father was the manager of a bank. We were not very rich, having about £400 a year on which to live. Many people would say that we were two fools to encounter such poverty together. I can only reply that since that day I have never been without money in my pocket, and that I soon acquired the means of paying what I owed. Nevertheless, more than twelve years had to pass over our heads before I received any payment for any literary work which afforded an appreciable increase to our income.

Immediately after our marriage, I left the west of Ireland and the hunting surveyor, and joined another in the south. It was a better district, and I was enabled to live at Clonmel, a town of some importance, instead of at Banagher, which is little more than a village. I had not felt myself to be comfortable in my old residence as a married man. On my arrival there as a bachelor I had been received most kindly, but when I brought my English wife I fancied that there was a feeling that I had behaved badly to Ireland generally. When a young man has been received hospitably in an Irish circle, I will not say that it is expected of him that he should marry some young lady in that society;—but it certainly is expected of him that he shall not marry any young lady out of it. I had given offence, and I was made to feel it.

There has taken place a great change in Ireland since the days in which I lived at Banagher, and a change so much for the better, that I have sometimes wondered at the obduracy with which people have spoken of the permanent ill condition

of the country. Wages are now nearly double
what they were then. The Post Office at any rate
is paying almost double for its rural labour,—
9s. a week when it used to pay 5s., and 12s. a week
when it used to pay 7s. Banks have sprung up
in almost every village. Rents are paid with more
than English punctuality. And the religious
enmity between the classes, though it is not yet
dead, is dying out. Soon after I reached Banagher
in 1841, I dined one evening with a Roman
Catholic. I was informed next day by a Protestant
gentleman who had been very hospitable to me
that I must choose my party. I could not sit both
at Protestant and Catholic tables. Such a caution
would now be impossible in any part of Ireland.
Home-rule no doubt is a nuisance,—and especially
a nuisance because the professors of the doctrine
do not at all believe it themselves. There are
probably no other twenty men in England or
Ireland who would be so utterly dumfounded and
prostrated were Home-rule to have its way as
the twenty Irish members who profess to support
it in the House of Commons. But it is not to be
expected that nuisances such as these should be
abolished at a blow. Home-rule is at any rate
better and more easily managed than the rebellion
at the close of the last century; it is better than
the treachery of the Union; less troublesome
than O'Connell's monster meetings; less dangerous
than Smith O'Brien and the battle of the cabbage-
garden at Ballingary; and very much less bloody
than Fenianism. The descent from O'Connell to
Mr. Butt has been the natural declension of a
political disease, which we had no right to hope
would be cured by any one remedy.

When I had been married a year my first novel was finished. In July 1845 I took it with me to the north of England, and intrusted the MS. to my mother to do with it the best she could among the publishers in London. No one had read it but my wife; nor, as far as I am aware, has any other friend of mine ever read a word of my writing before it was printed. She, I think, has so read almost everything, to my very great advantage in matters of taste. I am sure I have never asked a friend to read a line; nor have I ever read a word of my own writing aloud,—even to her. With one exception,—which shall be mentioned as I come to it,—I have never consulted a friend as to a plot, or spoken to any one of the work I have been doing. My first manuscript I gave up to my mother, agreeing with her that it would be as well that she should not look at it before she gave it to a publisher. I knew that she did not give me credit for the sort of cleverness necessary for such work. I could see in the faces and hear in the voices of those of my friends who were around me at the house in Cumberland— my mother, my sister, my brother-in-law, and, I think, my brother—that they had not expected me to come out as one of the family authors. There were three or four in the field before me, and it seemed to be almost absurd that another should wish to add himself to the number. My father had written much—those long ecclesiastical descriptions—quite unsuccessfully. My mother had become one of the popular authors of the day. My brother had commenced, and had been fairly well paid for his work. My sister, Mrs. Tilley, had also written a novel, which was at the time in manuscript—which was published afterwards without her name, and was called *Chollerton*. I could perceive that this attempt of mine was felt to be an unfortunate aggravation of the disease.

My mother however did the best she could for me, and soon reported that Mr. Newby of Mortimer Street was to publish the book. It was to be printed at his expense, and he was to give me half the profits. Half the profits! Many a young author expects much from such an undertaking. I can with truth declare that I expected nothing. And I got nothing. Nor did I expect fame, or even acknowledgment. I was sure that the book would fail, and it did fail most absolutely. I never heard of a person reading it in those days. If there was any notice taken of it by any critic of the day, I did not see it. I never asked any questions about it, or wrote a single letter on the subject to the publisher. I have Mr. Newby's agreement with me, in duplicate, and one or two preliminary notes; but beyond that I did not have a word from Mr. Newby. I am sure that he did not wrong me in that he paid me nothing. It is probable that he did not sell fifty copies of the work;—but of what he did sell he gave me no account.

I do not remember that I felt in any way disappointed or hurt. I am quite sure that no word of complaint passed my lips. I think I may say that after the publication I never said a word about the book, even to my wife. The fact that I had written and published it, and that I was writing another, did not in the least interfere with my life or with my determination to make the best I could of the Post Office. In Ireland, I think that no one knew that I had written a novel. But I went on writing. *The Macdermots* was published in 1847, and *The Kellys and the O'Kellys* followed in 1848. I changed my publisher, but did not change my fortune. This second Irish story was sent into the world by Mr. Colburn, who had long been my mother's publisher, who reigned in Great Marlborough Street, and I believe created the business which is now carried on by Messrs. Hurst & Blackett. He had previously been in partnership with Mr. Bentley in New Burlington Street. I made the same agreement as before as to half profits, and with precisely the same results. The book was not only not read, but was never heard of,—at any rate in Ireland. And yet it is a good Irish story, much inferior to *The Macdermots* as to plot, but superior in the mode of telling. Again I held my tongue, and not only said nothing but felt nothing. Any success would, I think, have carried me off my legs, but I was altogether prepared for failure. Though I thoroughly enjoyed the writing of these books, I did not imagine, when the time came for publishing them, that any one would condescend to read them.

But in reference to *The O'Kellys* there arose a circumstance which set my mind to work on a subject which has exercised it much ever since. I made my first acquaintance with criticism. A dear friend of mine to whom the book had been sent—as have all my books—wrote me word to Ireland that he had been dining at some club with a man high in authority among the gods of the *Times* newspaper, and that this special god had almost promised that *The O'Kellys* should be noticed in that most influential of ' organs '. The information moved me very much; but it set me thinking whether the notice, should it ever appear, would not have been more valuable, at any rate more honest, if it had been produced by other means;—if for instance the writer of the notice had been instigated by the merits or demerits of the book instead of by the friendship of a friend. And I made up my mind then that, should I continue this trade of authorship, I would have no dealings with any critic on my own behalf. I would neither ask for nor deplore criticism, nor would I ever thank a critic for praise, or quarrel with him, even in my own heart, for censure. To this rule I have adhered with absolute strictness, and this rule I would recommend to all young authors. What can be got by touting among the critics is never worth the ignominy. The same may of course be said of all things acquired by ignominious means. But in this matter it is so easy to fall into the dirt. *Facilis descensus Averni.* There seems to be but little fault in suggesting to a friend that a few words in this or that journal would be of service. But any praise so obtained must be an injustice to the public, for whose instruction, and not for the sustentation of the author, such notices are intended. And from such mild suggestion the descent to crawling at the critic's feet, to the sending of presents, and at last to a mutual understanding between critics and criticised, is only too easy. Other evils follow, for the denouncing of which this is hardly the place;—though I trust I may find such place before my work is finished. I took no notice of my friend's letter, but I was not the less careful in watching *The Times.* At last the review came,—a real review in

The Times. I learned it by heart, and can now give, if not the words, the exact purport. ' Of *The Kellys and the O'Kellys* we may say what the master said to his footman, when the man complained of the constant supply of legs of mutton on the kitchen table. "Well, John, legs of mutton are good substantial food;" and we may say also what John replied: "Substantial, sir;—yes, they are substantial, but a little coarse."' That was the review, and even that did not sell the book!

From Mr. Colburn I did receive an account, showing that 375 copies of the book had been printed, that 140 had been sold,—to those, I presume, who liked substantial food though it was coarse,—and that he had incurred a loss of £63, 10*s.* 1½*d.* The truth of the account I never for a moment doubted; nor did I doubt the wisdom of the advice given to me in the following letter, though I never thought of obeying it—

' GREAT MARLBOROUGH STREET,
November 11, 1848.

' MY DEAR SIR,—I am sorry to say that absence from town and other circumstances have prevented me from earlier inquiring into the results of the sale of *The Kellys and the O'Kellys*, with which the greatest efforts have been used, but in vain. The sale has been, I regret to say, so small that the loss upon the publication is very considerable; and it appears clear to me that, although in consequence of the great number of novels that are published, the sale of each, with some few exceptions, must be small, yet it is evident that readers do not like novels on Irish subjects as well as on others. Thus you will perceive it is impossible for me to give any encouragement to you to proceed in novel-writing.

'As, however, I understand you have nearly finished the novel *La Vendée*, perhaps you will favour me with a sight of it when convenient.— I remain, &c. &c.   H. COLBURN.'

This, though not strictly logical, was a rational letter, telling a plain truth plainly. I did not like the assurance that 'the greatest efforts had been used', thinking that any efforts which might be made for the popularity of a book ought to have come from the author ;—but I took in good part Mr. Colburn's assurance that he could not encourage me in the career I had commenced I would have bet twenty to one against my own success. But by continuing I could lose only pen and paper ; and if the one chance in twenty did turn up in my favour, then how much might I win !

CHAPTER V

MY FIRST SUCCESS

1849–1855

I HAD at once gone to work on a third novel, and had nearly completed it, when I was informed of the absolute failure of the former. I find however that the agreement for its publication was not made till 1850, by which time I imagine that Mr. Colburn must have forgotten the disastrous result of *The O'Kellys*, as he thereby agrees to give me £20 down for my 'new historical novel, to be called *La Vendée*'. He agreed also to pay me £30 more when he had sold 350 copies, and £50 more should he sell 450 within six months. I got my £20, and then heard no more of *La Vendée*, not even receiving any account. Perhaps the historical title had appeared more alluring to him than an Irish subject; though it was not long afterwards that I received a warning from the very same house of business against historical novels,—as I will tell at length when the proper time comes.

I have no doubt that the result of the sale of this story was no better than that of the two that had gone before. I asked no questions, however, and to this day have received no information. The story is certainly inferior to those which had gone before;—chiefly because I knew accurately the life of the people in Ireland, and knew, in truth, nothing of life in the La Vendée country, and also because the facts of the present time came more within the limits of my powers of story-telling than those of past years. But I read the book the other day, and am not ashamed of it. The conception as to the feeling of the people is, I think, true; the characters are distinct; and the tale is not dull. As far as I can remember, this morsel of criticism is the only one that was ever written on the book.

I had, however, received £20. Alas! alas! years were to roll by before I should earn by my pen another shilling. And, indeed, I was well aware that I had not earned that; but that the money had been 'talked out of' the worthy publisher by the earnestness of my brother, who made the bargain for me. I have known very much of publishers and have been surprised by much in their mode of business,—by the apparent lavishness and by the apparent hardness to authors in the same men;—but by nothing so much as by the ease with which they can occasionally be persuaded to throw away small sums of money. If you will only make the payment future instead of present, you may generally twist a few pounds in your own or your client's favour. 'You might as well promise her £20. This day six months will do very well.' The publisher, though he knows that the money will never come back to him, thinks it worth his while to rid himself of your importunity at so cheap a price.

But while I was writing La Vendée I made a literary attempt in another direction. In 1847 and 1848 there had come upon Ireland the desolation and destruction, first of the famine, and then of the pestilence which succeeded the famine. It was my duty at that time to be travelling constantly in those parts of Ireland in which the misery and troubles thence arising were, perhaps, at their worst. The western parts of Cork, Kerry, and Clare were pre-eminently unfortunate. The efforts—I may say the successful efforts—made by the Government to stay the hands of death will still be in the remembrance of many:—how Sir Robert Peel was instigated to repeal the Corn Laws; and how, subsequently, Lord John Russell took measures for employing the people, and supplying the country with Indian corn. The expediency of these latter measures was questioned by many. The people themselves wished of course to be fed without working; and the gentry, who were mainly responsible for the rates, were disposed to think that the management of affairs was taken too much out of their own hands. My mind at the time was busy with the matter, and, thinking that the Government was right, I was inclined to defend them as far as my small powers went. S. G. O. (Lord Sydney Godolphin Osborne) was at that time denouncing the Irish scheme of the Administration in the *Times*, using very strong language,—as those who remember his style will know. I fancied then—as I still think—that I understood the country much better than he did; and I was anxious to show that the steps taken for mitigating the terrible evil of the times were the best which the Minister of the day could have adopted. In 1848 I was in London, and, full of my purpose, I presented myself to Mr. John

Forster—who has since been an intimate and valued friend—but who was at that time the editor of the *Examiner*. I think that that portion of the literary world which understands the fabrication of newspapers will admit that neither before his time, nor since, has there been a more capable editor of a weekly newspaper. As a literary man, he was not without his faults. That which the cabman is reported to have said of him before the magistrate is quite true. He was always ' an arbitrary cove '. As a critic, he belonged to the school of Bentley and Gifford,—who would always bray in a literary mortar all critics who disagreed from them, as though such disagreement were a personal offence requiring personal castigation. But that very eagerness made him a good editor. Into whatever he did he put his very heart and soul. During his time the *Examiner* was almost all that a Liberal weekly paper should be. So to John Forster I went, and was shown into that room in Lincoln's Inn Fields in which, some three or four years earlier, Dickens had given that reading of which there is an illustration with portraits in the second volume of his life.

At this time I knew no literary men. A few I had met when living with my mother, but that had been now so long ago that all such acquaintance had died out. I knew who they were as far as a man could get such knowledge from the papers of the day, and felt myself as in part belonging to the guild, through my mother, and in some degree by my own unsuccessful efforts. But it was not probable that any one would admit my claim ;—nor on this occasion did I make any claim. I stated my name and official position, and the fact that opportunities had been given me of seeing the poor-houses in Ireland, and of making myself acquainted with the circumstances of the time. Would a series of letters on the subject be accepted by the *Examiner*? The great man, who loomed very large to me, was pleased to say that if the letters should recommend themselves by their style and matter, if they were not too long, and if—every reader will know how on such occasions an editor will guard himself— if this and if that, they should be favourably entertained. They were favourably entertained,— if printing and publication be favourable entertainment. But I heard no more of them. The world in Ireland did not declare that the Government had at last been adequately defended, nor did the treasurer of the *Examiner* send me a cheque in return.

Whether there ought to have been a cheque I do not even yet know. A man who writes a single letter to a newspaper of course is not paid for it,—nor for any number of letters on some point personal to himself. I have since written sets of letters to newspapers, and have been paid for them; but then I have bargained for a price. On this occasion I had hopes; but they never ran high, and I was not much disappointed. I have no copy now of those letters, and could not refer to them without much trouble; nor do I remember what I said. But I know that I did my best in writing them.

When my historical novel failed, as completely as had its predecessors, the two Irish novels, I began to ask myself whether, after all, that was my proper line. I had never thought of questioning the justice of the verdict expressed against me. The idea that I was the unfortunate owner of unappreciated genius never troubled me. I did not look at the books after they were published, feeling sure that they had been, as it were, damned with good reason. But still I was clear in my mind that I would not lay down my pen. Then and therefore I determined to change my hand, and to attempt a play. I did attempt the play, and in 1850 I wrote a comedy, partly in blank verse, and partly in prose, called *The Noble Jilt*. The plot I afterwards used in a novel called *Can You Forgive Her?* I believe that I did give the best of my intellect to the play, and I must own that when it was completed it pleased me much. I copied it, and re-copied it, touching it here and touching it there, and then sent it to my very old friend, George Bartley the actor, who had when I was in London been stage-manager of one of the great theatres, and who would I thought, for my own sake and for my mother's, give me the full benefit of his professional experience.

I have now before me the letter which he wrote to me,—a letter which I have read a score of times. It was altogether condemnatory. 'When I commenced,' he said, 'I had great hopes of your production. I did not think it opened dramatically, but that might have been remedied.' I knew then that it was all over. But, as my old friend warmed to the subject, the criticism became stronger and stronger, till my ears tingled. At last came the fatal blow. 'As to the character of your heroine, I felt at a loss how to describe it, but you have done it for me in the last speech of Madame Brudo.' Madame Brudo was the heroine's aunt.

' " Margaret, my child, never play the jilt again ;
'tis a most unbecoming character. Play it with
what skill you will, it meets but little sympathy."
And this, be assured, would be its effect upon an
audience. So that I must reluctantly add that, had
I been still a manager, *The Noble Jilt* is not a play
I could have recommended for production.' This
was a blow that I did feel. The neglect of a book
is a disagreeable fact which grows upon an author
by degrees. There is no special moment of agony,—
no stunning violence of condemnation. But a piece
of criticism such as this, from a friend, and from
a man undoubtedly capable of forming an opinion,
was a blow in the face ! But I accepted the
judgment loyally, and said not a word on the
subject to any one. I merely showed the letter
to my wife, declaring my conviction, that it must
be taken as gospel. And as critical gospel it has
since been accepted. In later days I have more
than once read the play, and I know that he was
right. The dialogue, however, I think to be good,
and I doubt whether some of the scenes be not
the brightest and best work I ever did.

Just at this time another literary project loomed
before my eyes, and for six or eight months had
considerable size. I was introduced to Mr. John
Murray, and proposed to him to write a handbook
for Ireland. I explained to him that I knew the
country better than most other people, perhaps
better than any other person, and could do it
well. He asked me to make a trial of my skill,
and to send him a certain number of pages, undertaking to give me an answer within a fortnight
after he should have received my work. I came
back to Ireland, and for some weeks I laboured

very hard. I 'did' the city of Dublin, and the county of Kerry, in which lies the lake scenery of Killarney; and I 'did' the route from Dublin to Killarney, altogether completing nearly a quarter of the proposed volume. The roll of MS. was sent to Albemarle Street,—but was never opened. At the expiration of nine months from the date on which it reached that time-honoured spot it was returned without a word, in answer to a very angry letter from myself. I insisted on having back my property,—and got it. I need hardly say that my property has never been of the slightest use to me. In all honesty I think that had he been less dilatory, John Murray would have got a very good Irish Guide at a cheap rate.

Early in 1851 I was sent upon a job of special official work, which for two years so completely absorbed my time that I was able to write nothing. A plan was formed for extending the rural delivery of letters, and for adjusting the work, which up to that time had been done in a very irregular manner. A country letter-carrier would be sent in one direction in which there were but few letters to be delivered, the arrangement having originated probably at the request of some influential person, while in another direction there was no letter-carrier because no influential person had exerted himself. It was intended to set this right throughout England, Ireland, and Scotland; and I quickly did the work in the Irish district to which I was attached. I was then invited to do the same in a portion of England, and I spent two of the happiest years of my life at the task. I began in Devonshire; and visited, I think I may say, every nook in that county, in Cornwall, Somerset-

shire, the greater part of Dorsetshire, the Channel
Islands, part of Oxfordshire, Wiltshire, Gloucester-
shire, Worcestershire, Herefordshire, Monmouth-
shire, and the six southern Welsh counties. In
this way I had an opportunity of seeing a considerable portion of Great Britain, with a minute-
ness which few have enjoyed. And I did my
business after a fashion in which no other official
man has worked, at least for many years. I went
almost everywhere on horseback. I had two
hunters of my own, and here and there, where
I could, I hired a third horse. I had an Irish
groom with me,—an old man, who has now been
in my service for thirty-five years ; and in this
manner I saw almost every house—I think I may
say every house of importance—in this large
district. The object was to create a postal net-
work which should catch all recipients of letters.
In France it was, and I suppose still is, the practice
to deliver every letter. Wherever the man may
live to whom a letter is addressed, it is the duty
of some letter-carrier to take that letter to his
house, sooner or later. But this, of course, must
be done slowly. With us a delivery much delayed
was thought to be worse than none at all. In some
places we did establish posts three times a week
and perhaps occasionally twice a week ; but such
halting arrangements were considered to be
objectionable, and we were bound down by
a salutary law as to expense, which came from
our masters at the Treasury. We were not
allowed to establish any messenger's walk on
which a sufficient number of letters would not be
delivered to pay the man's wages, counted at
a halfpenny a letter. But then the counting was

in our own hands, and an enterprising official
might be sanguine in his figures. I think I was
sanguine. I did not prepare false accounts; but
I fear that the postmasters and clerks who absolutely had the country to do became aware that
I was anxious for good results. It is amusing to
watch how a passion will grow upon a man.
During those two years it was the ambition of my
life to cover the country with rural letter-carriers.
I do not remember that in any case a rural post
proposed by me was negatived by the authorities;
but I fear that some of them broke down afterwards as being too poor, or because, in my anxiety
to include this house and that, I had sent the men
too far afield. Our law was that a man should
not be required to walk more than sixteen miles
a day. Had the work to be done been all on
a measured road, there would have been no need
for doubt as to the distances. But my letter-
carriers went here and there across the fields.
It was my special delight to take them by all
short cuts; and as I measured on horseback the
short cuts which they would have to make on
foot, perhaps I was sometimes a little unjust to
them.

All this I did on horseback, riding on an average
forty miles a day. I was paid sixpence a mile
for the distance travelled, and it was necessary
that I should at any rate travel enough to pay
for my equipage. This I did, and got my hunting
out of it also. I have often surprised some
small country postmaster, who had never seen or
heard of me before, by coming down upon him
at nine in the morning, with a red coat and boots
and breeches, and interrogating him as to the

disposal of every letter which came into his office. And in the same guise I would ride up to farm-houses, or parsonages, or other lone residences about the country, and ask the people how they got their letters, at what hour, and especially whether they were delivered free or at a certain charge. For a habit had crept into use, which came to be, in my eyes, at that time, the one sin for which there was no pardon, in accordance with which these rural letter-carriers used to charge a penny a letter, alleging that the house was out of their beat, and that they must be paid for their extra work. I think that I did stamp out that evil. In all these visits I was, in truth, a beneficent angel to the public, bringing every-where with me an earlier, cheaper, and much more regular delivery of letters. But not unfrequently the angelic nature of my mission was imperfectly understood. I was perhaps a little in a hurry to get on, and did not allow as much time as was necessary to explain to the wondering mistress of the house, or to an open-mouthed farmer, why it was that a man arrayed for hunting asked so many questions which might be considered impertinent, as applying to his or her private affairs. ' Good morning, sir. I have just called to ask a few questions. I am a surveyor of the Post Office. How do you get your letters ? As I am a little in a hurry, perhaps you can explain at once.' Then I would take out my pencil and note-book, and wait for information. And in fact there was no other way in which the truth could be ascertained. Unless I came down suddenly as a summer's storm upon them, the very people who were robbed by our messengers would not confess the robbery, fearing the ill-will of the men. It was necessary to startle them into the revelations which I required them to make for their own good. And I did startle them. I became thoroughly used to it, and soon lost my native bashfulness ;—but sometimes my visits astonished the retiring inhabitants of country houses. I did, however, do my work, and can look back upon what I did with thorough satisfaction. I was altogether in earnest ; and I believe that many a farmer now has his letters brought daily to his house free of charge, who but for me would still have had to send to the post-town for them twice a week, or to have paid a man for bringing them irregularly to his door.

This work took up my time so completely, and entailed upon me so great an amount of writing, that I was in fact unable to do any literary work. From day to day I thought of it, still purporting to make another effort, and often turning over in my head some fragment of a plot which had occurred to me. But the day did not come in which I could sit down with pen and paper and begin another novel. For, after all, what could it be but a novel ? The play had failed more absolutely than the novels, for the novels had attained the honour of print. The cause of this pressure of official work lay, not in the demands of the General Post Office, which more than once expressed itself as astonished by my celerity, but in the necessity which was incumbent on me to travel miles enough to pay for my horses, and upon the amount of correspondence, returns, figures, and reports which such an amount of daily travelling brought with it. I may boast that the

work was done very quickly and very thoroughly,—
with no fault but an over-eagerness to extend
postal arrangements far and wide.

In the course of the job I visited Salisbury, and
whilst wandering there one mid-summer evening
round the purlieus of the cathedral I conceived
the story of *The Warden*,—from whence came that
series of novels of which Barchester, with its
bishops, deans, and archdeacon, was the central
site. I may as well declare at once that no one
at their commencement could have had less
reason than myself to presume himself to be able
to write about clergymen. I have been often
asked in what period of my early life I had lived
so long in a cathedral city as to have become
intimate with the ways of a Close. I never lived
in any cathedral city,—except London, never knew
anything of any Close, and at that time had.
enjoyed no peculiar intimacy with any clergyman.
My archdeacon, who has been said to be life-like,
and for whom I confess that I have all a parent's
fond affection, was, I think, the simple result of
an effort of my moral consciousness. It was such
as that, in my opinion, that an archdeacon should
be,—or, at any rate, would be with such advantages
as an archdeacon might have ; and lo ! an archdeacon was produced, who has been declared by
competent authorities to be a real archdeacon
down to the very ground. And yet, as far as I can
remember, I had not then even spoken to an
archdeacon. I have felt the compliment to be
very great. The archdeacon came whole from
my brain after this fashion ;—but in writing about
clergymen generally, I had to pick up as I went
whatever I might know or pretend to know about

them. But my first idea had no reference to
clergymen in general. I had been struck by two
opposite evils,—or what seemed to me to be evils,—
and with an absence of all art-judgment in such
matters, I thought that I might be able to expose
them, or rather to describe them, both in one
and the same tale. The first evil was the possession
by the Church of certain funds and endowments
which had been intended for charitable purposes,
but which had been allowed to become incomes
for idle Church dignitaries. There had been more
than one such case brought to public notice at the
time, in which there seemed to have been an
egregious malversation of charitable purposes.
The second evil was its very opposite. Though
I had been much struck by the injustice above
described, I had also often been angered by the
undeserved severity of the newspapers towards
the recipients of such incomes, who could hardly
be considered to be the chief sinners in the matter.
When a man is appointed to a place, it is natural
that he should accept the income allotted to that
place without much inquiry. It is seldom that
he will be the first to find out that his services are
overpaid. Though he be called upon only to look
beautiful and to be dignified upon State occasions,
he will think £2000 a year little enough for such
beauty and dignity as he brings to the task.
I felt that there had been some tearing to pieces
which might have been spared. But I was
altogether wrong in supposing that the two things
could be combined. Any writer in advocating
a cause must do so after the fashion of an advocate,
—or his writing will be ineffective. He should
take up one side and cling to that, and then he

may be powerful. There should be no scruples of conscience. Such scruples make a man impotent for such work. It was open to me to have described a bloated parson, with a red nose and all other iniquities, openly neglecting every duty required from him, and living riotously on funds purloined from the poor,—defying as he did do so the moderate remonstrances of a virtuous press. Or I might have painted a man as good, as sweet, and as mild as my warden, who should also have been a hard-working, ill-paid minister of God's word, and might have subjected him to the rancorous venom of some daily Jupiter, who, without a leg to stand on, without any true case, might have been induced, by personal spite, to tear to rags the poor clergyman with poisonous, anonymous, and ferocious leading articles. But neither of these programmes recommended itself to my honesty. Satire, though it may exaggerate the vice it lashes, is not justified in creating it in order that it may be lashed. Caricature may too easily become a slander, and satire a libel. I believed in the existence neither of the red-nosed clerical cormorant, nor in that of the venomous assassin of the journals. I did believe that through want of care and the natural tendency of every class to take care of itself, money had slipped into the pockets of certain clergymen which should have gone elsewhere ; and I believed also that through the equally natural propensity of men to be as strong as they know how to be, certain writers of the press had allowed themselves to use language which was cruel, though it was in a good cause. But the two objects should not have been combined—and I now know myself well enough to be aware that I was not the man to have carried out either of them.

Nevertheless I thought much about it, and on the 29th of July 1853,—having been then two years without having made any literary effort,—I began *The Warden*, at Tenbury in Worcestershire. It was then more than twelve months since I had stood for an hour on the little bridge in Salisbury, and had made out to my own satisfaction the spot on which Hiram's hospital should stand. Certainly no work that I ever did took up so much of my thoughts. On this occasion I did no more than write the first chapter, even if so much. I had determined that my official work should be moderated, so as to allow me some time for writing; but then, just at this time, I was sent to take the postal charge of the northern counties in Ireland,—of Ulster, and the counties Meath and Louth. Hitherto in official language I had been a surveyor's clerk,—now I was to be a surveyor. The difference consisted mainly in an increase of income from about £450 to about £800;—for at that time the sum netted still depended on the number of miles travelled. Of course that English work to which I had become so warmly wedded had to be abandoned. Other parts of England were being done by other men, and I had nearly finished the area which had been entrusted to me. I should have liked to ride over the whole country, and to have sent a rural post letter-carrier to every parish, every village, every hamlet, and every grange in England.

We were at this time very much unsettled as regards any residence. While we were living at Clonmel two sons had been born, who certainly were important enough to have been mentioned sooner. At Clonmel we had lived in lodgings, and from there had moved to Mallow, a town in the county Cork, where we had taken a house. Mallow was in the centre of a hunting country, and had been very pleasant to me. But our house there had been given up when it was known that I should be detained in England ; and then we had wandered about in the western counties, moving our headquarters from one town to another. During this time we had lived at Exeter, at Bristol, at Caermarthen, at Cheltenham, and at Worcester. Now we again moved, and settled ourselves for eighteen months at Belfast. After that we took a house at Donnybrook, the well-known suburb of Dublin.

The work of taking up a new district, which requires not only that the man doing it should know the nature of the postal arrangements, but also the characters and the peculiarities of the postmasters and their clerks, was too heavy to allow of my going on with my book at once. It was not till the end of 1852 that I recommenced it, and it was in the autumn of 1853 that I finished the work. It was only one small volume, and in later days would have been completed in six weeks,—or in two months at the longest, if other work had pressed. On looking at the title-page, I find it was not published till 1855. I had made acquaintance, through my friend John Merivale, with William Longman the publisher, and had received from him an assurance that the manuscript should be ' looked at '. It was ' looked at ', and Messrs. Longman made me an offer to publish it at half profits. I had no reason to love ' half profits ', but I was very anxious to have my book published, and I acceded. It was now more than

ten years since I had commenced writing *The
Macdermots*, and I thought that if any success
was to be achieved, the time surely had come.
I had not been impatient; but, if there was to be
a time, surely it had come.

The novel-reading world did not go mad about
The Warden; but I soon felt that it had not
failed as the others had failed. There were
notices of it in the press, and I could discover
that people around me knew that I had written
a book. Mr. Longman was complimentary, and
after a while informed me that there would be
profits to divide. At the end of 1855 I received
a cheque for £9, 8s. 8d., which was the first money
I had ever earned by literary work;—that £20
which poor Mr. Colburn had been made to pay
certainly never having been earned at all. At the
end of 1856 I received another sum of £10, 15s. 1d.
The pecuniary success was not great. Indeed, as
regarded remuneration for the time, stone-breaking
would have done better. A thousand copies were
printed, of which, after a lapse of five or six years,
about 300 had to be converted into another form,
and sold as belonging to a cheap edition. In its
original form *The Warden* never reached the
essential honour of a second edition.

I have already said of the work that it failed
altogether in the purport for which it was intended.
But it has a merit of its own,—a merit by my own
perception of which I was enabled to see wherein
lay whatever strength I did possess. The characters of the bishop, of the archdeacon, of the
archdeacon's wife, and especially of the warden,
are all well and clearly drawn. I had realised to
myself a series of portraits, and had been able so
to put them on the canvas that my readers should

see that which I meant them to see. There is no
gift which an author can have more useful to him
than this. And the style of the English was good,
though from most unpardonable carelessness the
grammar was not unfrequently faulty. With such
results I had no doubt but that I would at once
begin another novel.

I will here say one word as a long-deferred
answer to an item of criticism which appeared
in the *Times* newspaper as to *The Warden*. In an
article—if I remember rightly, on *The Warden* and
Barchester Towers combined—which I would call
good-natured, but that I take it for granted that
the critics of the *Times* are actuated by higher
motives than good-nature, that little book and its
sequel are spoken of in terms which were very
pleasant to the author. But there was added to
this a gentle word of rebuke at the morbid condition of the author's mind which had prompted
him to indulge in personalities,—the personalities
in question having reference to some editor or
manager of the *Times* newspaper. For I had
introduced one Tom Towers as being potent
among the contributors to the *Jupiter*, under
which name I certainly did allude to the *Times*.
But at that time, living away in Ireland, I had
not even heard the name of any gentleman connected with the *Times* newspaper, and could not
have intended to represent any individual by
Tom Towers. As I had created an archdeacon,
so had I created a journalist, and the one creation
was no more personal or indicative of morbid
tendencies than the other. If Tom Towers was
at all like any gentleman then connected with
the *Times*, my moral consciousness must again
have been very powerful.

CHAPTER VI

'BARCHESTER TOWERS' AND
THE 'THREE CLERKS'

1855-1858

IT was, I think, before I started on my English
tours among the rural posts that I made my first
attempt at writing for a magazine. I had read,
soon after they came out, the two first volumes of
Charles Merivale's *History of the Romans under the
Empire*, and had got into some correspondence
with the author's brother as to the author's views
about Caesar. Hence arose in my mind a tendency
to investigate the character of probably the
greatest man who ever lived, which tendency in
after years produced a little book of which I shall
have to speak when its time comes,—and also
a taste generally for Latin literature, which has
been one of the chief delights of my later life.
And I may say that I became at this time as
anxious about Caesar, and as desirous of reaching the truth as to his character, as we have all
been in regard to Bismarck in these latter days.
I lived in Caesar, and debated with myself constantly whether he crossed the Rubicon as a
tyrant or as a patriot. In order that I might
review Mr. Merivale's book without feeling that
I was dealing unwarrantably with a subject beyond
me, I studied the Commentaries thoroughly, and

went through a mass of other reading which the object of a magazine article hardly justified,—but which has thoroughly justified itself in the subsequent pursuits of my life. I did write two articles, the first mainly on Julius Caesar, and the second on Augustus, which appeared in the *Dublin University Magazine*. They were the result of very much labour, but there came from them no pecuniary product. I had been very modest when I sent them to the editor, as I had been when I called on John Forster, not venturing to suggest the subject of money. After a while I did call upon the proprietor of the magazine in Dublin, and was told by him that such articles were generally written to oblige friends, and that articles written to oblige friends were not usually paid for. The Dean of Ely, as the author of the work in question now is, was my friend ; but I think I was wronged, as I certainly had no intention of obliging him by my criticism. Afterwards, when I returned to Ireland, I wrote other articles for the same magazine, one of which, intended to be very savage in its denunciation, was on an official blue-book just then brought out, preparatory to the introduction of competitive examinations for the Civil Service. For that and some other article, I now forget what, I was paid. Up to the end of 1857 I had received £55 for the hard work of ten years.

It was while I was engaged on *Barchester Towers* that I adopted a system of writing which, for some years afterwards, I found to be very serviceable to me. My time was greatly occupied in travelling, and the nature of my travelling was now changed. I could not any longer do it on horseback. Railroads afforded me my means of conveyance, and I

found that I passed in railway-carriages very
many hours of my existence. Like others, I
used to read,—though Carlyle has since told me
that a man when travelling should not read, but
' sit still and label his thoughts'. But if I intended
to make a profitable business out of my writing,
and, at the same time, to do my best for the Post
Office, I must turn these hours to more account
than I could do even by reading. I made for
myself therefore a little tablet, and found after
a few days' exercise that I could write as quickly
in a railway-carriage as I could at my desk. I
worked with a pencil, and what I wrote my wife
copied afterwards. In this way was composed the
greater part of *Barchester Towers* and of the novel
which succeeded it, and much also of others subsequent to them. My only objection to the practice
came from the appearance of literary ostentation,
to which I felt myself to be subject when going to
work before four or five fellow-passengers. But
I got used to it, as I had done to the amazement
of the west country farmers' wives when asking
them after their letters.

In the writing of *Barchester Towers* I took great
delight. The bishop and Mrs. Proudie were very
real to me, as were also the troubles of the archdeacon and the loves of Mr. Slope. When it was
done, Mr. W. Longman required that it should be
subjected to his reader; and he returned the MS.
to me, with a most laborious and voluminous
criticism,—coming from whom I never knew.
This was accompanied by an offer to print the
novel on the half-profit system, with a payment of
£100 in advance out of my half-profits,—on condition that I would comply with the suggestions

made by his critic. One of these suggestions required that I should cut the novel down to two volumes. In my reply, I went through the criticisms, rejecting one and accepting another, almost alternately, but declaring at last that no consideration should induce me to put out a third of my work. I am at a loss to know how such a task could be performed. I could burn the MS., no doubt, and write another book on the same story; but how two words out of six are to be withdrawn from a written novel, I cannot conceive. I believe such tasks have been attempted—perhaps performed; but I refused to make even the attempt. Mr. Longman was too gracious to insist on his critic's terms; and the book was published, certainly none the worse, and I do not think much the better, for the care that had been taken with it.

The work succeeded just as *The Warden* had succeeded. It achieved no great reputation, but it was one of the novels which novel readers were called upon to read. Perhaps I may be assuming upon myself more than I have a right to do in saying now that *Barchester Towers* has become one of those novels which do not die quite at once, which live and are read for perhaps a quarter of a century; but if that be so, its life has been so far prolonged by the vitality of some of its younger brothers. *Barchester Towers* would hardly be so well known as it is had there been no *Framley Parsonage* and no *Last Chronicle of Barset*.

I received my £100, in advance, with profound delight. It was a positive and most welcome increase to my income, and might probably be regarded as a first real step on the road to sub-

stantial success. I am well aware that there are
many who think that an author in his authorship
should not regard money,—nor a painter, or
sculptor, or composer in his art. I do not know
that this unnatural self-sacrifice is supposed to
extend itself further. A barrister, a clergyman,
a doctor, an engineer, and even actors and archi-
tects, may without disgrace follow the bent of
human nature, and endeavour to fill their bellies
and clothe their backs, and also those of their wives
and children, as comfortably as they can by the
exercise of their abilities and their crafts. They
may be as rationally realistic, as may the butchers
and the bakers ; but the artist and the author forget the high glories of their calling if they condescend to make a money return a first object.
They who preach this doctrine will be much
offended by my theory, and by this book of mine,
if my theory and my book come beneath their
notice. They require the practice of a so-called
virtue which is contrary to nature, and which, in
my eyes, would be no virtue if it were practised.
They are like clergymen who preach sermons
against the love of money, but who know that the
love of money is so distinctive a characteristic of
humanity that such sermons are mere platitudes
called for by customary but unintelligent piety.
All material progress has come from man's desire
to do the best he can for himself and those about
him, and civilisation and Christianity itself have
been made possible by such progress. Though
we do not all of us argue this matter out within
our breasts, we do all feel it ; and we know that
the more a man earns the more useful he is to his
fellow-men. The most useful lawyers, as a rule,

have been those who have made the greatest
incomes,—and it is the same with the doctors. It
would be the same in the Church if they who have
the choosing of bishops always chose the best man.
And it has in truth been so too in art and authorship. Did Titian or Rubens disregard their
pecuniary rewards ? As far as we know, Shakespeare worked always for money, giving the best of
his intellect to support his trade as an actor. In
our own century what literary names stand higher
than those of Byron, Tennyson, Scott, Dickens,
Macaulay, and Carlyle ? And I think I may say
that none of those great men neglected the
pecuniary result of their labours. Now and then
a man may arise among us who in any calling,
whether it be in law, in physic, in religious teaching,
in art, or literature, may in his professional
enthusiasm utterly disregard money. All will
honour his enthusiasm, and if he be wifeless and
childless, his disregard of the great object of men's
work will be blameless. But it is a mistake to
suppose that a man is a better man because he
despises money. Few do so, and those few in
doing so suffer a defeat. Who does not desire to
be hospitable to his friends, generous to the poor,
liberal to all, munificent to his children, and to be
himself free from the carking fear which poverty
creates ? The subject will not stand an argument ;
—and yet authors are told that they should disregard payment for their work, and be content to
devote their unbought brains to the welfare of the
public. Brains that are unbought will never serve
the public much. Take away from English authors
their copyrights, and you would very soon take
away from England her authors.

I say this here, because it is my purpose as I go on to state what to me has been the result of my profession in the ordinary way in which professions are regarded, so that by my example may be seen what prospect there is that a man devoting himself to literature with industry, perseverance, certain necessary aptitudes, and fair average talents, may succeed in gaining a livelihood, as another man does in another profession. The result with me has been comfortable but not splendid, as I think was to have been expected from the combination of such gifts.

I have certainly always had also before my eyes the charms of reputation. Over and above the money view of the question, I wished from the beginning to be something more than a clerk in the Post Office. To be known as somebody,—to be Anthony Trollope if it be no more,—is to me much. The feeling is a very general one, and I think beneficent. It is that which has been called the ' last infirmity of noble mind.' The infirmity is so human that the man who lacks it is either above or below humanity. I own to the infirmity. But I confess that my first object in taking to literature as a profession was that which is common to the barrister when he goes to the Bar, and to the baker when he sets up his oven. I wished to make an income on which I and those belonging to me might live in comfort.

If indeed a man writes his books badly, or paints his pictures badly, because he can make his money faster in that fashion than by doing them well, and at the same time proclaims them to be the best he can do,—if in fact he sells shoddy for broadcloth,—he is dishonest, as is any other

fraudulent dealer. So may be the barrister who
takes money that he does not earn, or the clergyman who is content to live on a sinecure. No doubt
the artist or the author may have a difficulty which
will not occur to the seller of cloth, in settling
within himself what is good work and what is bad,—
when labour enough has been given, and when
the task has been scamped. It is a danger as to
which he is bound to be severe with himself—in
which he should feel that his conscience should be
set fairly in the balance against the natural bias of
his interest. If he do not do so, sooner or later his
dishonesty will be discovered, and will be estimated
accordingly. But in this he is to be governed
only by the plain rules of honesty which should
govern us all. Having said so much, I shall not
scruple as I go on to attribute to the pecuniary
result of my labours all the importance which I felt
them to have at the time.

Barchester Towers, for which I had received £100
in advance, sold well enough to bring me further
payments—moderate payments—from the publishers. From that day up to this very time in
which I am writing, that book and *The Warden*
together have given me almost every year some
small income. I get the accounts very regularly,
and I find that I have received £727, 11s. 3d. for
the two. It is more than I got for the three or
four works that came afterwards, but the payments
have been spread over twenty years.

When I went to Mr. Longman with my next
novel, *The Three Clerks*, in my hand, I could not
induce him to understand that a lump sum down
was more pleasant than a deferred annuity. I
wished him to buy it from me at a price which he

might think to be a fair value, and I argued with him that as soon as an author has put himself into a position which insures a sufficient sale of his works to give a profit, the publisher is not entitled to expect the half of such proceeds. While there is a pecuniary risk, the whole of which must be borne by the publisher, such division is fair enough; but such a demand on the part of the publisher is monstrous as soon as the article produced is known to be a marketable commodity. I thought that I had now reached that point, but Mr. Longman did not agree with me. And he endeavoured to convince me that I might lose more than I gained, even though I should get more money by going elsewhere. ‘It is for you,’ said he, ‘to think whether our names on your little page are not worth more to you than the increased payment.’ This seemed to me to savour of that high-flown doctrine of the contempt of money which I have never admired. I did think much of Messrs. Longman's name, but I liked it best at the bottom of a cheque.

I was also scared from the august columns of Paternoster Row by a remark made to myself by one of the firm, which seemed to imply that they did not much care for works of fiction. Speaking of a fertile writer of tales who was not then dead, he declared that——(naming the author in question) had spawned upon them (the publishers) three novels a year! Such language is perhaps justifiable in regard to a man who shows so much of the fecundity of the herring; but I did not know how fruitful might be my own muse, and I thought that I had better go elsewhere.

I had then written *The Three Clerks*, which, when

I could not sell it to Messrs. Longman, I took in the
first instance to Messrs. Hurst & Blackett, who had
become successors to Mr. Colburn. I had made an
appointment with one of the firm, which, however,
that gentleman was unable to keep. I was on my
way from Ireland to Italy, and had but one
day in London in which to dispose of my manuscript. I sat for an hour in Great Marlborough
Street, expecting the return of the peccant publisher who had broken his tryst, and I was about
to depart with my bundle under my arm when the
foreman of the house came to me. He seemed to
think it a pity that I should go, and wished me
to leave my work with him. This, however, I
would not do, unless he would undertake to buy
it then and there. Perhaps he lacked authority.
Perhaps his judgment was against such purchase.
But while we debated the matter, he gave me some
advice. 'I hope it's not historical, Mr. Trollope?'
he said. 'Whatever you do, don't be historical;
your historical novel is not worth a damn.' Thence
I took *The Three Clerks* to Mr. Bentley; and on the
same afternoon succeeded in selling it to him for
£250. His son still possesses it, and the firm has,
I believe, done very well with the purchase. It
was certainly the best novel I had as yet written.
The plot is not so good as that of the *Macdermots*;
nor are there any characters in the book equal to
those of Mrs. Proudie and the Warden; but the
work has a more continued interest, and contains
the first well-described love-scene that I ever
wrote. The passage in which Kate Woodward,
thinking that she will die, tries to take leave of the
lad she loves, still brings tears to my eyes when
I read it. I had not the heart to kill her. I never

could do that. And I do not doubt but that they are living happily together to this day.

The lawyer Chaffanbrass made his first appearance in this novel, and I do not think that I have cause to be ashamed of him. But this novel now is chiefly noticeable to me from the fact that in it I introduced a character under the name of Sir Gregory Hardlines, by which I intended to lean very heavily on that much loathed scheme of competitive examination, of which at that time Sir Charles Trevelyan was the great apostle. Sir Gregory Hardlines was intended for Sir Charles Trevelyan,—as any one at the time would know who had taken an interest in the Civil Service. ' We always call him Sir Gregory,' Lady Trevelyan said to me afterwards, when I came to know her and her husband. I never learned to love competitive examination ; but I became, and am, very fond of Sir Charles Trevelyan. Sir Stafford Northcote, who is now Chancellor of the Exchequer, was then leagued with his friend Sir Charles, and he too appears in *The Three Clerks* under the feebly facetious name of Sir Warwick West End.

But for all that *The Three Clerks* was a good novel.

When that sale was made I was on my way to Italy with my wife, paying a third visit there to my mother and brother. This was in 1857, and she had then given up her pen. It was the first year in which she had not written, and she expressed to me her delight that her labours should be at an end, and that mine should be beginning in the same field. In truth they had already been continued for a dozen years, but a man's career will generally be held to date itself from the commencement

of his success. On those foreign tours I always
encountered adventures, which, as I look back upon
them now, tempt me almost to write a little book
of my long past Continental travels. On this
occasion, as we made our way slowly through
Switzerland and over the Alps, we encountered
again and again a poor forlorn Englishman, who
had no friend and no aptitude for travelling. He
was always losing his way, and finding himself
with no seat in the coaches and no bed at the inns.
On one occasion I found him at Coire seated at
5 a.m. in the *coupé* of a diligence which was
intended to start at noon for the Engadine, while
it was his purpose to go over the Alps in another
which was to leave at 5.30, and which was already
crowded with passengers. ' Ah ! ' he said, ' I am
in time now, and nobody shall turn me out of this
seat,' alluding to former little misfortunes of which
I had been a witness. When I explained to him
his position, he was as one to whom life was too
bitter to be borne. But he made his way into Italy,
and encountered me again at the Pitti Palace in
Florence. ' Can you tell me something ? ' he said
to me in a whisper, having touched my shoulder.
' The people are so ill-natured I don't like to ask
them. Where is it they keep the Medical Venus ? '
I sent him to the Uffizzi, but I fear he was disappointed.

We ourselves, however, on entering Milan had
been in quite as much distress as any that he
suffered. We had not written for beds, and on
driving up to a hotel at ten in the evening found it
full. Thence we went from one hotel to another,
finding them all full. The misery is one well known
to travellers, but I never heard of another case in

which a man and his wife were told at midnight to get out of the conveyance into the middle of the street because the horse could not be made to go any further. Such was our condition. I induced the driver, however, to go again to the hotel which was nearest to him, and which was kept by a German. Then I bribed the porter to get the master to come down to me; and, though my French is ordinarily very defective, I spoke with such eloquence to that German innkeeper that he, throwing his arms round my neck in a transport of compassion, swore that he would never leave me nor my wife till he had put us to bed. And he did so; but, ah! there were so many in those beds! It is such an experience as this which teaches a travelling foreigner how different on the Continent is the accommodation provided for him, from that which is supplied for the inhabitants of the country.

It was on a previous visit to Milan, when the telegraph-wires were only just opened to the public by the Austrian authorities, that we had decided one day at dinner that we would go to Verona that night. There was a train at six, reaching Verona at midnight, and we asked some servant of the hotel to telegraph for us, ordering supper and beds. The demand seemed to create some surprise; but we persisted, and were only mildly grieved when we found ourselves charged twenty zwanzigers for the message. Telegraphy was new at Milan, and the prices were intended to be almost prohibitory. We paid our twenty zwanzigers and went on, consoling ourselves with the thought of our ready supper and our assured beds. When we reached Verona, there arose a great cry along the platform for Signor Trollopè. I put out my head and declared my identity, when I was waited upon by a glorious personage dressed like a beau for a ball, with half-a-dozen others almost as glorious behind him, who informed me, with his hat in his hand, that he was the landlord of the 'Due Torre'. It was a heating moment, but it became more hot when he asked me after my people,—'mes gens'. I could only turn round, and point to my wife and brother-in-law. I had no other 'people'. There were three carriages provided for us, each with a pair of grey horses. When we reached the house it was all lit up. We were not allowed to move without an attendant with a lighted candle. It was only gradually that the mistake came to be understood. On us there was still the horror of the bill, the extent of which could not be known till the hour of departure had come. The landlord, however, had acknowledged to himself that his inductions had been ill-founded, and he treated us with clemency. He had never before received a telegram.

I apologise for these tales, which are certainly outside my purpose, and will endeavour to tell no more that shall not have a closer relation to my story. I had finished *The Three Clerks* just before I left England, and when in Florence was cudgelling my brain for a new plot. Being then with my brother, I asked him to sketch me a plot, and he drew out that of my next novel, called *Doctor Thorne*. I mention this particularly, because it was the only occasion in which I have had recourse to some other source than my own brains for the thread of a story. How far I may unconsciously have adopted incidents from what I have read,—

either from history or from works of imagination,—
I do not know. It is beyond question that a man
employed as I have been must do so. But when
doing it I have not been aware that I have done it.
I have never taken another man's work, and
deliberately framed my work upon it. I am far
from censuring this practice in others. Our greatest
masters in works of imagination have obtained
such aid for themselves. Shakespeare dug out of
such quarries wherever he could find them. Ben
Jonson, with heavier hand, built up his structures
on his studies of the classics, not thinking it
beneath him to give, without direct acknowledgment, whole pieces translated both from poets and
historians. But in those days no such acknowledgment was usual. Plagiary existed, and was
very common, but was not known as a sin. It is
different now ; and I think that an author, when
he uses either the words or the plot of another,
should own as much, demanding to be credited
with no more of the work than he has himself produced. I may say also that I have never printed
as my own a word that has been written by others.[1]
It might probably have been better for my readers
had I done so, as I am informed that *Doctor Thorne*,
the novel of which I am now speaking, has a larger
sale than any other book of mine.

Early in 1858, while I was writing *Doctor Thorne*,
I was asked by the great men at the General Post
Office to go to Egypt to make a treaty with the

---

[1] I must make one exception to this declaration. The
legal opinion as to heirlooms in *The Eustace Diamonds*
was written for me by Charles Merewether, the present
Member for Northampton. I am told that it has become the
ruling authority on the subject.

Pasha for the conveyance of our mails through that country by railway. There was a treaty in existence, but that had reference to the carriage of bags and boxes by camels from Alexandria to Suez. Since its date the railway had grown, and was now nearly completed, and a new treaty was wanted. So I came over from Dublin to London, on my road, and again went to work among the publishers. The other novel was not finished; but I thought I had now progressed far enough to arrange a sale while the work was still on the stocks. I went to Mr. Bentley and demanded £400,—for the copyright. He acceded, but came to me the next morning at the General Post Office to say that it could not be. He had gone to work at his figures after I had left him, and had found that £300 would be the outside value of the novel. I was intent upon the larger sum ; and in furious haste,—for I had but an hour at my disposal,—I rushed to Chapman & Hall in Piccadilly, and said what I had to say to Mr. Edward Chapman in a quick torrent of words. They were the first of a great many words which have since been spoken by me in that back-shop. Looking at me as he might have done at a highway robber who had stopped him on Hounslow Heath, he said that he supposed he might as well do as I desired. I considered this to be a sale, and it was a sale. I remember that he held the poker in his hand all the time that I was with him ;—but in truth, even though he had declined to buy the book, there would have been no danger.

CHAPTER VII

'DOCTOR THORNE'—'THE BERTRAMS'— 'THE WEST INDIES AND THE SPANISH MAIN'

As I journeyed across France to Marseilles, and made thence a terribly rough voyage to Alexandria, I wrote my allotted number of pages every day. On this occasion more than once I left my paper on the cabin table, rushing away to be sick in the privacy of my state room. It was February, and the weather was miserable; but still I did my work. *Labor omnia vincit improbus.* I do not say that to all men has been given physical strength sufficient for such exertion as this, but I do believe that real exertion will enable most men to work at almost any season. I had previously to this arranged a system of task-work for myself, which I would strongly recommend to those who feel as I have felt, that labour, when not made absolutely obligatory by the circumstances of the hour, should never be allowed to become spasmodic. There was no day on which it was my positive duty to write for the publishers, as it was my duty to write reports for the Post Office. I was free to be idle if I pleased. But as I had made up my mind to undertake this second profession, I found it to be expedient to bind myself by certain self-imposed laws. When I have com-

menced a new book, I have always prepared
a diary, divided into weeks, and carried it on for
the period which I have allowed myself for the
completion of the work. In this I have entered,
day by day, the number of pages I have written,
so that if at any time I have slipped into idleness
for a day or two, the record of that idleness has
been there, staring me in the face, and demanding
of me increased labour, so that the deficiency
might be supplied. According to the circumstances
of the time,—whether my other business might
be then heavy or light, or whether the book
which I was writing was or was not wanted with
speed,—I have allotted myself so many pages
a week. The average number has been about 40.
It has been placed as low as 20, and has risen to
112. And as a page is an ambiguous term, my
page has been made to contain 250 words; and
as words, if not watched, will have a tendency to
straggle, I have had every word counted as I went.
In the bargains I have made with publishers
I have,—not, of course, with their knowledge,
but in my own mind,—undertaken always to
supply them with so many words, and I have
never put a book out of hand short of the number
by a single word. I may also say that the excess
has been very small. I have prided myself on
completing my work exactly within the proposed
dimensions. But I have prided myself especially
in completing it within the proposed time,—and
I have always done so. There has ever been the
record before me, and a week passed with an
insufficient number of pages has been a blister
to my eye, and a month so disgraced would have
been a sorrow to my heart.

I have been told that such appliances are beneath the notice of a man of genius. I have never fancied myself to be a man of genius, but had I been so I think I might well have subjected myself to these trammels. Nothing surely is so potent as a law that may not be disobeyed. It has the force of the water-drop that hollows the stone. A small daily task, if it be really daily, will beat the labours of a spasmodic Hercules. It is the tortoise which always catches the hare. The hare has no chance. He loses more time in glorifying himself for a quick spurt than suffices for the tortoise to make half his journey.

I have known authors whose lives have always been troublesome and painful because their tasks have never been done in time. They have ever been as boys struggling to learn their lesson as they entered the school gates. Publishers have distrusted them, and they have failed to write their best because they have seldom written at ease. I have done double their work,—though burdened with another profession,—and have done it almost without an effort. I have not once, through all my literary career, felt myself even in danger of being late with my task. I have known no anxiety as to ' copy '. The needed pages far ahead—very far ahead—have almost always been in the drawer beside me. And that little diary, with its dates and ruled spaces, its record that must be seen, its daily, weekly demand upon my industry, has done all that for me.

There are those who would be ashamed to subject themselves to such a taskmaster, and who think that the man who works with his imagination should allow himself to wait till—

inspiration moves him. When I have heard such doctrine preached, I have hardly been able to repress my scorn. To me it would not be more absurd if the shoemaker were to wait for inspiration, or the tallow-chandler for the divine moment of melting. If the man whose business it is to write has eaten too many good things, or has drunk too much, or smoked too many cigars,—as men who write sometimes will do,—then his condition may be unfavourable for work; but so will be the condition of a shoemaker who has been similarly imprudent. I have sometimes thought that the inspiration wanted has been the remedy which time will give to the evil results of such imprudence.—*Mens sana in corpore sano*. The author wants that as does every other workman,—that and a habit of industry. I was once told that the surest aid to the writing of a book was a piece of cobbler's wax on my chair. I certainly believe in the cobbler's wax much more than the inspiration.

It will be said, perhaps, that a man whose work has risen to no higher pitch than mine has attained, has no right to speak of the strains and impulses to which real genius is exposed. I am ready to admit the great variations in brain power which are exhibited by the products of different men, and am not disposed to rank my own very high; but my own experience tells me that a man can always do the work for which his brain is fitted if he will give himself the habit of regarding his work as a normal condition of his life. I therefore venture to advise young men who look forward to authorship as the business of their lives, even when they propose that that authorship be of the highest class known, to avoid enthusiastic rushes with their pens, and to seat themselves at their desks day by day as though they were lawyers' clerks;—and so let them sit until the allotted task shall be accomplished.

While I was in Egypt, I finished *Doctor Thorne*, and on the following day began *The Bertrams*. I was moved now by a determination to excel, if not in quality, at any rate in quantity. An ignoble ambition for an author, my readers will no doubt say. But not, I think, altogether ignoble, if an author can bring himself to look at his work as does any other workman. This had become my task, this was the furrow in which my plough was set, this was the thing the doing of which had fallen into my hands, and I was minded to work at it with a will. It is not on my conscience that I have ever scamped my work. My novels, whether good or bad, have been as good as I could make them. Had I taken three months of idleness between each they would have been no better. Feeling convinced of that, I finished *Doctor Thorne* on one day, and began *The Bertrams* on the next.

I had then been nearly two months in Egypt, and had at last succeeded in settling the terms of a postal treaty. Nearly twenty years have passed since that time, and other years may yet run on before these pages are printed. I trust I may commit no official sin by describing here the nature of the difficulty which met me. I found, on my arrival, that I was to communicate with an officer of the Pasha, who was then called Nubar Bey. I presume him to have been the gentleman who has lately dealt with our Government as to the Suez Canal shares, and who is now well known to the political world as Nubar Pasha. I found him a most courteous gentleman, an Armenian. I never went to his office, nor do I know that he had an office. Every other day he would come to me at my hotel, and bring with him servants, and pipes, and coffee. I enjoyed his coming greatly; but there was one point on which we could not agree. As to money and other details, it seemed as though he could hardly accede fast enough to the wishes of the Postmaster-General; but on one point he was firmly opposed to me. I was desirous that the mails should be carried through Egypt in twenty-four hours, and he thought that forty-eight hours should be allowed. I was obstinate, and he was obstinate; and for a long time we could come to no agreement. At last his oriental tranquillity seemed to desert him, and he took upon himself to assure me, with almost more than British energy, that, if I insisted on the quick transit, a terrible responsibility would rest on my head. I made this mistake, he said,—that I supposed that a rate of travelling which would be easy and secure in England could be attained with safety in Egypt. ' The Pasha, his master, would,' he said, ' no doubt accede to any terms demanded by the British Post Office, so great was his reverence for everything British. In that case he, Nubar, would at once resign his position, and retire into obscurity. He would be ruined; but the loss of life and blood-shed which would certainly follow so rash an attempt should not be on his head.' I smoked my pipe, or rather his, and drank his coffee, with oriental quiescence but British firmness. Every

now and again, through three or four visits,
I renewed the expression of my opinion that the
transit could easily be made in twenty-four hours.
At last he gave way,—and astonished me by the
cordiality of his greeting.   There was no longer
any question of bloodshed or of resignation of
office, and he assured me, with energetic complai-
sance, that it should be his care to see that the time
was punctually kept.   It was punctually kept,
and, I believe, is so still. I must confess, however,
that my persistency was not the result of any
courage specially personal to myself. While the
matter was being debated, it had been whispered
to me that the Peninsular and Oriental Steamship
Company had conceived that forty-eight hours
would suit the purposes of their traffic better than
twenty-four, and that, as they were the great pay-
masters on the railway, the Minister of the
Egyptian State, who managed the railway, might
probably wish to accommodate them.   I often
wondered who originated that frightful picture
of blood and desolation. That it came from an
English heart and an English hand I was always
sure.

From Egypt I visited the Holy Land, and on
my way inspected the Post Offices at Malta and
Gibraltar.   I could fill a volume with true tales
of my adventures. The *Tales of All Countries*
have, most of them, some foundation in such
occurrences. There is one called *John Bull on the
Guadalquivir*, the chief incident in which occurred
to me and a friend of mine on our way up that
river to Seville. We both of us handled the gold
ornaments of a man whom we believed to be a bull-
fighter, but who turned out to be a duke,—and

a duke, too, who could speak English! How gracious he was to us, and yet how thoroughly he covered us with ridicule!

On my return home I received £400 from Messrs. Chapman & Hall for *Doctor Thorne*, and agreed to sell them *The Bertrams* for the same sum. This latter novel was written under very vagrant circumstances,—at Alexandria, Malta, Gibraltar, Glasgow, then at sea, and at last finished in Jamaica. Of my journey to the West Indies I will say a few words presently, but I may as well speak of these two novels here. *Doctor Thorne* has, I believe, been the most popular book that I have written,—if I may take the sale as a proof of comparative popularity. *The Bertrams* has had quite an opposite fortune. I do not know that I have ever heard it well spoken of even by my friends, and I cannot remember that there is any character in it that has dwelt in the minds of novel-readers. I myself think that they are of about equal merit, but that neither of them is good. They fall away very much from *The Three Clerks*, both in pathos and humour. There is no personage in either of them comparable to Chaffanbrass the lawyer. The plot of *Doctor Thorne* is good, and I am led therefore to suppose that a good plot,—which, to my own feeling, is the most insignificant part of a tale,—is that which will most raise it or most condemn it in the public judgment. The plots of *Tom Jones* and of *Ivanhoe* are almost perfect, and they are probably the most popular novels of the schools of the last and of this century; but to me the delicacy of Amelia, and the rugged strength of Burley and Meg Merrilies, say more for the power of those great novelists than the gift of construction shown in the two works I have named. A novel should give a picture of common life enlivened by humour and sweetened by pathos. To make that picture worthy of attention, the canvas should be crowded with real portraits, not of individuals known to the world or to the author, but of created personages impregnated with traits of character which are known. To my thinking, the plot is but the vehicle for all this; and when you have the vehicle without the passengers, a story of mystery in which the agents never spring to life, you have but a wooden show. There must, however, be a story. You must provide a vehicle of some sort. That of *The Bertrams* was more than ordinarily bad; and as the book was relieved by no special character, it failed. Its failure never surprised me; but I have been surprised by the success of *Doctor Thorne*.

At this time there was nothing in the success of the one or the failure of the other to affect me very greatly. The immediate sale, and the notices elicited from the critics, and the feeling which had now come to me of a confident standing with the publishers, all made me know that I had achieved my object. If I wrote a novel, I could certainly sell it. And if I could publish three in two years,—confining myself to half the fecundity of that terrible author of whom the publisher in Paternoster Row had complained to me,—I might add £600 a-year to my official income. I was still living in Ireland, and could keep a good house over my head, insure my life, educate my two boys, and hunt perhaps twice a-week, on £1400 a-year. If more should come, it would be

well;—but £600 a-year I was prepared to reckon
as success. It had been slow in coming, but was
very pleasant when it came.

On my return from Egypt I was sent down to
Scotland to revise the Glasgow Post Office. I
almost forget now what it was that I had to do
there, but I know that I walked all over the city
with the letter-carriers, going up to the top flats
of the houses, as the men would have declared me
incompetent to judge the extent of their labours
had I not trudged every step with them. It was
midsummer, and wearier work I never performed.
The men would grumble, and then I would think
how it would be with them if they had to go home
afterwards and write a love-scene. But the love-
scenes written in Glasgow, all belonging to *The
Bertrams*, are not good.

Then in the autumn of that year, 1858, I was
asked to go to the West Indies, and cleanse the
Augean stables of our Post Office system there.
Up to that time, and at that time, our Colonial
Post Offices generally were managed from home,
and were subject to the British Postmaster-
General. Gentlemen were sent out from England
to be postmasters, surveyors, and what not;
and as our West Indian islands have never been
regarded as being of themselves happily situated
for residence, the gentlemen so sent were sometimes
more conspicuous for want of income than for
official zeal and ability. Hence the stables had
become Augean. I was also instructed to carry
out in some of the islands a plan for giving up
this postal authority to the island Governor, and
in others to propose some such plan. I was then
to go on to Cuba, to make a postal treaty with

the Spanish authorities, and to Panama for the
same purpose with the Government of New
Grenada. All this work I performed to my
satisfaction, and I hope to that of my masters
in St. Martin's le Grand.

But the trip is at the present moment of importance to my subject, as having enabled me
to write that which, on the whole, I regard as
the best book that has come from my pen. It
is short, and, I think I may venture to say,
amusing, useful, and true. As soon as I had
learned from the secretary at the General Post
Office that this journey would be required,
I proposed the book to Messrs. Chapman & Hall,
demanding £250 for a single volume. The contract
was made without any difficulty, and when I
returned home the work was complete in my desk.
I began it on board the ship in which I left
Kingston, Jamaica, for Cuba,—and from week to
week I carried it on as I went. From Cuba I made
my way to St. Thomas, and through the island down
to Demerara, then back to St. Thomas,—which is
the starting-point for all places in that part of the
globe,—to Santa Martha, Carthagena, Aspinwall,
over the Isthmus to Panama, up the Pacific to
a little harbour on the coast of Costa Rica, thence
across Central America, through Costa Rica, and
down the Nicaragua river to the Mosquito coast,
and after that home by Bermuda and New York.
Should any one want further details of the voyage,
are they not written in my book ? The fact
memorable to me now is that I never made a single
note while writing or preparing it. Preparation,
indeed, there was none. The descriptions and
opinions came hot on to the paper from their causes.

I will not say that this is the best way of writing a book intended to give accurate information. But it is the best way of producing to the eye of the reader, and to his ear, that which the eye of the writer has seen and his ear heard. There are two kinds of confidence which a reader may have in his author,—which two kinds the reader who wishes to use his reading well should carefully discriminate. There is a confidence in facts and a confidence in vision. The one man tells you accurately what has been. The other suggests to you what may, or perhaps what must have been, or what ought to have been. The former requires simple faith. The latter calls upon you to judge for yourself, and form your own conclusions. The former does not intend to be prescient, nor the latter accurate. Research is the weapon used by the former ; observation by the latter. Either may be false,—wilfully false ; as also may either be steadfastly true. As to that, the reader must judge for himself. But the man who writes *currente calamo*, who works with a rapidity which will not admit of accuracy, may be as true, and in one sense as trustworthy, as he who bases every word upon a rock of facts. I have written very much as I have travelled about ; and though I have been very inaccurate, I have always written the exact truth as I saw it ;—and I have, I think, drawn my pictures correctly.

The view I took of the relative position in the West Indies of black men and white men was the view of the *Times* newspaper at that period ; and there appeared three articles in that journal, one closely after another, which made the fortune of the book. Had it been very bad, I suppose its fortune could not have been made for it even by the *Times* newspaper. I afterwards became acquainted with the writer of those articles, the contributor himself informing me that he had written them. I told him that he had done me a greater service than can often be done by one man to another, but that I was under no obligation to him. I do not think that he saw the matter quite in the same light.

I am aware that by that criticism I was much raised in my position as an author. Whether such lifting up by such means is good or bad for literature is a question which I hope to discuss in a future chapter. But the result was immediate to me, for I at once went to Chapman & Hall and successfully demanded £000 for my next novel.

CHAPTER VIII

THE 'CORNHILL MAGAZINE' AND 'FRAMLEY PARSONAGE'

Soon after my return from the West Indies I was enabled to change my district in Ireland for one in England. For some time past my official work had been of a special nature, taking me out of my own district; but through all that, Dublin had been my home, and there my wife and children had lived. I had often sighed to return to England,—with a silly longing. My life in England for twenty-six years from the time of my birth to the day on which I left it, had been wretched. I had been poor, friendless, and joyless. In Ireland it had constantly been happy. I had achieved the respect of all with whom I was concerned, I had made for myself a comfortable home, and I had enjoyed many pleasures. Hunting itself was a great delight to me; and now, as I contemplated a move to England, and a house in the neighbourhood of London, I felt that hunting must be abandoned.[1] Nevertheless I thought that a man who could write books ought not to live in Ireland,—ought to live within the reach of the publishers, the clubs, and the dinner-

[1] It was not abandoned till sixteen more years had passed away.

parties of the metropolis. So I made my request at headquarters, and with some little difficulty got myself appointed to the Eastern District of England,—which comprised Essex, Suffolk, Norfolk, Cambridgeshire, Huntingdonshire, and the greater part of Hertfordshire.

At this time I did not stand very well with the dominant interest at the General Post Office. My old friend Colonel Maberly had been, some time since, squeezed into, and his place was filled by Mr. Rowland Hill, the originator of the penny post. With him I never had any sympathy, nor he with me. In figures and facts he was most accurate, but I never came across any one who so little understood the ways of men,—unless it was his brother Frederic. To the two brothers the servants of the Post Office,—men numerous enough to have formed a large army in old days,—were so many machines who could be counted on for their exact work without deviation, as wheels may be counted on, which are kept going always at the same pace and always by the same power. Rowland Hill was an industrious public servant, anxious for the good of his country ; but he was a hard taskmaster, and one who would, I think, have put the great department with which he was concerned altogether out of gear by his hardness, had he not been at last controlled. He was the Chief Secretary, my brother-in-law—who afterwards succeeded him—came next to him, and Mr. Hill's brother was the Junior Secretary. In the natural course of things, I had not, from my position, anything to do with the management of affairs ;—but from time to time I found myself more or less mixed up in it. I was known to be a thoroughly efficient public servant; I am sure I may say so much of myself without fear of contradiction from any one who has known the Post Office;—I was very fond of the department, and when matters came to be considered, I generally had an opinion of my own. I have no doubt that I often made myself very disagreeable. I know that I sometimes tried to do so. But I could hold my own because I knew my business and was useful. I had given official offence by the publication of *The Three Clerks*. I afterwards gave greater offence by a lecture on The Civil Service which I delivered in one of the large rooms at the General Post Office to the clerks there. On this occasion, the Postmaster-General, with whom personally I enjoyed friendly terms, sent for me and told me that Mr. Hill had told him that I ought to be dismissed. When I asked his lordship whether he was prepared to dismiss me, he only laughed. The threat was no threat to me, as I knew myself to be too good to be treated in that fashion. The lecture had been permitted, and I had disobeyed no order. In the lecture which I delivered, there was nothing to bring me to shame,—but it advocated the doctrine that a civil servant is only a servant as far as his contract goes, and that he is beyond that entitled to be as free a man in politics, as free in his general pursuits, and as free in opinion, as those who are in open professions and open trades. All this is very nearly admitted now, but it certainly was not admitted then. At that time no one in the Post Office could even vote for a Member of Parliament.

Through my whole official life I did my best

to improve the style of official writing. I have
written, I should think, some thousands of reports,
—many of them necessarily very long ; some of
them dealing with subjects so absurd as to allow
a touch of burlesque ; some few in which a spark
of indignation or a slight glow of pathos might
find an entrance. I have taken infinite pains with
these reports, habituating myself always to write
them in the form in which they should be sent,—
without a copy. It is by writing thus that a man
can throw on to his paper the exact feeling with
which his mind is impressed at the moment.
A rough copy, or that which is called a draft,
is written in order that it may be touched and
altered and put upon stilts. The waste of time,
moreover, in such an operation, is terrible. If
a man knows his craft with his pen, he will have
learned to write without the necessity of changing
his words or the form of his sentences. I had
learned so to write my reports that they who read
them should know what it was that I meant them
to understand. But I do not think that they
were regarded with favour. I have heard horror
expressed because the old forms were disregarded
and language used which had no savour of red-
tape. During the whole of this work in the Post
Office it was my principle always to obey authority
in everything instantly, but never to allow my
mouth to be closed as to the expression of my
opinion. They who had the ordering of me very
often did not know the work as I knew it,—could
not tell as I could what would be the effect of
this or that change. When carrying out instructions which I knew should not have been given,
I never scrupled to point out the fatuity of the

improper order in the strongest language that
I could decently employ. I have revelled in these
official correspondences, and look back to some
of them as the greatest delights of my life. But
I am not sure that they were so delightful to
others.

I succeeded, however, in getting the English
district,—which could hardly have been refused
to me,—and prepared to change our residence
towards the end of 1859. At the time I was
writing *Castle Richmond*, the novel which I had
sold to Messrs. Chapman & Hall for £600. But
there arose at this time a certain literary project
which probably had a great effect upon my career.
Whilst travelling on postal service abroad, or
riding over the rural districts in England, or
arranging the mails in Ireland,—and such for the
last eighteen years had now been my life,—I had
no opportunity of becoming acquainted with
literary life in London. It was probably some
feeling of this which had made me anxious to
move my penates back to England. But even
in Ireland, where I was still living in October
1859, I had heard of the *Cornhill Magazine*, which
was to come out on the 1st of January 1860, under
the editorship of Thackeray.

I had at this time written from time to time
certain short stories, which had been published
in different periodicals, and which in due time
were republished under the name of *Tales of
All Countries*. On the 23rd of October 1859
I wrote to Thackeray, whom I had, I think, never
then seen, offering to send him for the magazine
certain of these stories. In reply to this I received
two letters,—one from Messrs. Smith & Elder, the

proprietors of the *Cornhill*, dated 26th of October, and the other from the editor, written two days later. That from Mr. Thackeray was as follows :—

' 36 ONSLOW SQUARE, S.W.,
October 28*th*.

' MY DEAR MR. TROLLOPE,—Smith & Elder have sent you their proposals ; and the business part done, let me come to the pleasure, and say how very glad indeed I shall be to have you as a co-operator in our new magazine. And looking over the annexed programme, you will see whether you can't help us in many other ways besides tale-telling. Whatever a man knows about life and its doings, that let us hear about. You must have tossed a good deal about the world, and have countless sketches in your memory and your portfolio. Please to think if you can furbish up any of these besides a novel. When events occur, and you have a good lively tale, bear us in mind. One of our chief objects in this magazine is the getting out of novel spinning, and back into the world. Don't understand me to disparage our craft, especially *your* wares. I often say I am like the pastrycook, and don't care for tarts, but prefer bread and cheese ; but the public love the tarts (luckily for us), and we must bake and sell them. There was quite an excitement in my family one evening when Paterfamilias (who goes to sleep on a novel almost always when he tries it after dinner) came up-stairs into the drawing-room wide awake and calling for the second volume of *The Three Clerks*. I hope the *Cornhill Magazine* will have as pleasant a story. And the Chapmans, if they are

the honest men I take them to be, I've no doubt
have told you with what sincere liking your works
have been read by yours very faithfully,

W. M. THACKERAY.'

This was very pleasant, and so was the letter
from Smith & Elder offering me £1000 for the
copyright of a three-volume novel, to come out
in the new magazine,—on condition that the first
portion of it should be in their hands by December 12th.   There was much in all this that astonished me;—in the first place the price, which
was more than double what I had yet received,
and nearly double that which I was about to
receive from Messrs. Chapman & Hall.   Then there
was the suddenness of the call.   It was already
the end of October, and a portion of the work was
required to be in the printer's hands within six
weeks.   *Castle Richmond* was indeed half written,
but that was sold to Chapman.   And it had already
been a principle with me in my art, that no part of
a novel should be published till the entire story
was completed.   I knew, from what I read from
month to month, that this hurried publication of
incompleted work was frequently, I might perhaps
say always, adopted by the leading novelists of the
day.   That such has been the case, is proved by
the fact that Dickens, Thackeray, and Mrs. Gaskell
died with unfinished novels, of which portions had
been already published.   I had not yet entered
upon the system of publishing novels in parts,
and therefore had never been tempted.   But I
was aware that an artist should keep in his hand
the power of fitting the beginning of his work to
the end.   No doubt it is his first duty to fit the

end to the beginning, and he will endeavour to do
so. But he should still keep in his hands the
power of remedying any defect in this respect.

> ' Servetur ad imum
> Qualis ab incepto processerit,'

should be kept in view as to every character
and every string of action. Your Achilles should
all through, from beginning to end, be ' impatient,
fiery, ruthless, keen.' Your Achilles, such as he
is, will probably keep up his character. But your
Davus also should be always Davus, and that is
more difficult. The rustic driving his pigs to
market cannot always make them travel by the
exact path which he has intended for them. When
some young lady at the end of a story cannot be
made quite perfect in her conduct, that vivid
description of angelic purity with which you laid
the first lines of her portrait should be slightly
toned down. I had felt that the rushing mode of
publication to which the system of serial stories
had given rise, and by which small parts as they
were written were sent hot to the press, was
injurious to the work done. If I now complied
with the proposition made to me, I must act
against my own principle. But such a principle
becomes a tyrant if it cannot be superseded on a
just occasion. If the reason be ' tanti', the
principle should for the occasion be put in abey-
ance. I sat as judge, and decreed that the present
reason was ' tanti'. On this my first attempt at
a serial story, I thought it fit to break my own
rule. I can say, however, that I have never
broken it since.

But what astonished me most was the fact that

at so late a day this new *Cornhill Magazine* should
be in want of a novel ! Perhaps some of my future
readers will be able to remember the great expectations which were raised as to this periodical.
Thackeray's was a good name with which to con-
jure. The proprietors, Messrs. Smith & Elder, were
most liberal in their manner of initiating the work,
and were able to make an expectant world of
readers believe that something was to be given
them for a shilling very much in excess of anything they had ever received for that or double
the money. Whether these hopes were or were
not fulfilled it is not for me to say, as, for the
first few years of the magazine's existence, I wrote
for it more than any other one person. But such
was certainly the prospect ;—and how had it come
to pass that, with such promises made, the editor
and the proprietors were, at the end of October,
without anything fixed as to what must be
regarded as the chief dish in the banquet to be
provided ?

I fear that the answer to this question must
be found in the habits of procrastination which
had at that time grown upon the editor. He
had, I imagine, undertaken the work himself,
and had postponed its commencement till there
was left to him no time for commencing. There
was still, it may be said, as much time for him as
for me. I think there was,—for though he had his
magazine to look after, I had the Post Office. But
he thought, when unable to trust his own energy,
that he might rely upon that of a new recruit. He
was but four years my senior in life, but he was at
the top of the tree, while I was still at the bottom.

Having made up my mind to break my principle,

I started at once from Dublin to London. I arrived there on the morning of Thursday, 3d of November, and left it on the evening of Friday. In the meantime I had made my agreement with Messrs. Smith & Elder, and had arranged my plot. But when in London, I first went to Edward Chapman, at 193 Piccadilly. If the novel I was then writing for him would suit the *Cornhill*, might I consider my arrangement with him to be at an end ? Yes ; I might. But if that story would not suit the *Cornhill*, was I to consider my arrangement with him as still standing,—that agreement requiring that my MS. should be in his hands in the following March ? As to that, I might do as I pleased. In our dealings together Mr. Edward Chapman always acceded to every suggestion made to him. He never refused a book, and never haggled at a price. Then I hurried into the City, and had my first interview with Mr. George Smith. When he heard that *Castle Richmond* was an Irish story, he begged that I would endeavour to frame some other for his magazine. He was sure that an Irish story would not do for a commencement ;—and he suggested the Church, as though it were my peculiar subject. I told him that *Castle Richmond* would have to ' come out ' while any other novel that I might write for him would be running through the magazine ;—but to that he expressed himself altogether indifferent. He wanted an English tale, on English life, with a clerical flavour. On these orders I went to work, and framed what I suppose I must call the plot of *Framley Parsonage*.

On my journey back to Ireland, in the railway carriage, I wrote the first few pages of that story.

I had got into my head an idea of what I meant
to write,—a morsel of the biography of an English
clergyman who should not be a bad man, but one
led into temptation by his own youth and by the
unclerical accidents of the life of those around
him. The love of his sister for the young lord
was an adjunct necessary, because there must be
love in a novel. And then by placing Framley
Parsonage near Barchester, I was able to fall back
upon my old friends Mrs. Proudie and the archdeacon. Out of these slight elements I fabricated
a hodge-podge in which the real plot consisted at
last simply of a girl refusing to marry the man she
loved till the man's friends agreed to accept her
lovingly. Nothing could be less efficient or artistic.
But the characters were so well handled, that the
work from the first to the last was popular,—and
was received as it went on with still increasing
favour by both editor and proprietor of the magazine. The story was thoroughly English. There
was a little fox-hunting and a little tuft-hunting,
some Christian virtue and some Christian cant.
There was no heroism and no villainy. There was
much Church, but more love-making. And it was
downright honest love,—in which there was no
pretence on the part of the lady that she was too
ethereal to be fond of a man, no half-and-half inclination on the part of the man to pay a certain
price and no more for a pretty toy. Each of
them longed for the other, and they were not
ashamed to say so. Consequently they in England
who were living, or had lived, the same sort of
life, liked *Framley Parsonage*. I think myself that
Lucy Robarts is perhaps the most natural English
girl that I ever drew,—the most natural, at any

rate, of those who have been good girls. She was not as dear to me as Kate Woodward in *The Three Clerks*, but I think she is more like real human life. Indeed I doubt whether such a character could be made more lifelike than Lucy Robarts.

And I will say also that in this novel there is no very weak part,—no long succession of dull pages. The production of novels in serial form forces upon the author the conviction that he should not allow himself to be tedious in any single part. I hope no reader will misunderstand me. In spite of that conviction, the writer of stories in parts will often be tedious. That I have been so myself is a fault that will lie heavy on my tombstone. But the writer when he embarks in such a business should feel that he cannot afford to have many pages skipped out of the few which are to meet the reader's eye at the same time. Who can imagine the first half of the first volume of *Waverley* coming out in shilling numbers ? I had realised this when I was writing *Framley Parsonage* ; and working on the conviction which had thus come home to me, I fell into no bathos of dulness.

I subsequently came across a piece of criticism which was written on me as a novelist by a brother novelist very much greater than myself, and whose brilliant intellect and warm imagination led him to a kind of work the very opposite of mine. This was Nathaniel Hawthorne, the American, whom I did not then know, but whose works I knew. Though it praises myself highly, I will insert it here, because it certainly is true in its nature : ' It is odd enough,' he says, ' that my own individual taste is for quite another class of works than those which I myself am able to write. If

I were to meet with such books as mine by another
writer, I don't believe I should be able to get
through them. Have you ever read the novels of
Anthony Trollope? They precisely suit my taste,—
solid and substantial, written on the strength of
beef and through the inspiration of ale, and just
as real as if some giant had hewn a great lump
out of the earth and put it under a glass case, with
all its inhabitants going about their daily business,
and not suspecting that they were being made
a show of. And these books are just as English
as a beef-steak. Have they ever been tried in
America? It needs an English residence to make
them thoroughly comprehensible; but still I
should think that human nature would give them
success anywhere.'

This was dated early in 1860, and could have
had no reference to *Framley Parsonage*; but it
was as true of that work as of any that I have
written. And the criticism, whether just or unjust,
describes with wonderful accuracy the purport
that I have ever had in view in my writing. I have
always desired to ' hew out some lump of the earth',
and to make men and women walk upon it just as
they do walk here among us,—with not more of
excellence, nor with exaggerated baseness,—so that
my readers might recognise human beings like to
themselves, and not feel themselves to be carried
away among gods or demons. If I could do this,
then I thought I might succeed in impregnating
the mind of the novel-reader with a feeling that
honesty is the best policy; that truth prevails
while falsehood fails; that a girl will be loved as
she is pure, and sweet, and unselfish; that a man
will be honoured as he is true, and honest, and

brave of heart ; that things meanly done are ugly
and odious, and things nobly done beautiful and
gracious. I do not say that lessons such as these
may not be more grandly taught by higher flights
than mine. Such lessons come to us from our
greatest poets. But there are so many who will
read novels and understand them, who either do
not read the works of our great poets, or reading
them miss the lesson ! And even in prose fiction
the character whom the fervid imagination of the
writer has lifted somewhat into the clouds, will
hardly give so plain an example to the hasty
normal reader as the humbler personage whom
that reader unconsciously feels to resemble himself or herself. I do think that a girl would more
probably dress her own mind after Lucy Robarts
than after Flora Macdonald.

There are many who would laugh at the idea
of a novelist teaching either virtue or nobility,—
those, for instance, who regard the reading of
novels as a sin, and those also who think it to be
simply an idle pastime. They look upon the tellers
of stories as among the tribe of those who pander
to the wicked pleasures of a wicked world. I have
regarded my art from so different a point of view
that I have ever thought of myself as a preacher
of sermons, and my pulpit as one which I could
make both salutary and agreeable to my audience.
I do believe that no girl has risen from the reading
of my pages less modest than she was before,
and that some may have learned from them that
modesty is a charm well worth preserving. I think
that no youth has been taught that in falseness
and flashness is to be found the road to manliness ;
but some may perhaps have learned from me that

it is to be found in truth and a high but gentle spirit. Such are the lessons I have striven to teach ; and I have thought it might best be done by representing to my readers characters like themselves,—or to which they might liken themselves.

Framley Parsonage—or, rather, my connection with the *Cornhill*—was the means of introducing me very quickly to that literary world from which I had hitherto been severed by the fact of my residence in Ireland. In December 1859, while I was still very hard at work on my novel, I came over to take charge of the Eastern District, and settled myself at a residence about twelve miles from London, in Hertfordshire, but on the borders both of Essex and Middlesex,—which was somewhat too grandly called Waltham House. This I took on lease, and subsequently bought after I had spent about £1000 on improvements. From hence I was able to make myself frequent both in Cornhill and Piccadilly, and to live, when the opportunity came, among men of my own pursuit.

It was in January 1860 that Mr. George Smith—to whose enterprise we owe not only the *Cornhill Magazine* but the *Pall Mall Gazette*—gave a sumptuous dinner to his contributors. It was a memorable banquet in many ways, but chiefly so to me because on that occasion I first met many men who afterwards became my most intimate associates. It can rarely happen that one such occasion can be the first starting-point of so many friendships. It was at that table, and on that day, that I first saw Thackeray, Charles Taylor (Sir)—than whom in latter life I have loved no man better,—Robert Bell, G. H. Lewes, and John Everett Millais. With all these men I afterwards lived on affectionate terms;—but I will here speak specially of the last, because from that time he was joined with me in so much of the work that I did.

Mr. Millais was engaged to illustrate *Framley Parsonage*, but this was not the first work he did for the magazine. In the second number there is a picture of his accompanying Monckton Milnes' *Unspoken Dialogue*. The first drawing he did for *Framley Parsonage* did not appear till after the dinner of which I have spoken, and I do not think that I knew at the time that he was engaged on my novel. When I did know it, it made me very proud. He afterwards illustrated *Orley Farm, The Small House of Allington, Rachel Ray*, and *Phineas Finn*. Altogether he drew from my tales eighty-seven drawings, and I do not think that more conscientious work was ever done by man. Writers of novels know well—and so ought readers of novels to have learned—that there are two modes of illustrating, either of which may be adopted equally by a bad and by a good artist. To which class Mr. Millais belongs I need not say ; but, as a good artist, it was open to him simply to make a pretty picture, or to study the work of the author from whose writing he was bound to take his subject. I have too often found that the former alternative has been thought to be the better, as it certainly is the easier method. An artist will frequently dislike to subordinate his ideas to those of an author, and will sometimes be too idle to find out what those ideas are. But this artist was neither proud nor idle. In every figure that he drew it was his object to promote the views of the writer whose work he had undertaken to illustrate, and he never spared himself any pains in studying that work, so as to enable him to do so. I have carried on some of those characters from book to book, and have had my own early ideas impressed indelibly on my memory by the excellence of his delineations. Those illustrations were commenced fifteen years ago, and from that time up to this day my affection for the man of whom I am speaking has increased. To see him has always been a pleasure. His voice has been a sweet sound in my ears. Behind his back I have never heard him praised without joining the eulogist; I have never heard a word spoken against him without opposing the censurer. These words, should he ever see them, will come to him from the grave, and will tell him of my regard,—as one living man never tells another.

Sir Charles Taylor, who carried me home in his brougham that evening, and thus commenced an intimacy which has since been very close, was born to wealth, and was therefore not compelled by the necessities of a profession to enter the lists as an author. But he lived much with those who did so,—and could have done it himself had want or ambition stirred him. He was our king at the Garrick Club, to which, however, I did not yet belong. He gave the best dinners of my time, and was,—happily I may say is,[1]—the best giver of dinners. A man rough of tongue, brusque in his manners, odious to those who dislike him, somewhat inclined to tyranny, he is the prince of friends, honest as the sun, and as open-handed as Charity itself.

Robert Bell has now been dead nearly ten

[1] Alas! within a year of the writing of this he went from us.

years. As I look back over the interval and
remember how intimate we were, it seems odd
to me that we should have known each other
for no more than six years. He was a man who
had lived by his pen from his very youth ; and
was so far successful that I do not think that
want ever came near him. But he never made
that mark which his industry and talents would
have seemed to ensure. He was a man well known
to literary men, but not known to readers. As
a journalist he was useful and conscientious, but
his plays and novels never made themselves
popular. He wrote a life of Canning, and he
brought out an annotated edition of the British
poets ; but he achieved no great success. I have
known no man better read in English literature.
Hence his conversation had a peculiar charm, but
he was not equally happy with his pen. He will
long be remembered at the Literary Fund Com-
mittees, of which he was a staunch and most
trusted supporter. I think it was he who first
introduced me to that board. It has often been
said that literary men are peculiarly apt to think
that they are slighted and unappreciated. Robert
Bell certainly never achieved the position in
literature which he once aspired to fill, and which
he was justified in thinking that he could earn for
himself. I have frequently discussed these subjects with him, but I never heard from his mouth
a word of complaint as to his own literary fate.
He liked to hear the chimes go at midnight,
and he loved to have ginger hot in his mouth.
On such occasions no sound ever came out of
a man's lips sweeter than his wit and gentle
revelry.

George Lewes,—with his wife, whom all the world knows as George Eliot,—has also been and still is one of my dearest friends. He is, I think, the acutest critic I know,—and the severest. His severity, however, is a fault. His intention to be honest, even when honesty may give pain, has caused him to give pain when honesty has not required it. He is essentially a doubter, and has encouraged himself to doubt till the faculty of trusting has almost left him. I am not speaking of the personal trust which one man feels in another, but of that confidence in literary excellence, which is, I think, necessary for the full enjoyment of literature. In one modern writer he did believe thoroughly. Nothing can be more charming than the unstinted admiration which he has accorded to everything that comes from the pen of the wonderful woman to whom his lot has been united. To her name I shall recur again when speaking of the novelists of the present day.

Of 'Billy Russell', as we always used to call him, I may say that I never knew but one man equal to him in the quickness and continuance of witty speech. That one man was Charles Lever—also an Irishman—whom I had known from an earlier date, and also with close intimacy. Of the two, I think that Lever was perhaps the more astounding producer of good things. His manner was perhaps a little the happier, and his turns more sharp and unexpected. But ' Billy ' also was marvellous. Whether abroad as special correspondent, or at home amidst the flurry of his newspaper work, he was a charming companion ; his ready wit always gave him the last word.

Of Thackeray I will speak again when I record his death.

There were many others whom I met for the first time at George Smith's table. Albert Smith, for the first, and indeed for the last time, as he died soon after; Higgins, whom all the world knew as Jacob Omnium, a man I greatly regarded; Dallas, who for a time was literary critic to the *Times*, and who certainly in that capacity did better work than has appeared since in the same department; George Augustus Sala, who, had he given himself fair play, would have risen to higher eminence than that of being the best writer in his day of sensational leading articles; and Fitz-James Stephen, a man of very different calibre, who has not yet culminated, but who, no doubt, will culminate among our judges. There were many others;—but I cannot now recall their various names as identified with those banquets.

Of *Framley Parsonage* I need only further say, that as I wrote it I became more closely than ever acquainted with the new shire which I had added to the English counties. I had it all in my mind,—its roads and railroads, its towns and parishes, its members of Parliament, and the different hunts which rode over it. I knew all the great lords and their castles, the squires and their parks, the rectors and their churches. This was the fourth novel of which I had placed the scene in Barsetshire, and as I wrote it I made a map of the dear county. Throughout these stories there has been no name given to a fictitious site which does not represent to me a spot of which I know all the accessories, as though I had lived and wandered there.

CHAPTER IX

'CASTLE RICHMOND;' 'BROWN, JONES, AND ROBINSON;' 'NORTH AMERICA;' 'ORLEY FARM'

WHEN I had half-finished *Framley Parsonage*, I went back to my other story, *Castle Richmond*, which I was writing for Messrs. Chapman & Hall, and completed that. I think that this was the only occasion on which I have had two different novels in my mind at the same time. This, however, did not create either difficulty or confusion. Many of us live in different circles; and when we go from our friends in the town to our friends in the country, we do not usually fail to remember the little details of the one life or the other. The parson at Rusticum, with his wife and his wife's mother, and all his belongings; and our old friend, the Squire, with his family history; and Farmer Mudge, who has been cross with us, because we rode so unnecessarily over his barley; and that rascally poacher, once a gamekeeper, who now traps all the foxes; and pretty Mary Cann, whose marriage with the wheelwright we did something to expedite;—though we are alive to them all, do not drive out of our brain the club gossip, or the memories of last season's dinners, or any incident of our London intimacies. In our lives we are always weaving novels, and we manage to

keep the different tales distinct. A man does,
in truth, remember that which it interests him
to remember; and when we hear that memory
has gone as age has come on, we should understand
that the capacity for interest in the matter concerned has perished. A man will be generally very
old and feeble before he forgets how much money
he has in the funds. There is a good deal to be
learned by any one who wishes to write a novel
well; but when the art has been acquired, I do
not see why two or three should not be well written
at the same time. I have never found myself
thinking much about the work that I had to do till
I was doing it. I have indeed for many years
almost abandoned the effort to think, trusting
myself, with the narrowest thread of a plot, to
work the matter out when the pen is in my hand.
But my mind is constantly employing itself on the
work I have done. Had I left either *Framley
Parsonage* or *Castle Richmond* half-finished fifteen
years ago, I think I could complete the tales now
with very little trouble. I have not looked at
Castle Richmond since it was published; and poor
as the work is, I remember all the incidents.

Castle Richmond certainly was not a success,
—though the plot is a fairly good plot, and is
much more of a plot than I have generally been
able to find. The scene is laid in Ireland, during
the famine; and I am well aware now that
English readers no longer like Irish stories. I cannot understand why it should be so, as the Irish
character is peculiarly well fitted for romance.
But Irish subjects generally have become distasteful. This novel, however, is of itself a weak
production. The characters do not excite sym-

pathy. The heroine has two lovers, one of whom is a scamp and the other a prig. As regards the scamp, the girl's mother is her own rival. Rivalry of the same nature has been admirably depicted by Thackeray in his *Esmond*; but there the mother's love seems to be justified by the girl's indifference. In *Castle Richmond* the mother strives to rob her daughter of the man's love. The girl herself has no character ; and the mother, who is strong enough, is almost revolting. The dialogue is often lively, and some of the incidents are well told ; but the story as a whole was a failure. I cannot remember, however, that it was roughly handled by the critics when it came out ; and I much doubt whether anything so hard was said of it then as that which I have said here.

I was now settled at Waltham Cross, in a house in which I could entertain a few friends modestly, where we grew our cabbages and strawberries, made our own butter, and killed our own pigs. I occupied it for twelve years, and they were years to me of great prosperity. In 1861 I became a member of the Garrick Club, with which institution I have since been much identified. I had belonged to it about two years, when, on Thackeray's death, I was invited to fill his place on the Committee, and I have been one of that august body ever since. Having up to that time lived very little among men, having known hitherto nothing of clubs, having even as a boy been banished from social gatherings, I enjoyed infinitely at first the gaiety of the Garrick. It was a festival to me to dine there—which I did indeed but seldom ; and a great delight to play a rubber in the little room up-stairs of an afternoon. I am speaking now of the old club in King Street. This playing of whist before dinner has since that become a habit with me, so that unless there be something else special to do—unless there be hunting, or I am wanted to ride in the park by the young tyrant of my household—it is ' my custom always in the afternoon '. I have sometimes felt sore with myself for this persistency, feeling that I was making myself a slave to an amusement which has not after all very much to recommend it. I have often thought that I would break myself away from it, and ' swear off', as Rip Van Winkle says. But my swearing off has been like that of Rip Van Winkle. And now, as I think of it coolly, I do not know but that I have been right to cling to it. As a man grows old he wants amusement, more even than when he is young ; and then it becomes so difficult to find amusement. Reading should, no doubt, be the delight of men's leisure hours. Had I to choose between books and cards, I should no doubt take the books. But I find that I can seldom read with pleasure for above an hour and a half at a time, or more than three hours a day. As I write this I am aware that hunting must soon be abandoned. After sixty it is given but to few men to ride straight across country, and I cannot bring myself to adopt any other mode of riding. I think that without cards I should now be much at a loss. When I began to play at the Garrick, I did so simply because I liked the society of the men who played.

I think that I became popular among those with whom I associated. I have long been aware of a certain weakness in my own character, which I may call a craving for love. I have ever had a wish to be liked by those around me,—a wish that during the first half of my life was never gratified. In my school-days no small part of my misery came from the envy with which I regarded the popularity of popular boys. They seemed to me to live in a social paradise, while the desolation of my pandemonium was complete. And afterwards, when I was in London as a young man, I had but few friends. Among the clerks in the Post Office I held my own fairly for the first two or three years; but even then I regarded myself as something of a pariah. My Irish life had been much better. I had had my wife and children, and had been sustained by a feeling of general respect. But even in Ireland I had in truth lived but little in society. Our means had been sufficient for our wants, but insufficient for entertaining others. It was not till we had settled ourselves at Waltham that I really began to live much with others. The Garrick Club was the first assemblage of men at which I felt myself to be popular.

I soon became a member of other clubs. There was the Arts Club in Hanover Square, of which I saw the opening, but from which, after three or four years, I withdrew my name, having found that during these three or four years I had not once entered the building. Then I was one of the originators of the Civil Service Club—not from judgment, but instigated to do so by others. That also I left for the same reason. In 1864 I received the honour of being elected by the Committee at the Athenæum. For this I was indebted to the kindness of Lord Stanhope; and I never was more surprised than when I was informed of the fact. About the same time I became a member of the Cosmopolitan, a little club that meets twice a week in Charles Street, Berkeley Square, and supplies to all its members, and its members' friends, tea and brandy and water without charge ! The gatherings there I used to think very delightful. One met Jacob Omnium, Monckton Milnes, Tom Hughes, William Stirling, Henry Reeve, Arthur Russell, Tom Taylor, and such like ; and generally a strong political element, thoroughly well mixed, gave a certain spirit to the place. Lord Ripon, Lord Stanley, William Forster, Lord Enfield, Lord Kimberley, George Bentinck, Vernon Harcourt, Bromley Davenport, Knatchbull Hugessen, with many others, used to whisper the secrets of Parliament with free tongues. Afterwards I became a member of the Turf, which I found to be serviceable—or the reverse—only for the playing of whist at high points.

In August 1861 I wrote another novel for the *Cornhill Magazine*. It was a short story, about one volume in length, and was called *The Struggles of Brown, Jones, and Robinson*. In this I attempted a style for which I certainly was not qualified, and to which I never had again recourse. It was meant to be funny, was full of slang, and was intended as a satire on the ways of trade. Still I think that there is some good fun in it, but I have heard no one else express such an opinion. I do not know that I ever heard any opinion expressed on it, except by the publisher, who kindly remarked that he did not think it was equal to my usual work. Though he had purchased the copyright, he did not republish the story in a book form till 1870, and then it passed into the world of letters *sub silentio*. I do not know that it was ever criticised or ever read. I received £600 for it. From that time to this I have been paid at about that rate for my work—£600 for the quantity contained in an ordinary novel volume, or £3000 for a long tale published in twenty parts, which is equal in length to five such volumes. I have occasionally, I think, received something more than this, never I think less for any tale, except when I have published my work anonymously.[1] Having said so much, I need not further specify the prices as I mention the books as they were written. I will, however, when I am completing this memoir, give a list of all the sums I have received for my literary labours. I think that *Brown, Jones, and Robinson* was the hardest bargain I ever sold to a publisher.

In 1861 the War of Secession had broken out in America, and from the first I interested myself much in the question. My mother had thirty years previously written a very popular, but, as I had thought, a somewhat unjust book about our cousins over the water. She had seen what was distasteful in the manners of a young people, but had hardly recognised their energy. I had entertained for many years an ambition to follow her footsteps there, and to write another book. I had already paid a short visit to New York City and State on my way home from the West Indies, but had not seen enough then to justify me in the expression of any opinion. The breaking out of the war did not make me think that the time was peculiarly fit for such inquiry as I wished to make, but it did represent itself as an occasion on which a book might be popular. I consequently

[1] Since the date at which this was written I have encountered a diminution in price.

consulted the two great powers with whom I was concerned. Messrs. Chapman & Hall, the publishers, were one power, and I had no difficulty in arranging my affairs with them. They agreed to publish the book on my terms, and bade me Godspeed on my journey. The other power was the Postmaster-General and Mr. Rowland Hill, the Secretary of the Post Office. I wanted leave of absence for the unusual period of nine months, and fearing that I should not get it by the ordinary process of asking the Secretary, I went direct to his lordship. ' Is it on the plea of ill-health ? ' he asked, looking into my face, which was then that of a very robust man. His lordship knew the Civil Service as well as any one living, and must have seen much of falseness and fraudulent pretence, or he could not have asked that question. I told him that I was very well, but that I wanted to write a book. ' Had I any special ground to go upon in asking for such indulgence ? ' I had, I said, done my duty well by the service. There was a good deal of demurring, but I got my leave for nine months,—and I knew that I had earned it. Mr. Hill attached to the minute granting me the leave an intimation that it was to be considered as a full equivalent for the special services rendered by me to the department. I declined, however, to accept the grace with such a stipulation, and it was withdrawn by the directions of the Postmaster-General.[1]

[1] During the period of my service in the Post Office I did very much special work for which I never asked any remuneration,—and never received any, though payments for special services were common in the department at that time. But if there was to be a question of such remunera-

I started for the States in August and returned
in the following May. The war was raging during
the time that I was there, and the country was full
of soldiers. A part of the time I spent in Virginia,
Kentucky, and Missouri, among the troops, along
the line of attack. I visited all the States (except-
ing California) which had not then seceded,—
failing to make my way into the seceding States
unless I was prepared to visit them with an amount
of discomfort I did not choose to endure. I worked
very hard at the task I had assigned to myself,
and did, I think, see much of the manners and
institutions of the people. Nothing struck me
more than their persistence in the ordinary
pursuits of life in spite of the war which was
around them. Neither industry nor amusement
seemed to meet with any check. Schools, hospitals,
and institutes were by no means neglected because
new regiments were daily required. The truth,
I take it, is that we, all of us, soon adapt ourselves
to the circumstances around us. Though three
parts of London were in flames I should no doubt
expect to have my dinner served to me if I lived in
the quarter which was free from fire.

The book I wrote was very much longer than
that on the West Indies, but was also written
almost without a note. It contained much
information, and, with many inaccuracies, was
a true book. But it was not well done. It is
tedious and confused, and will hardly, I think,
be of future value to those who wish to make
themselves acquainted with the United States.
It was published about the middle of the war,—

tion, I did not choose that my work should be valued at
the price put upon it by Mr. Hill.

just at the time in which the hopes of those who
loved the South were most buoyant, and the fears
of those who stood by the North were the strongest.
But it expressed an assured confidence—which
never quavered in a page or in a line—that the
North would win. This assurance was based on the
merits of the Northern cause, on the superior
strength of the Northern party, and on a conviction that England would never recognise the
South, and that France would be guided in her
policy by England. I was right in my prophecies,
and right, I think, on the grounds on which they
were made. The Southern cause was bad. The
South had provoked the quarrel because its
political supremacy was checked by the election of
Mr. Lincoln to the Presidency. It had to fight
as a little man against a big man, and fought
gallantly. That gallantry,—and a feeling based on
a misconception as to American character that the
Southerners are better gentlemen than their
Northern brethren,—did create great sympathy
here ; but I believe that the country was too just
to be led into political action by a spirit of romance,
and I was warranted in that belief. There was
a moment in which the Northern cause was in
danger, and the danger lay certainly in the
prospect of British interference. Messrs. Slidell and
Mason,—two men insignificant in themselves,—
had been sent to Europe by the Southern party,
and had managed to get on board the British mail
steamer called 'The Trent', at the Havannah.
A most undue importance was attached to this
mission by Mr. Lincoln's government, and efforts
were made to stop them. A certain Commodore
Wilkes, doing duty as policeman on the seas,

did stop the Trent, and took the men out. They were carried, one to Boston and one to New York, and were incarcerated, amidst the triumph of the nation. Commodore Wilkes, who had done nothing in which a brave man could take glory, was made a hero and received a prize sword. England of course demanded her passengers back, and the States for a while refused to surrender them. But Mr. Seward was at that time the Secretary of State, and Mr. Seward, with many political faults, was a wise man. I was at Washington at the time, and it was known there that the contest among the leading Northerners was very sharp on the matter. Mr. Sumner and Mr. Seward were, under Mr. Lincoln, the two chiefs of the party. It was understood that Mr. Sumner was opposed to the rendition of the men, and Mr. Seward in favour of it. Mr. Seward's counsels at last prevailed with the President, and England's declaration of war was prevented. I dined with Mr. Seward on the day of the decision, meeting Mr. Sumner at his house, and was told as I left the dining-room what the decision had been. During the afternoon I and others had received intimation through the embassy that we might probably have to leave Washington at an hour's notice. This, I think, was the severest danger that the Northern cause encountered during the war.

But my book, though it was right in its views on this subject,—and wrong in none other as far as I know,—was not a good book. I can recommend no one to read it now in order that he may be either instructed or amused,—as I can do that on the West Indies. It served its purpose at the time, and was well received by the public and by the critics.

Before starting to America I had completed *Orley Farm*, a novel which appeared in shilling numbers,—after the manner in which *Pickwick*, *Nicholas Nickleby*, and many others had been published. Most of those among my friends who talk to me now about my novels, and are competent to form an opinion on the subject, say that this is the best I have written. In this opinion I do not coincide. I think that the highest merit which a novel can have consists in perfect delineation of character, rather than in plot, or humour, or pathos, and I shall before long mention a subsequent work in which I think the main character of the story is so well developed as to justify me in asserting its claim above the others. The plot of *Orley Farm* is probably the best I have ever made ; but it has the fault of declaring itself, and thus coming to an end too early in the book. When Lady Mason tells her ancient lover that she did forge the will, the plot of *Orley Farm* has unravelled itself ;—and this she does in the middle of the tale. Independently, however, of this the novel is good. Sir Peregrine Orme, his grandson, Madeline Stavely, Mr. Furnival, Mr. Chaffanbrass, and the commercial gentlemen, are all good. The hunting is good. The lawyer's talk is good. Mr. Moulder carves his turkey admirably, and Mr. Kantwise sells his tables and chairs with spirit. I do not know that there is a dull page in the book. I am fond of *Orley Farm* ;—and am especially fond of its illustrations by Millais, which are the best I have seen in any novel in any language.

I now felt that I had gained my object. In 1862 I had achieved that which I contemplated when I went to London in 1834, and towards which

I made my first attempt when I began the *Macdermots* in 1843. I had created for myself a position among literary men, and had secured to myself an income on which I might live in ease and comfort,—which ease and comfort have been made to include many luxuries. From this time for a period of twelve years my income averaged £4500 a year. Of this I spent about two-thirds, and put by one. I ought perhaps to have done better,—to have spent one-third, and put by two ; but I have ever been too well inclined to spend freely that which has come easily.

This, however, has been so exactly the life which my thoughts and aspirations had marked out,—thoughts and aspirations which used to cause me to blush with shame because I was so slow in forcing myself to the work which they demanded,—that I have felt some pride in having attained it. I have before said how entirely I fail to reach the altitude of those who think that a man devoted to letters should be indifferent to the pecuniary results for which work is generally done. An easy income has always been regarded by me as a great blessing. Not to have to think of sixpences, or very much of shillings ; not to be unhappy because the coals have been burned too quickly, and the house linen wants renewing ; not to be debarred by the rigour of necessity from opening one's hands, perhaps foolishly, to one's friends ;—all this to me has been essential to the comfort of life. I have enjoyed the comfort for I may almost say the last twenty years, though no man in his youth had less prospect of doing so, or would have been less likely at twenty-five to have had such luxuries foretold to him by his friends.

But though the money has been sweet, the respect, the friendships, and the mode of life which has been achieved, have been much sweeter. In my boyhood, when I would be crawling up to school with dirty boots and trousers through the muddy lanes, I was always telling myself that the misery of the hour was not the worst of it, but that the mud and solitude and poverty of the time would insure me mud and solitude and poverty through my life. Those lads about me would go into Parliament, or become rectors and deans, or squires of parishes, or advocates thundering at the Bar. They would not live with me now,—but neither should I be able to live with them in after years. Nevertheless I have lived with them. When, at the age in which others go to the universities, I became a clerk in the Post Office, I felt that my old visions were being realised. I did not think it a high calling. I did not know then how very much good work may be done by a member of the Civil Service who will show himself capable of doing it. The Post Office at last grew upon me and forced itself into my affections. I became intensely anxious that people should have their letters delivered to them punctually. But my hope to rise had always been built on the writing of novels, and at last by the writing of novels I had risen.

I do not think that I ever toadied any one, or that I have acquired the character of a tuft-hunter. But here I do not scruple to say that I prefer the society of distinguished people, and that even the distinction of wealth confers many advantages. The best education is to be had at a price as well as the best broadcloth. The son of a peer is more likely to rub his shoulders against well-informed men than the son of a tradesman. The graces come easier to the wife of him who has had great-grandfathers than they do to her whose husband has been less,—or more fortunate, as he may think it. The discerning man will recognise the information and the graces when they are achieved without such assistance, and will honour the owners of them the more because of the difficulties they have overcome;—but the fact remains that the society of the well-born and of the wealthy will as a rule be worth seeking. I say this now, because these are the rules by which I have lived, and these are the causes which have instigated me to work.

I have heard the question argued—On what terms should a man of inferior rank live with those who are manifestly superior to him ? If a marquis or an earl honour me, who have no rank, with his intimacy, am I in my intercourse with him to remember our close acquaintance or his high rank ? I have always said that where the difference in position is quite marked, the overtures to intimacy should always come from the higher rank ; but if the intimacy be ever fixed, then that rank should be held of no account. It seems to me that intimate friendship admits of no standing but that of equality. I cannot be the Sovereign's friend, nor probably the friend of many very much beneath the Sovereign, because such equality is impossible.

When I first came to Waltham Cross in the winter of 1859–1860, I had almost made up my mind that my hunting was over. I could not then count upon an income which would enable me to

carry on an amusement which I should doubtless
find much more expensive in England than in
Ireland. I brought with me out of Ireland one
mare, but she was too light for me to ride in the
hunting-field. As, however, the money came in,
I very quickly fell back into my old habits. First
one horse was bought, then another, and then
a third, till it became established as a fixed rule
that I should not have less than four hunters in the
stable. Sometimes when my boys have been
at home I have had as many as six. Essex was the
chief scene of my sport, and gradually I became
known there almost as well as though I had been
an Essex squire, to the manner born. Few have
investigated more closely than I have done the
depth, and breadth, and water-holding capacities
of an Essex ditch. It will, I think, be accorded
to me by Essex men generally that I have ridden
hard. The cause of my delight in the amusement
I have never been able to analyse to my own
satisfaction. In the first place, even now, I know
very little about hunting,—though I know very
much of the accessories of the field. I am too
blind to see hounds turning, and cannot therefore
tell whether the fox has gone this way or that.
Indeed all the notice I take of hounds is not to ride
over them. My eyes are so constituted that I can
never see the nature of a fence. I either follow
some one, or ride at it with the full conviction that
I may be going into a horse-pond or a gravel-pit.
I have jumped into both one and the other.
I am very heavy, and have never ridden expensive
horses. I am also now old for such work, being so
stiff that I cannot get on to my horse without the
aid of a block or a bank. But I ride still after the

same fashion, with a boy's energy, determined to get ahead if it may possibly be done, hating the roads, despising young men who ride them, and with a feeling that life can not, with all her riches, have given me anything better than when I have gone through a long run to the finish, keeping a place, not of glory, but of credit, among my juniors.

CHAPTER X

'THE SMALL HOUSE AT ALLINGTON', 'CAN YOU FORGIVE HER?' 'RACHEL RAY', AND THE 'FORTNIGHTLY REVIEW'

DURING the early months of 1862 *Orley Farm* was still being brought out in numbers, and at the same time *Brown, Jones, and Robinson* was appearing in the *Cornhill Magazine*. In September 1862 the *Small House at Allington* began its career in the same periodical. The work on North America had also come out in 1862. In August 1863 the first number of *Can You Forgive Her?* was published as a separate serial, and was continued through 1864. In 1863 a short novel was produced in the ordinary volume form, called *Rachel Ray*. In addition to these I published during the time two volumes of stories called *The Tales of all Countries*. In the early spring of 1865 *Miss Mackenzie* was issued in the same form as *Rachel Ray*; and in May of the same year *The Belton Estate* was commenced with the commencement of the *Fortnightly Review*, of which periodical I will say a few words in this chapter.

I quite admit that I crowded my wares into the market too quickly, because the reading world could not want such a quantity of matter from the hands of one author in so short a space of time. I had not been quite so fertile as the unfor-

tunate gentleman who disgusted the publisher in
Paternoster Row,—in the story of whose produc-
tiveness I have always thought there was a touch
of romance,—but I had probably done enough to
make both publishers and readers think that I was
coming too often beneath their notice. Of publishers, however, I must speak collectively, as
my sins were, I think, chiefly due to the encouragement which I received from them individually.
What I wrote for the *Cornhill Magazine*, I always
wrote at the instigation of Mr. Smith. My other
works were published by Messrs. Chapman & Hall,
in compliance with contracts made by me with
them, and always made with their good-will.
Could I have been two separate persons at one
and the same time, of whom one might have been
devoted to Cornhill and the other to the interests
of the firm in Piccadilly, it might have been very
well;—but as I preserved my identity in both
places, I myself became aware that my name was
too frequent on title-pages.

Critics, if they ever trouble themselves with
these pages, will, of course, say that in what I have
now said I have ignored altogether the one great
evil of rapid production,—namely, that of inferior
work. And of course if the work was inferior
because of the too great rapidity of production,
the critics would be right. Giving to the subject
the best of my critical abilities, and judging of
my own work as nearly as possible as I would that
of another, I believe that the work which has been
done quickest has been done the best. I have
composed better stories—that is, have created
better plots—than those of *The Small House at
Allington* and *Can You Forgive Her?* and I have

portrayed two or three better characters than are
to be found in the pages of either of them; but
taking these books all through, I do not think
that I have ever done better work. Nor would
these have been improved by any effort in the art
of story telling, had each of these been the isolated
labour of a couple of years. How short is the time
devoted to the manipulation of a plot can be
known only to those who have written plays
and novels;—I may say also, how very little time
the brain is able to devote to such wearing work.
There are usually some hours of agonising doubt,
almost of despair,—so at least it has been with me,—
or perhaps some days. And then, with nothing
settled in my brain as to the final development
of events, with no capability of settling anything
but with a most distinct conception of some
character or characters, I have rushed at the work
as a rider rushes at a fence which he does not see.
Sometimes I have encountered what, in hunting
language, we call a cropper. I had such a fall in
two novels of mine, of which I have already spoken
—*The Bertrams* and *Castle Richmond*. I shall
have to speak of other such troubles. But these
failures have not arisen from over-hurried work.
When my work has been quicker done,—and it has
sometimes been done very quickly—the rapidity
has been achieved by hot pressure, not in the
conception, but in the telling of the story. Instead
of writing eight pages a day, I have written
sixteen; instead of working five days a week,
I have worked seven. I have trebled my usual
average, and have done so in circumstances which
have enabled me to give up all my thoughts for
the time to the book I have been writing. This

has generally been done at some quiet spot among
the mountains,—where there has been no society,
no hunting, no whist, no ordinary household
duties. And I am sure that the work so done
has had in it the best truth and the highest spirit
that I have been able to produce. At such times
I have been able to imbue myself thoroughly with
the characters I have had in hand. I have
wandered alone among the rocks and woods, crying
at their grief, laughing at their absurdities, and
thoroughly enjoying their joy. I have been impregnated with my own creations till it has been
my only excitement to sit with the pen in my
hand, and drive my team before me at as quick
a pace as I could make them travel.

The critics will again say that all this may
be very well as to the rough work of the author's
own brain, but it will be very far from well in
reference to the style in which that work has been
given to the public. After all, the vehicle which
a writer uses for conveying his thoughts to the
public should not be less important to him than
the thoughts themselves. An author can hardly
hope to be popular unless he can use popular
language. That is quite true ; but then comes the
question of achieving a popular—in other words,
I may say, a good and lucid style. How may an
author best acquire a mode of writing which shall
be agreeable and easily intelligible to the reader ?
He must be correct, because without correctness
he can be neither agreeable nor intelligible.
Readers will expect him to obey those rules which
they, consciously or unconsciously, have been
taught to regard as binding on language ; and
unless he does obey them, he will disgust. Without

much labour, no writer will achieve such a style. He has very much to learn; and, when he has learned that much, he has to acquire the habit of using what he has learned with ease. But all this must be learned and acquired,—not while he is writing that which shall please, but long before. His language must come from him as music comes from the rapid touch of the great performer's fingers; as words come from the mouth of the indignant orator; as letters fly from the fingers of the trained compositor; as the syllables tinkled out by little bells form themselves to the ear of the telegraphist. A man who thinks much of his words as he writes them will generally leave behind him work that smells of oil. I speak here, of course, of prose; for in poetry we know what care is necessary, and we form our taste accordingly.

Rapid writing will no doubt give rise to inaccuracy,—chiefly because the ear, quick and true as may be its operation, will occasionally break down under pressure, and, before a sentence be closed, will forget the nature of the composition with which it was commenced. A singular nominative will be disgraced by a plural verb, because other pluralities have intervened and have tempted the ear into plural tendencies. Tautologies will occur, because the ear, in demanding fresh emphasis, has forgotten that the desired force has been already expressed. I need not multiply these causes of error, which must have been stumbling-blocks indeed when men wrote in the long sentences of Gibbon, but which Macaulay, with his multiplicity of divisions, has done so much to enable us to avoid. A rapid writer will hardly

avoid these errors altogether. Speaking of myself,
I am ready to declare that, with much training,
I have been unable to avoid them. But the writer
for the press is rarely called upon—a writer of
books should never be called upon—to send his
manuscript hot from his hand to the printer.
It has been my practice to read everything four
times at least—thrice in manuscript and once in
print. Very much of my work I have read twice
in print. In spite of this I know that inaccuracies
have crept through,—not single spies, but in
battalions. From this I gather that the super-
vision has been insufficient, not that the work
itself has been done too fast. I am quite sure that
those passages which have been written with the
greatest stress of labour, and consequently with
the greatest haste, have been the most effective
and by no means the most inaccurate.

The Small House at Allington redeemed my
reputation with the spirited proprietor of the
Cornhill, which must, I should think, have been
damaged by *Brown, Jones, and Robinson*. In it
appeared Lily Dale, one of the characters which
readers of my novels have liked the best. In the
love with which she has been greeted I have hardly
joined with much enthusiasm, feeling that she is
somewhat of a French prig. She became first
engaged to a snob, who jilted her ; and then,
though in truth she loved another man who was
hardly good enough, she could not extricate
herself sufficiently from the collapse of her first
great misfortune to be able to make up her mind
to be the wife of one whom, though she loved him,
she did not altogether reverence. Prig as she
was, she made her way into the hearts of many

readers, both young and old ; so that, from that time to this, I have been continually honoured with letters, the purport of which has always been to beg me to marry Lily Dale to Johnny Eames. Had I done so, however, Lily would never have so endeared herself to these people as to induce them to write letters to the author concerning her fate. It was because she could not get over her troubles that they loved her. Outside Lily Dale and the chief interest of the novel, *The Small House at Allington* is, I think, good. The De Courcy family are alive, as is also Sir Raffle Buffle, who is a hero of the Civil Service. Sir Raffle was intended to represent a type, not a man ; but the man for the picture was soon chosen, and I was often assured that the portrait was very like. I have never seen the gentleman with whom I am supposed to have taken the liberty. There is also an old squire down at Allington, whose life as a country gentleman with rather straitened means is, I think, well described.

Of *Can you Forgive Her ?* I cannot speak with too great affection, though I do not know that of itself it did very much to increase my reputation. As regards the story, it was formed chiefly on that of the play which my friend Mr. Bartley had rejected long since, the circumstances of which the reader may perhaps remember. The play had been called *The Noble Jilt* ; but I was afraid of the name for a novel, lest the critics might throw a doubt on the nobility. There was more of tentative humility in that which I at last adopted. The character of the girl is carried through with considerable strength, but is not attractive. The humorous characters, which are also taken from

the play,—a buxom widow who with her eyes open
chooses the most scampish of two selfish suitors
because he is the better looking,—are well done.
Mrs. Greenow, between Captain Bellfield and
Mr. Cheeseacre, is very good fun—as far as the
fun of novels is. But that which endears the
book to me is the first presentation which I made
in it of Plantagenet Palliser, with his wife, Lady
Glencora.

By no amount of description or asseveration
could I succeed in making any reader understand
how much these characters with their belongings
have been to me in my latter life ; or how frequently I have used them for the expression of my
political or social convictions. They have been
as real to me as free trade was to Mr. Cobden, or
the dominion of a party to Mr. Disraeli ; and as
I have not been able to speak from the benches of
the House of Commons, or to thunder from plat-
forms, or to be efficacious as a lecturer, they have
served me as safety-valves by which to deliver
my soul. Mr. Plantagenet Palliser had appeared
in *The Small House at Allington*, but his birth
had not been accompanied by many hopes. In
the last pages of that novel he is made to seek
a remedy for a foolish false step in life by marrying
the grand heiress of the day ;—but the personage
of the great heiress does not appear till she comes
on the scene as a married woman in *Can You Forgive Her ?* He is the nephew and heir to a duke—
the Duke of Omnium—who was first introduced
in *Doctor Thorne*, and afterwards in *Framley
Parsonage*, and who is one of the belongings of
whom I have spoken. In these personages and
their friends, political and social, I have endea-

voured to depict the faults and frailties and vices,—
as also the virtues, the graces, and the strength
of our highest classes ; and if I have not made
the strength and virtues predominant over the
faults and vices, I have not painted the picture
as I intended. Plantagenet Palliser I think to
be a very noble gentleman,—such a one as justifies
to the nation the seeming anomaly of an hereditary
peerage and of primogeniture. His wife is in all
respects very inferior to him ; but she, too, has,
or has been intended to have, beneath the thin
stratum of her follies a basis of good principle,
which enabled her to live down the conviction of the
original wrong which was done to her, and taught
her to endeavour to do her duty in the position to
which she was called. She had received a great
wrong,—having been made, when little more than
a child, to marry a man for whom she cared
nothing ;—when, however, though she was little
more than a child, her love had been given elsewhere. She had very heavy troubles, but they did
not overcome her.

As to the heaviest of these troubles, I will say
a word in vindication of myself and of the way
I handled it in my work. In the pages of *Can
You Forgive Her ?* the girl's first love is introduced,
—beautiful, well-born, and utterly worthless. To
save a girl from wasting herself, and an heiress
from wasting her property on such a scamp, was
certainly the duty of the girl's friends. But it
must ever be wrong to force a girl into a marriage
with a man she does not love,—and certainly the
more so when there is another whom she does
love. In my endeavour to teach this lesson
I subjected the young wife to the terrible danger

of overtures from the man to whom her heart had been given. I was walking no doubt on ticklish ground, leaving for a while a doubt on the question whether the lover might or might not succeed. Then there came to me a letter from a distinguished dignitary of our Church, a man whom all men honoured, treating me with severity for what I was doing. It had been one of the innocent joys of his life, said the clergyman, to have my novels read to him by his daughters. But now I was writing a book which caused him to bid them close it! Must I also turn away to vicious sensation such as this? Did I think that a wife contemplating adultery was a character fit for my pages? I asked him in return, whether from his pulpit, or at any rate from his communion-table, he did not denounce adultery to his audience; and if so, why should it not be open to me to preach the same doctrine to mine. I made known nothing which the purest girl could not but have learned, and ought not to have learned, elsewhere, and I certainly lent no attraction to the sin which I indicated. His rejoinder was full of grace, and enabled him to avoid the annoyance of argumentation without abandoning his cause. He said that the subject was so much too long for letters; that he hoped I would go and stay a week with him in the country,—so that we might have it out. That opportunity, however, has never yet arrived.

Lady Glencora overcomes that trouble, and is brought, partly by her own sense of right and wrong, and partly by the genuine nobility of her husband's conduct, to attach herself to him after a certain fashion. The romance of her life is gone, but there remains a rich reality of which she is fully able to taste the flavour. She loves her rank and becomes ambitious, first of social, and then of political ascendancy. He is thoroughly true to her, after his thorough nature, and she, after her less perfect nature, is imperfectly true to him.

In conducting these characters from one story to another I realised the necessity, not only of consistency,—which, had it been maintained by a hard exactitude, would have been untrue to nature,—but also of those changes which time always produces. There are, perhaps, but few of us who, after the lapse of ten years, will be found to have changed our chief characteristics. The selfish man will still be selfish, and the false man false. But our manner of showing or of hiding these characteristics will be changed,—as also our power of adding to or diminishing their intensity. It was my study that these people, as they grew in years, should encounter the changes which come upon us all ; and I think that I have succeeded. The Duchess of Omnium, when she is playing the part of Prime Minister's wife, is the same woman as that Lady Glencora who almost longs to go off with Burgo Fitzgerald, but yet knows that she will never do so ; and the Prime Minister Duke, with his wounded pride and sore spirit, is he who, for his wife's sake, left power and place when they were first offered to him ;—but they have undergone the changes which a life so stirring as theirs would naturally produce. To do all this thoroughly was in my heart from first to last ; but I do not know that the game has been worth the candle. To carry out my scheme I have had to spread my picture over so wide a canvas that I cannot expect that any lover of such art should trouble himself to look at it as a whole. Who will read *Can You Forgive Her? Phineas Finn, Phineas Redux,* and *The Prime Minister* consecutively, in order that they may understand the characters of the Duke of Omnium, of Plantagenet Palliser, and of Lady Glencora ? Who will ever know that they should be so read ? But in the performance of the work I had much gratification, and was enabled from time to time to have in this way that fling at the political doings of the day which every man likes to take, if not in one fashion then in another. I look upon this string of characters,—carried sometimes into other novels than those just named,—as the best work of my life. Taking him altogether, I think that Plantagenet Palliser stands more firmly on the ground than any other personage I have created.

On Christmas Day 1863 we were startled by the news of Thackeray's death. He had then for many months given up the editorship of the *Cornhill Magazine,*—a position for which he was hardly fitted either by his habits or temperament,—but was still employed in writing for its pages. I had known him only for four years, but had grown into much intimacy with him and his family. I regard him as one of the most tender-hearted human beings I ever knew, who, with an exaggerated contempt for the foibles of the world at large, would entertain an almost equally exaggerated sympathy with the joys and troubles of individuals around him. He had been unfor-tunate in early life—unfortunate in regard to money—unfortunate with an afflicted wife—unfortunate in having his home broken up before

his children were fit to be his companions. This
threw him too much upon clubs, and taught him
to dislike general society. But it never affected
his heart, or clouded his imagination. He could
still revel in the pangs and joys of fictitious life,
and could still feel—as he did to the very last—
the duty of showing to his readers the evil consequences of evil conduct. It was perhaps his
chief fault as a writer that he could never abstain
from that dash of satire which he felt to be
demanded by the weaknesses which he saw around
him. The satirist who writes nothing but satire
should write but little,—or it will seem that his
satire springs rather from his own caustic nature
than from the sins of the world in which he lives.
I myself regard *Esmond* as the greatest novel in
the English language, basing that judgment upon
the excellence of its language, on the clear individuality of the characters, on the truth of its
delineations in regard to the time selected, and on
its great pathos. There are also in it a few scenes
so told that even Scott has never equalled the
telling. Let any one who doubts this read the
passage in which Lady Castlewood induces the
Duke of Hamilton to think that his nuptials
with Beatrice will be honoured if Colonel Esmond
will give away the bride. When he went from us
he left behind living novelists with great names ;
but I think that they who best understood the
matter felt that the greatest master of fiction of
this age had gone.

Rachel Ray underwent a fate which no other
novel of mine has encountered. Some years
before this a periodical called *Good Words* had
been established under the editorship of my

friend Dr. Norman Macleod, a well-known Presby-
terian pastor in Glasgow. In 1863 he asked me
to write a novel for his magazine, explaining
to me that his principles did not teach him to
confine his matter to religious subjects, and
paying me the compliment of saying that he
would feel himself quite safe in my hands. In
reply I told him I thought he was wrong in his
choice ; that though he might wish to give a novel
to the readers of *Good Words*, a novel from me
would hardly be what he wanted, and that I could
not undertake to write either with any specially
religious tendency, or in any fashion different
from that which was usual to me. As worldly
and—if any one thought me wicked—as wicked
as I had heretofore been, I must still be, should
I write for *Good Words*. He persisted in his
request, and I came to terms as to a story for the
periodical. I wrote it and sent it to him, and
shortly afterwards received it back—a considerable
portion having been printed—with an intimation
that it would not do. A letter more full of wailing
and repentance no man ever wrote. It was, he
said, all his own fault. He should have taken my
advice. He should have known better. But the
story, such as it was, he could not give to his
readers in the pages of *Good Words*. Would I forgive him ? Any pecuniary loss to which his
decision might subject me the owner of the
publication would willingly make good. There
was some loss—or rather would have been—and
that money I exacted, feeling that the fault had
in truth been with the editor. There is the tale
now to speak for itself. It is not brilliant, nor in
any way very excellent ; but it certainly is not

very wicked. There is some dancing in one of the early chapters, described, no doubt, with that approval of the amusement which I have always entertained; and it was this to which my friend demurred. It is more true of novels than perhaps of anything else, that one man's food is another man's poison.

Miss Mackenzie was written with a desire to prove that a novel may be produced without any love; but even in this attempt it breaks down before the conclusion. In order that I might be strong in my purpose, I took for my heroine a very unattractive old maid, who was overwhelmed with money troubles; but even she was in love before the end of the book, and made a romantic marriage with an old man. There is in this story an attack upon charitable bazaars, made with a violence which will, I think, convince any reader that such attempts at raising money were at the time very odious to me. I beg to say that since that I have had no occasion to alter my opinion. *Miss Mackenzie* was published in the early spring of 1865.

At the same time I was engaged with others in establishing a periodical Review, in which some of us trusted much, and from which we expected great things. There was, however, in truth so little combination of idea among us, that we were not justified in our trust or in our expectations. And yet we were honest in our purpose, and have, I think, done some good by our honesty. The matter on which we were all agreed was freedom of speech, combined with personal responsibility. We would be neither conservative nor liberal, neither religious nor free-thinking, neither popular nor exclusive ;—but we would let any man who had a thing to say, and knew how to say it, speak freely. But he should always speak with the responsibility of his name attached. In the very beginning I militated against this impossible negation of principles,—and did so most irrationally, seeing that I had agreed to the negation of principles,—by declaring that nothing should appear denying or questioning the divinity of Christ. It was a most preposterous claim to make for such a publication as we proposed, and it at once drove from us one or two who had proposed to join us. But we went on, and our company—limited—was formed. We subscribed, I think, £1250 each. I at least subscribed that amount, and—having agreed to bring out our publication every fortnight, after the manner of the well-known French publication,—we called it *The Fortnightly*. We secured the services of G. H. Lewes as our editor. We agreed to manage our finances by a Board, which was to meet once a fortnight, and of which I was the Chairman. And we determined that the payments for our literature should be made on a liberal and strictly ready-money system. We carried out our principles till our money was all gone, and then we sold the copyright to Messrs. Chapman & Hall for a trifle. But before we parted with our property we found that a fortnightly issue was not popular with the trade through whose hands the work must reach the public ; and, as our periodical had not become sufficiently popular itself to bear down such opposition, we succumbed, and brought it out once a month. Still it was *The Fortnightly*, and still it is *The Fortnightly*. Of all the serial publications of the day, it probably is the most serious, the most earnest, the least devoted to amusement, the least flippant, the least jocose,—and yet it has the face to show itself month after month to the world, with so absurd a misnomer! It is, as all who know the laws of modern literature are aware, a very serious thing to change the name of a periodical. By doing so you begin an altogether new enterprise. Therefore should the name be well chosen;—whereas this was very ill chosen, a fault for which I alone was responsible.

That theory of eclecticism was altogether impracticable. It was as though a gentleman should go into the House of Commons determined to support no party, but to serve his country by individual utterances. Such gentlemen have gone into the House of Commons, but they have not served their country much. Of course the project broke down. Liberalism, free-thinking, and open inquiry will never object to appear in company with their opposites, because they have the conceit to think that they can quell those opposites; but the opposites will not appear in conjunction with liberalism, free-thinking, and open inquiry. As a natural consequence, our new publication became an organ of liberalism, free-thinking, and open inquiry. The result has been good; and though there is much in the now established principles of *The Fortnightly* with which I do not myself agree, I may safely say that the publication has assured an individuality, and asserted for itself a position in our periodical literature, which is well understood and highly respected.

As to myself and my own hopes in the matter, —I was craving after some increase in literary honesty, which I think is still desirable, but which is hardly to be attained by the means which then recommended themselves to me. In one of the early numbers I wrote a paper advocating the signature of the authors to periodical writing, admitting that the system should not be extended to journalistic articles on political subjects. I think that I made the best of my case ; but further consideration has caused me to doubt whether the reasons which induced me to make an exception in favour of political writing do not extend themselves also to writing on other subjects. Much of the literary criticism which we now have is very bad indeed ;—so bad as to be open to the charge both of dishonesty and incapacity. Books are criticised without being read,—are criticised by favour,—and are trusted by editors to the criticism of the incompetent. If the names of the critics were demanded, editors would be more careful. But I fear the effect would be that we should get but little criticism, and that the public would put but little trust in that little. An ordinary reader would not care to have his books recommended to him by Jones ; but the recommendation of the great unknown comes to him with all the weight of the *Times*, the *Spectator*, or the *Saturday*.

Though I admit so much, I am not a recreant from the doctrine I then preached. I think that the name of the author does tend to honesty, and that the knowledge that it will be inserted adds much to the author's industry and care. It debars him also from illegitimate license and dishonest assertions. A man should never be ashamed to acknowledge that which he is not ashamed to publish. In *The Fortnightly* everything has been signed, and in this way good has, I think, been done. Signatures to articles in other periodicals have become much more common since *The Fortnightly* was commenced.

After a time Mr. Lewes retired from the editorship, feeling that the work pressed too severely on his moderate strength. Our loss in him was very great, and there was considerable difficulty in finding a successor. I must say that the present proprietor has been fortunate in the choice he did make. Mr. John Morley has done the work with admirable patience, zeal, and capacity. Of course he has got around him a set of contributors whose modes of thought are what we may call much advanced; he being 'much advanced' himself, would not work with other aids. The periodical has a peculiar tone of its own; but it holds its own with ability, and though there are many who perhaps hate it, there are none who despise it. When the company sold it, having spent about £9000 on it, it was worth little or nothing. Now I believe it to be a good property.

My own last personal concern with it was on a matter of fox-hunting.[1] There came out in it an article from the pen of Mr. Freeman the historian, condemning the amusement, which I love, on the grounds of cruelty and general brutality. Was it possible, asked Mr. Freeman, quoting from Cicero, that any educated man should find delight in so coarse a pursuit? Always

[1] I have written various articles for it since, especially two on Cicero, to which I devoted great labour.

bearing in mind my own connection with *The Fortnightly*, I regarded this almost as a rising of a child against the father. I felt at any rate bound to answer Mr. Freeman in the same columns, and I obtained Mr. Morley's permission to do so. I wrote my defence of fox-hunting, and there it is. In regard to the charge of cruelty, Mr. Freeman seems to assert that nothing unpleasant should be done to any of God's creatures except for a useful purpose. The protection of a lady's shoulders from the cold is a useful purpose; and therefore a dozen fur-bearing animals may be snared in the snow and left to starve to death in the wires, in order that the lady may have the tippet, —though a tippet of wool would serve the purpose as well as a tippet of fur. But the congregation and healthful amusement of one or two hundred persons, on whose behalf a single fox may or may not be killed, is not a useful purpose. I think that Mr. Freeman has failed to perceive that amusement is as needful and almost as necessary as food and raiment. The absurdity of the further charge as to the general brutality of the pursuit, and its consequent unfitness for an educated man, is to be attributed to Mr. Freeman's ignorance of what is really done and said in the hunting-field,— perhaps to his misunderstanding of Cicero's words. There was a rejoinder to my answer, and I asked for space for further remarks. I could have it, the editor said, if I much wished it; but he preferred that the subject should be closed. Of course I was silent. His sympathies were all with Mr. Freeman,—and against the foxes, who, but for foxhunting, would cease to exist in England. And I felt that *The Fortnightly* was hardly the place for the defence of the sport. Afterwards Mr. Freeman kindly suggested to me that he would be glad to publish my article in a little book to be put out by him condemnatory of fox-hunting generally. He was to have the last word and the first word, and that power of picking to pieces which he is known to use in so masterly a manner, without any reply from me! This I was obliged to decline. If he would give me the last word, as he would have the first, then, I told him, I should be proud to join him in the book. This offer did not however meet his views.

It had been decided by the Board of Management, somewhat in opposition to my own ideas on the subject, that the *Fortnightly Review* should always contain a novel. It was of course natural that I should write the first novel, and I wrote *The Belton Estate*. It is similar in its attributes to *Rachel Ray* and to *Miss Mackenzie*. It is readable, and contains scenes which are true to life; but it has no peculiar merits, and will add nothing to my reputation as a novelist. I have not looked at it since it was published; and now turning back to it in my memory, I seem to remember almost less of it than of any book that I have written.

END OF THE FIRST VOLUME

CHAPTER XI

'THE CLAVERINGS,' THE 'PALL MALL GAZETTE,' 'NINA BALATKA,' AND 'LINDA TRESSEL'

The Claverings, which came out in 1866 and 1867, was the last novel which I wrote for the *Cornhill*; and it was for this that I received the highest rate of pay that was ever accorded to me. It was the same length as *Framley Parsonage*, and the price was £2800. Whether much or little, it was offered by the proprietor of the magazine, and was paid in a single cheque.

In the *Claverings* I did not follow the habit which had now become very common to me, of introducing personages whose names are already known to the readers of novels, and whose characters were familiar to myself. If I remember rightly, no one appears here who had appeared before or who has been allowed to appear since. I consider the story as a whole to be good, though I am not aware that the public has ever corroborated that verdict. The chief character is that of a young woman who has married manifestly for money and rank,—so manifestly that she does not herself pretend, even while she is making the marriage, that she has any other reason. The man is old, disreputable, and a worn-out debauchee. Then comes the punishment natural to the offence.

When she is free, the man whom she had loved, and who had loved her, is engaged to another woman. He vacillates and is weak,—in which weakness is the fault of the book, as he plays the part of hero. But she is strong—strong in her purpose, strong in her desires, and strong in her consciousness that the punishment which comes upon her has been deserved.

But the chief merit of *The Claverings* is in the genuine fun of some of the scenes. Humour has not been my forte, but I am inclined to think that the characters of Captain Boodle, Archie Clavering, and Sophie Gordeloup are humorous. Count Pateroff, the brother of Sophie, is also good, and disposes of the young hero's interference in a somewhat masterly manner. In *The Claverings*, too, there is a wife whose husband is a brute to her, who loses an only child—his heir—and who is rebuked by her lord because the boy dies. Her sorrow is, I think, pathetic. From beginning to end the story is well told. But I doubt now whether any one reads *The Claverings*. When I remember how many novels I have written, I have no right to expect that above a few of them shall endure even to the second year beyond publication. This story closed my connection with the *Cornhill Magazine*;—but not with its owner, Mr. George Smith, who subsequently brought out a further novel of mine in a separate form, and who about this time established the *Pall Mall Gazette*, to which paper I was for some years a contributor.

It was in 1865 that the *Pall Mall Gazette* was commenced, the name having been taken from a fictitious periodical, which was the offspring of

Thackeray's brain. It was set on foot by the unassisted energy and resources of George Smith, who had succeeded by means of his magazine and his publishing connection in getting around him a society of literary men who sufficed, as far as literary ability went, to float the paper at once under favourable auspices. His two strongest staffs probably were 'Jacob Omnium', whom I regard as the most forcible newspaper writer of my days, and Fitz-James Stephen, the most conscientious and industrious. To them the *Pall Mall Gazette* owed very much of its early success,— and to the untiring energy and general ability of its proprietor. Among its other contributors were George Lewes, Hannay,—who, I think, came up from Edinburgh for employment on its columns,— Lord Houghton, Lord Strangford, Charles Merivale, Greenwood the present editor, Greg, myself, and very many others ;—so many others, that I have met at a Pall Mall dinner a crowd of guests who would have filled the House of Commons more respectably than I have seen it filled even on important occasions. There are many who now remember—and no doubt when this is published there will be left some to remember—the great stroke of business which was done by the revelations of a visitor to one of the casual wards in London. A person had to be selected who would undergo the misery of a night among the usual occupants of a casual ward in a London poorhouse, and who should at the same time be able to record what he felt and saw. The choice fell upon Mr. Greenwood's brother, who certainly possessed the courage and the powers of endurance. The description, which was very well given, was

I think, chiefly written by the brother of the Casual himself. It had a great effect, which was increased by secrecy as to the person who encountered all the horrors of that night. I was more than once assured that Lord Houghton was the man. I heard it asserted also that I myself had been the hero. At last the unknown one could no longer endure that his honours should be hidden, and revealed the truth,—in opposition, I fear, to promises to the contrary, and instigated by a conviction that if known he could turn his honours to account. In the meantime, however, that record of a night passed in a workhouse had done more to establish the sale of the journal than all the legal lore of Stephen, or the polemical power of Higgins, or the critical acumen of Lewes.

My work was very various. I wrote much on the subject of the American War, on which my feelings were at the time very keen,—subscribing, if I remember right, my name to all that I wrote. I contributed also some sets of sketches, of which those concerning hunting found favour with the public. They were republished afterwards, and had a considerable sale, and may, I think, still be recommended to those who are fond of hunting, as being accurate in their description of the different classes of people who are to be met in the hunting-field. There was also a set of clerical sketches, which was considered to be of sufficient importance to bring down upon my head the critical wrath of a great dean of that period. The most ill-natured review that was ever written upon any work of mine appeared in the *Contemporary Review* with reference to these Clerical Sketches. The critic told me that I did not

understand Greek. That charge has been made
not unfrequently by those who have felt themselves
strong in that pride-producing language. It is
much to read Greek with ease, but it is not disgraceful to be unable to do so. To pretend to
read it without being able,—that is disgraceful.
The critic, however, had been driven to wrath by
my saying that Deans of the Church of England
loved to revisit the glimpses of the metropolitan
moon.

I also did some critical work for the *Pall Mall*,—
as I did also for *The Fortnightly*. It was not to
my taste, but was done in conformity with strict
conscientious scruples. I read what I took in
hand, and said what I believed to be true,—
always giving to the matter time altogether
incommensurate with the pecuniary result to
myself. In doing this for the *Pall Mall*, I fell
into great sorrow. A gentleman, whose wife was
dear to me as if she were my own sister, was in
some trouble as to his conduct in the public
service. He had been blamed, as he thought
unjustly, and vindicated himself in a pamphlet.
This he handed to me one day, asking me to read
it, and express my opinion about it if I found that
I had an opinion. I thought the request inju-
dicious, and I did not read the pamphlet. He
met me again, and, handing me a second pamphlet,
pressed me very hard. I promised him that
I would read it, and that if I found myself able
I would express myself;—but that I must say not
what I wished to think, but what I did think.
To this of course he assented. I then went very
much out of my way to study the subject,—which
was one requiring study. I found, or thought

that I found, that the conduct of the gentleman in his office had been indiscreet; but that charges made against himself affecting his honour were baseless. This I said, emphasising much more strongly than was necessary the opinion which I had formed of his indiscretion,—as will so often be the case when a man has a pen in his hand. It is like a club or a sledge-hammer,—in using which, either for defence or attack, a man can hardly measure the strength of the blows he gives. Of course there was offence,—and a breaking off of intercourse between loving friends,—and a sense of wrong received, and I must own, too, of wrong done. It certainly was not open to me to white-wash with honesty him whom I did not find to be white; but there was no duty incumbent on me to declare what was his colour in my eyes,—no duty even to ascertain. But I had been ruffled by the persistency of the gentleman's request,—which should not have been made,—and I punished him for his wrong-doing by doing a wrong myself. I must add, that before he died his wife succeeded in bringing us together.

In the early days of the paper, the proprietor, who at that time acted also as chief editor, asked me to undertake a duty,—of which the agony would indeed at no one moment have been so sharp as that endured in the casual ward, but might have been prolonged until human nature sank under it. He suggested to me that I should during an entire season attend the May meetings in Exeter Hall, and give a graphic and, if possible, amusing description of the proceedings. I did attend one,—which lasted three hours,—and wrote a paper which I think was called *A Zulu in Search of a Religion.* But when the meeting was over I went to that spirited proprietor, and begged him to impose upon me some task more equal to my strength. Not even on behalf of the *Pall Mall Gazette,* which was very dear to me, could I go through a second May meeting,—much less endure a season of such martyrdom.

I have to acknowledge that I found myself unfit for work on a newspaper. I had not taken to it early enough in life to learn its ways and bear its trammels. I was fidgety when any word was altered in accordance with the judgment of the editor, who, of course, was responsible for what appeared. I wanted to select my own subjects,— not to have them selected for me ; to write when I pleased,—and not when it suited others. As a permanent member of a staff I was no use, and after two or three years I dropped out of the work.

From the commencement of my success as a writer, which I date from the beginning of the *Cornhill Magazine,* I had always felt an injustice in literary affairs which had never afflicted me or even suggested itself to me while I was unsuccessful. It seemed to me that a name once earned carried with it too much favour. I indeed had never reached a height to which praise was awarded as a matter of course ; but there were others who sat on higher seats to whom the critics brought unmeasured incense and adulation, even when they wrote, as they sometimes did write, trash which from a beginner would not have been thought worthy of the slightest notice. I hope no one will think that in saying this I am actuated by jealousy of others. Though I never reached that height, still I had so far progressed that that which I wrote was received with too much favour. The injustice which struck me did not consist in that which was withheld from me, but in that which was given to me. I felt that aspirants coming up below me might do work as good as mine, and probably much better work, and yet fail to have it appreciated. In order to test this, I determined to be such an aspirant myself, and to begin a course of novels anonymously, in order that I might see whether I could obtain a second identity,—whether as I had made one mark by such literary ability as I possessed, I might succeed in doing so again. In 1865 I began a short tale called *Nina Balatka*, which in 1866 was published anonymously in *Blackwood's Magazine*. In 1867 this was followed by another of the same length, called *Linda Tressel*. I will speak of them together, as they are of the same nature and of nearly equal merit. Mr. Blackwood, who himself read the MS. of *Nina Balatka*, expressed an opinion that it would not from its style be discovered to have been written by me ; —but it was discovered by Mr. Hutton of the *Spectator*, who found the repeated use of some special phrase which had rested upon his ear too frequently when reading for the purpose of criticism other works of mine. He declared in his paper that *Nina Balatka* was by me, showing I think more sagacity than good nature. I ought not, however, to complain of him, as of all the critics of my work he has been the most observant, and generally the most eulogistic. *Nina Balatka* never rose sufficiently high in reputation to make its detection a matter of any importance. Once or twice I heard the story mentioned by readers who did not know me to be the author, and always with praise ; but it had no real success. The same may be said of *Linda Tressel*. Blackwood, who of course knew the author, was willing to publish them, trusting that works by an experienced writer would make their way, even without the writer's name, and he was willing to pay me for them, perhaps half what they would have fetched with my name. But he did not find the speculation answer, and declined a third attempt, though a third such tale was written for him.

Nevertheless I am sure that the two stories are good. Perhaps the first is somewhat the better, as being the less lachrymose. They were both written very quickly, but with a considerable amount of labour ; and both were written immediately after visits to the towns in which the scenes are laid,—Prague, mainly, and Nuremburg. Of course I had endeavoured to change not only my manner of language, but my manner of story-telling also ; and in this, *pace* Mr. Hutton, I think that I was successful. English life in them there was none. There was more of romance proper than had been usual with me. And I made an attempt at local colouring, at descriptions of scenes and places, which has not been usual with me. In all this I am confident that I was in a measure successful. In the loves, and fears, and hatreds, both of Nina and of Linda, there is much that is pathetic. Prague is Prague, and Nuremburg is Nuremburg. I know that the stories are good, but they missed the object with which they had been written. Of course there is not in this any evidence that I might not have succeeded a second time as I succeeded before, had I gone on with the same dogged perseverance. Mr. Blackwood, had I still further reduced my price, would probably have continued the experiment. Another ten years of unpaid unflagging labour might have built up a second reputation. But this at any rate did seem clear to me, that with all the increased advantages which practice in my art must have given me, I could not at once induce English readers to read what I gave to them, unless I gave it with my name.

I do not wish to have it supposed from this that I quarrel with public judgment in affairs of literature. It is a matter of course that in all things the public should trust to established reputation. It is as natural that a novel reader wanting novels should send to a library for those by George Eliot or Wilkie Collins, as that a lady when she wants a pie for a picnic should go to Fortnum & Mason. Fortnum & Mason can only make themselves Fortnum & Mason by dint of time and good pies combined. If Titian were to send us a portrait from the other world, as certain dead poets send their poetry, by means of a medium, it would be some time before the art critic of the *Times* would discover its value. We may sneer at the want of judgment thus displayed, but such slowness of judgment is human and has always existed. I say all this here because my thoughts on the matter have forced upon me the conviction that very much consideration is due to the bitter feelings of disappointed authors.

We who have succeeded are so apt to tell new aspirants not to aspire, because the thing to be done may probably be beyond their reach. ' My dear young lady, had you not better stay at home and darn your stockings?' 'As, sir, you have asked for my candid opinion, I can only counsel you to try some other work of life which may be better suited to your abilities.' What old-established successful author has not said such words as these to humble aspirants for critical advice, till they have become almost formulas? No doubt there is cruelty in such answers; but the man who makes them has considered the matter within himself, and has resolved that such cruelty is the best mercy. No doubt the chances against literary aspirants are very great. It is so easy to aspire,—and to begin! A man cannot make a watch or a shoe without a variety of tools and many materials. He must also have learned much. But any young lady can write a book who has a sufficiency of pens and paper. It can be done anywhere; in any clothes—which is a great thing; at any hours—to which happy accident in literature I owe my success. And the success, when achieved, is so pleasant! The aspirants, of course, are very many; and the experienced councillor, when asked for his candid judgment as to this or that effort, knows that among every hundred efforts there will be ninety-nine failures. Then the answer is so ready: 'My dear young lady, do darn your stockings; it will be for the best.' Or perhaps, less tenderly, to the male aspirant: 'You must earn some money, you say. Don't you think that a stool in a counting-house might be better?' The advice will probably be good advice,—probably, no doubt, as may be proved by the terrible majority of failures. But who is to be sure that he is not expelling an angel from the heaven to which, if less roughly treated, he would soar,—that he is not dooming some Milton to be mute and inglorious, who, but for such cruel ill-judgment, would become vocal to all ages?

The answer to all this seems to be ready enough. The judgment, whether cruel or tender, should not be ill-judgment. He who consents to sit as judge should have capacity for judging. But in this matter no accuracy of judgment is possible. It may be that the matter subjected to the critic is so bad or so good as to make an assured answer possible. ' You, at any rate, cannot make this your vocation ; ' or ' You, at any rate, can succeed, if you will try.' But cases as to which such certainty can be expressed are rare. The critic who wrote the article on the early verses of Lord Byron, which produced the *English Bards and Scotch Reviewers*, was justified in his criticism by the merits of the *Hours of Idleness*. The lines had nevertheless been written by that Lord Byron who became our Byron. In a little satire called *The Biliad*, which, I think, nobody knows, are the following well-expressed lines :—

' When Payne Knight's *Taste* was issued to the town,
A few Greek verses in the text set down
Were torn to pieces, mangled into hash,
Doomed to the flames as execrable trash,—
In short, were butchered rather than dissected,
And several false quantities detected,—
Till, when the smoke had vanished from the cinders,
'Twas just discovered that—*the lines were Pindar's !* '

There can be no assurance against cases such as these ; and yet we are so free with our advice, always bidding the young aspirant to desist.

There is perhaps no career of life so charming as that of a successful man of letters. Those little

unthought of advantages which I just now named
are in themselves attractive. If you like the town,
live in the town, and do your work there ; if you
like the country, choose the country. It may be
done on the top of a mountain or in the bottom
of a pit. It is compatible with the rolling of the sea
and the motion of a railway. The clergyman,
the lawyer, the doctor, the member of Parliament,
the clerk in a public office, the tradesman, and
even his assistant in the shop, must dress in
accordance with certain fixed laws ; but the
author need sacrifice to no grace, hardly even to
Propriety. He is subject to no bonds such as
those which bind other men. Who else is free
from all shackle as to hours ? The judge must sit
at ten, and the attorney-general, who is making
his £20,000 a year, must be there with his bag.
The Prime Minister must be in his place on that
weary front bench shortly after prayers, and must
sit there, either asleep or awake, even though
—— or —— should be addressing the House.
During all that Sunday which he maintains should
be a day of rest, the active clergyman toils like
a galley-slave. The actor, when eight o'clock
comes, is bound to his footlights. The Civil
Service clerk must sit there from ten till four,—
unless his office be fashionable, when twelve to six
is just as heavy on him. The author may do his
work at five in the morning when he is fresh from
his bed, or at three in the morning before he goes
there. And the author wants no capital, and
encounters no risks. When once he is afloat, the
publisher finds all that ;—and indeed, unless he be
rash, finds it whether he be afloat or not. But it
is in the consideration which he enjoys that the

successful author finds his richest reward. He is, if not of equal rank, yet of equal standing with the highest; and if he be open to the amenities of society, may choose his own circles. He without money can enter doors which are closed against almost all but him and the wealthy. I have often heard it said that in this country the man of letters is not recognised. I believe the meaning of this to be that men of letters are not often invited to be knights and baronets. I do not think that they wish it;—and if they had it they would, as a body, lose much more than they would gain. I do not at all desire to have letters put after my name, or to be called Sir Anthony, but if my friends Tom Hughes and Charles Reade became Sir Thomas and Sir Charles, I do not know how I might feel,—or how my wife might feel, if we were left unbedecked. As it is, the man of letters who would be selected for titular honour, if such bestowal of honours were customary, receives from the general respect of those around him a much more pleasant recognition of his worth.

If this be so,—if it be true that the career of the successful literary man be thus pleasant,—it is not wonderful that many should attempt to win the prize. But how is a man to know whether or not he has within him the qualities necessary for such a career? He makes an attempt, and fails; repeats his attempt, and fails again! So many have succeeded at last who have failed more than once or twice! Who will tell him the truth as to himself? Who has power to find out that truth? The hard man sends him off without a scruple to that office-stool; the soft man assures him that there is much merit in his MS.

Oh, my young aspirant,—if ever such a one should read these pages,—be sure that no one can tell you! To do so it would be necessary not only to know what there is now within you, but also to foresee what time will produce there. This, however, I think may be said to you, without any doubt as to the wisdom of the counsel given, that if it be necessary for you to live by your work, do not begin by trusting to literature. Take the stool in the office as recommended to you by the hard man; and then, in such leisure hours as may belong to you, let the praise which has come from the lips of that soft man induce you to persevere in your literary attempts. Should you fail, then your failure will not be fatal,—and what better could you have done with the leisure hours had you not so failed? Such double toil, you will say, is severe. Yes; but if you want this thing, you must submit to severe toil.

Sometime before this I had become one of the Committee appointed for the distribution of the moneys of the Royal Literary Fund, and in that capacity I heard and saw much of the sufferings of authors. I may in a future chapter speak further of this Institution, which I regard with great affection, and in reference to which I should be glad to record certain convictions of my own; but I allude to it now, because the experience I have acquired in being active in its cause forbids me to advise any young man or woman to enter boldly on a literary career in search of bread. I know how utterly I should have failed myself had my bread not been earned elsewhere while I was making my efforts. During ten years of work, which I commenced with some aid from

the fact that others of my family were in the same
profession, I did not earn enough to buy me the
pens, ink, and paper which I was using ; and then
when, with all my experience in my art, I began
again as from a new springing point, I should
have failed again unless again I could have given
years to the task. Of course there have been
many who have done better than I,—many whose
powers have been infinitely greater. But then,
too, I have seen the failure of many who were
greater.

The career, when success has been achieved, is
certainly very pleasant ; but the agonies which
are endured in the search for that success are
often terrible. And the author's poverty is,
I think, harder to be borne than any other poverty.
The man, whether rightly or wrongly, feels that
the world is using him with extreme injustice.
The more absolutely he fails, the higher, it is
probable, he will reckon his own merits ; and
the keener will be the sense of injury in that he
whose work is of so high a nature cannot get
bread, while they whose tasks are mean are lapped
in luxury. ' I, with my well-filled mind, with my
clear intellect, with all my gifts, cannot earn a poor
crown a day, while that fool, who simpers in
a little room behind a shop, makes his thousands
every year.' The very charity, to which he too
often is driven, is bitterer to him than to others.
While he takes it he almost spurns the hand that
gives it to him, and every fibre of his heart within
him is bleeding with a sense of injury.

The career, when successful, is pleasant enough
certainly ; but when unsuccessful, it is of all
careers the most agonising.

CHAPTER XII

ON NOVELS AND THE ART OF WRITING
THEM

It is nearly twenty years since I proposed to myself to write a history of English prose fiction. I shall never do it now, but the subject is so good a one that I recommend it heartily to some man of letters, who shall at the same time be indefatigable and light-handed. I acknowledge that I broke down in the task, because I could not endure the labour in addition to the other labours of my life. Though the book might be charming, the work was very much the reverse. It came to have a terrible aspect to me, as did that proposition that I should sit out all the May meetings of a season. According to my plan of such a history it would be necessary to read an infinity of novels, and not only to read them, but so to read them as to point out the excellences of those which are most excellent, and to explain the defects of those which, though defective, had still reached sufficient reputation to make them worthy of notice. I did read many after this fashion,—and here and there I have the criticisms which I wrote. In regard to many, they were written on some blank page within the book. I have not, however, even a list of the books so criticised. I think that the *Arcadia* was the first, and *Ivanhoe* the last. My plan, as I settled it at last, had been to begin with *Robinson Crusoe*, which is the earliest really popular novel which we have in our language, and to continue the review so as to include the works of all English novelists of reputation, except those who might still be living when my task should be completed. But when Dickens and Bulwer died, my spirit flagged, and that which I had already found to be very difficult had become almost impossible to me at my then period of life.

I began my own studies on the subject with works much earlier than *Robinson Crusoe*, and made my way through a variety of novels which were necessary for my purpose, but which in the reading gave me no pleasure whatever. I never worked harder than at the *Arcadia*, or read more detestable trash than the stories written by Mrs. Aphra Behn; but these two were necessary to my purpose, which was not only to give an estimate of the novels as I found them, but to describe how it had come to pass that the English novels of the present day have become what they are, to point out the effects which they have produced, and to inquire whether their great popularity has on the whole done good or evil to the people who read them. I still think that the book is one well worthy to be written.

I intended to write that book to vindicate my own profession as a novelist, and also to vindicate that public taste in literature which has created and nourished the profession which I follow. And I was stirred up to make such an attempt by a conviction that there still exists among us Englishmen a prejudice in respect to novels which might, perhaps, be lessened by such a work. This prejudice

is not against the reading of novels, as is proved
by their general acceptance among us. But it
exists strongly in reference to the appreciation in
which they are professed to be held ; and it robs
them of much of that high character which they
may claim to have earned by their grace, their
honesty, and good teaching.

No man can work long at any trade without being
brought to consider much whether that which he
is daily doing tends to evil or to good. I have
written many novels, and have known many
writers of novels, and I can assert that such
thoughts have been strong with them and with
myself. But in acknowledging that these writers
have received from the public a full measure of
credit for such genius, ingenuity, or perseverance
as each may have displayed, I feel that there is
still wanting to them a just appreciation of the
excellence of their calling, and a general understanding of the high nature of the work which
they perform.

By the common consent of all mankind who
have read, poetry takes the highest place in
literature. That nobility of expression, and all but
divine grace of words, which she is bound to attain
before she can make her footing good, is not compatible with prose. Indeed it is that which turns
prose into poetry. When that has been in truth
achieved, the reader knows that the writer has
soared above the earth, and can teach his lessons
somewhat as a god might teach. He who sits
down to write his tale in prose makes no such
attempt, nor does he dream that the poet's
honour is within his reach ;—but his teaching is of
the same nature, and his lessons all tend to the

same end. By either, false sentiments may be fostered ; false notions of humanity may be engendered ; false honour, false love, false worship may be created ; by either, vice instead of virtue may be taught. But by each, equally, may true honour, true love, true worship, and true humanity be inculcated ; and that will be the greatest teacher who will spread such truth the widest. But at present, much as novels, as novels, are bought and read, there exists still an idea, a feeling which is very prevalent, that novels at their best are but innocent. Young men and women,—and old men and women too,—read more of them than of poetry, because such reading is easier than the reading of poetry ; but they read them,—as men eat pastry after dinner,—not without some inward conviction that the taste is vain if not vicious. I take upon myself to say that it is neither vicious nor vain.

But all writers of fiction who have desired to think well of their own work, will probably have had doubts on their minds before they have arrived at this conclusion. Thinking much of my own daily labour and of its nature, I felt myself at first to be much afflicted and then to be deeply grieved by the opinion expressed by wise and thinking men as to the work done by novelists. But when, by degrees, I dared to examine and sift the sayings of such men, I found them to be sometimes silly and often arrogant. I began to inquire what had been the nature of English novels since they first became common in our own language, and to be desirous of ascertaining whether they had done harm or good. I could well remember that, in my own young days, they had not taken that undisputed possession of drawing-rooms which they now hold. Fifty years ago, when George IV was king, they were not indeed treated as Lydia had been forced to treat them in the preceding reign, when, on the approach of elders, *Peregrine Pickle* was hidden beneath the bolster, and *Lord Ainsworth* put away under the sofa. But the families in which an unrestricted permission was given for the reading of novels were very few, and from many they were altogether banished. The high poetic genius and correct morality of Walter Scott had not altogether succeeded in making men and women understand that lessons which were good in poetry could not be bad in prose. I remember that in those days an embargo was laid upon novel-reading, as a pursuit, which was to the novelist a much heavier tax than that want of full appreciation of which I now complain.

There is, we all know, no such embargo now. May we not say that people of an age to read have got too much power into their own hands to endure any very complete embargo ? Novels are read right and left, above stairs and below, in town houses and in country parsonages, by young countesses and by farmer's daughters, by old lawyers and by young students. It has not only come to pass that a special provision of them has to be made for the godly, but that the provision so made must now include books which a few years since the godly would have thought to be profane. It was this necessity which, a few years since, induced the editor of *Good Words* to apply to me for a novel,—which, indeed, when supplied was rejected, but which now, probably, owing to further change in the same direction, would have been accepted.

If such be the case—if the extension of novel-reading be so wide as I have described it—then very much good or harm must be done by novels. The amusement of the time can hardly be the only result of any book that is read, and certainly not so with a novel, which appeals especially to the imagination, and solicits the sympathy of the young. A vast proportion of the teaching of the day,—greater probably than many of us have acknowledged to ourselves,—comes from these books, which are in the hands of all readers. It is from them that girls learn what is expected from them, and what they are to expect when lovers come; and also from them that young men unconsciously learn what are, or should be, or may be, the charms of love,—though I fancy that few young men will think so little of their natural instincts and powers as to believe that I am right in saying so. Many other lessons also are taught. In these times, when the desire to be honest is pressed so hard, is so violently assaulted by the ambition to be great; in which riches are the easiest road to greatness; when the temptations to which men are subjected dull their eyes to the perfected iniquities of others; when it is so hard for a man to decide vigorously that the pitch, which so many are handling, will defile him if it be touched;—men's conduct will be actuated much by that which is from day to day depicted to them as leading to glorious or inglorious results. The woman who is described as having obtained all that the world holds to be precious, by lavishing her charms and her caresses unworthily and heart-lessly, will induce other women to do the same with theirs,—as will she who is made interesting by exhibitions of bold passion teach others to be spuriously passionate. The young man who in a novel becomes a hero, perhaps a Member of Parliament, and almost a Prime Minister, by trickery, falsehood, and flash cleverness, will have many followers, whose attempts to rise in the world ought to lie heavily on the conscience of the novelists who create fictitious Cagliostros. There are Jack Sheppards other than those who break into houses and out of prisons,—Macheaths, who deserve the gallows more than Gay's hero.

Thinking of all this, as a novelist surely must do, —as I certainly have done through my whole career,—it becomes to him a matter of deep conscience how he shall handle those characters by whose words and doings he hopes to interest his readers. It will very frequently be the case that he will be tempted to sacrifice something for effect, to say a word or two here, or to draw a picture there, for which he feels that he has the power, and which when spoken or drawn would be alluring. The regions of absolute vice are foul and odious. The savour of them, till custom has hardened the palate and the nose, is disgusting. In these he will hardly tread. But there are outskirts on these regions, on which sweet-smelling flowers seem to grow, and grass to be green. It is in these border-lands that the danger lies. The novelist may not be dull. If he commit that fault he can do neither harm nor good. He must please, and the flowers and the grass in these neutral territories sometimes seem to give him so easy an opportunity of pleasing!

The writer of stories must please, or he will be nothing. And he must teach whether he wish to

teach or no. How shall he teach lessons of virtue
and at the same time make himself a delight to his
readers ? That sermons are not in themselves
often thought to be agreeable we all know. Nor
are disquisitions on moral philosophy supposed to
be pleasant reading for our idle hours. But the
novelist, if he have a conscience, must preach his
sermons with the same purpose as the clergyman,
and must have his own system of ethics. If he can
do this efficiently, if he can make virtue alluring and
vice ugly, while he charms his readers instead of
wearying them, then I think Mr. Carlyle need not
call him distressed, nor talk of that long ear of
fiction, nor question whether he be or not the most
foolish of existing mortals.

I think that many have done so ; so many that
we English novelists may boast as a class that such
has been the general result of our own work.
Looking back to the past generation, I may say
with certainty that such was the operation of the
novels of Miss Edgeworth, Miss Austen, and
Walter Scott. Coming down to my own times,
I find such to have been the teaching of
Thackeray, of Dickens, and of George Eliot.
Speaking, as I shall speak to any who may
read these words, with that absence of self-
personality which the dead may claim, I will boast
that such has been the result of my own writing.
Can any one by search through the works of the six
great English novelists I have named, find a scene,
a passage, or a word that would teach a girl to be
immodest, or a man to be dishonest ? When men
in their pages have been described as dishonest
and women as immodest, have they not ever been
punished ? It is not for the novelist to say, baldly

and simply : ' Because you lied here, or were heartless there, because you Lydia Bennet forgot the lessons of your honest home, or you Earl Leicester were false through your ambition, or you Beatrix loved too well the glitter of the world, therefore you shall be scourged with scourges either in this world or in the next ; ' but it is for him to show, as he carries on his tale, that his Lydia, or his Leicester, or his Beatrix, will be dishonoured in the estimation of all readers by his or her vices. Let a woman be drawn clever, beautiful, attractive, —so as to make men love her, and women almost envy her,—and let her be made also heartless, unfeminine, and ambitious of evil grandeur, as was Beatrix, what a danger is there not in such a character ! To the novelist who shall handle it, what peril of doing harm ! But if at last it have been so handled that every girl who reads of Beatrix shall say : ' Oh ! not like that ;—let me not be like that ! ' and that every youth shall say : ' Let me not have such a one as that to press my bosom, anything rather than that ! '—then will not the novelist have preached his sermon as perhaps no clergyman can preach it ?

Very much of a novelist's work must appertain to the intercourse between young men and young women. It is admitted that a novel can hardly be made interesting or successful without love. Some few might be named, but even in those the attempt breaks down, and the softness of love is found to be necessary to complete the story. *Pickwick* has been named as an exception to the rule, but even in *Pickwick* there are three or four sets of lovers, whose little amatory longings give a softness to the work. I tried it once with

Miss Mackenzie, but I had to make her fall in love at last. In this frequent allusion to the passion which most stirs the imagination of the young, there must be danger. Of that the writer of fiction is probably well aware. Then the question has to be asked, whether the danger may not be so averted that good may be the result,—and to be answered.

In one respect the necessity of dealing with love is advantageous,—advantageous from the very circumstance which has made love necessary to all novelists. It is necessary because the passion is one which interests or has interested all. Every one feels it, has felt it, or expects to feel it,—or else rejects it with an eagerness which still perpetuates the interest. If the novelist, therefore, can so handle the subject as to do good by his handling, as to teach wholesome lessons in regard to love, the good which he does will be very wide. If I can teach politicians that they can do their business better by truth than by falsehood, I do a great service ; but it is done to a limited number of persons. But if I can make young men and women believe that truth in love will make them happy, then, if my writings be popular, I shall have a very large class of pupils. No doubt the cause for that fear which did exist as to novels arose from an idea that the matter of love would be treated in an inflammatory and generally unwholesome manner. 'Madam,' says Sir Anthony in the play, ' a circulating library in a town is an evergreen tree of diabolical knowledge. It blossoms through the year ; and depend on it, Mrs. Malaprop, that they who are so fond of handling the leaves will long for the fruit at last.' Sir Anthony was no doubt right. But he takes it

for granted that the longing for the fruit is an evil.
The novelist who writes of love thinks differently,
and thinks that the honest love of an honest man
is a treasure which a good girl may fairly hope to
win,—and that if she can be taught to wish only for
that, she will have been taught to entertain only
wholesome wishes.

I can easily believe that a girl should be taught
to wish to love by reading how Laura Bell loved
Pendennis. Pendennis was not in truth a very
worthy man, nor did he make a very good husband ;
but the girl's love was so beautiful, and the wife's
love when she became a wife so womanlike, and
at the same time so sweet, so unselfish, so wifely,
so worshipful,—in the sense in which wives are told
that they ought to worship their husbands,—that
I cannot believe that any girl can be injured, or
even not benefited, by reading of Laura's love.

There once used to be many who thought, and
probably there still are some, even here in England,
who think that a girl should hear nothing of love
till the time come in which she is to be married.
That, no doubt, was the opinion of Sir Anthony
Absolute and of Mrs. Malaprop. But I am hardly
disposed to believe that the old system was more
favourable than ours to the purity of manners.
Lydia Languish, though she was constrained by
fear of her aunt to hide the book, yet had *Peregrine
Pickle* in her collection. While human nature
talks of love so forcibly it can hardly serve our
turn to be silent on the subject. 'Naturam
expellas furcâ, tamen usque recurret.' There are
countries in which it has been in accordance with
the manners of the upper classes that the girl
should be brought to marry the man almost out of

the nursery—or rather perhaps out of the convent
—without having enjoyed that freedom of thought
which the reading of novels and of poetry will
certainly produce ; but I do not know that the
marriages so made have been thought to be happier
than our own.

Among English novels of the present day, and
among English novelists, a great division is made.
There are sensational novels and anti-sensational,
sensational novelists and anti-sensational ; sensational readers and anti-sensational. The novelists
who are considered to be anti-sensational are
generally called realistic. I am realistic. My
friend Wilkie Collins is generally supposed to be
sensational The readers who prefer the one are
supposed to take delight in the elucidation of
character. Those who hold by the other are
charmed by the continuation and gradual development of a plot. All this is, I think, a mistake,—
which mistake arises from the inability of the
imperfect artist to be at the same time realistic
and sensational. A good novel should be both,
and both in the highest degree. If a novel fail
in either, there is a failure in art. Let those readers
who believe that they do not like sensational
scenes in novels think of some of those passages
from our great novelists which have charmed them
most :—of Rebecca in the castle with Ivanhoe ; of
Burley in the cave with Morton ; of the mad lady
tearing the veil of the expectant bride, in *Jane
Eyre* ; of Lady Castlewood as, in her indignation,
she explains to the Duke of Hamilton Henry
Esmond's right to be present at the marriage of his
Grace with Beatrix ;—may I add, of Lady Mason,
as she makes her confession at the feet of Sir

Peregrine Orme ? Will any one say that the authors
of these passages have sinned in being over-
sensational ?   No doubt, a string of horrible
incidents, bound together without truth in detail,
and told as affecting personages without character,
—wooden blocks, who cannot make themselves
known to the reader as men and women,—does not
instruct or amuse, or even fill the mind with awe.
Horrors heaped upon horrors, and which are horrors
only in themselves, and not as touching any
recognised and known person, are not tragic, and
soon cease even to horrify.   And such would-be
tragic elements of a story may be increased without
end, and without difficulty.   I may tell you of a
woman murdered,—murdered in the same street
with you, in the next house,—that she was a wife
murdered by her husband,—a bride not yet a week
a wife.   I may add to it for ever.   I may say that
the murderer roasted her alive.   There is no end to
it.   I may declare that a former wife was treated
with equal barbarity ; and may assert that, as the
murderer was led away to execution, he declared
his only sorrow, his only regret to be, that he could
not live to treat a third wife after the same fashion.
There is nothing so easy as the creation and the
cumulation of fearful incidents after this fashion.
If such creation and cumulation be the beginning
and the end of the novelist's work,—and novels
have been written which seem to be without other
attractions,—nothing can be more dull or more
useless.   But not on that account are we averse to
tragedy in prose fiction.   As in poetry, so in prose,
he who can deal adequately with tragic elements
is a greater artist and reaches a higher aim than
the writer whose efforts never carry him above the

mild walks of everyday life. The *Bride of Lammermoor* is a tragedy throughout, in spite of its comic elements. The life of Lady Castlewood, of whom I have spoken, is a tragedy. Rochester's wretched thraldom to his mad wife, in *Jane Eyre*, is a tragedy. But these stories charm us not simply because they are tragic, but because we feel that men and women with flesh and blood, creatures with whom we can sympathise, are struggling amidst their woes. It all lies in that. No novel is anything, for the purposes either of comedy or tragedy, unless the reader can sympathise with the characters whose names he finds upon the pages. Let an author so tell his tale as to touch his reader's heart and draw his tears, and he has, so far, done his work well. Truth let there be,—truth of description, truth of character, human truth as to men and women. If there be such truth, I do not know that a novel can be too sensational.

I did intend when I meditated that history of English fiction to include within its pages some rules for the writing of novels ;—or I might perhaps say, with more modesty, to offer some advice on the art to such tyros in it as might be willing to take advantage of the experience of an old hand. But the matter would, I fear, be too long for this episode, and I am not sure that I have as yet got the rules quite settled in my own mind. I will, however, say a few words on one or two points which my own practice has pointed out to me.

I have from the first felt sure that the writer, when he sits down to commence his novel, should do so, not because he has to tell a story, but because he has a story to tell. The novelist's first novel will generally have sprung from the right cause. Some series of events, or some development of character, will have presented itself to his imagination,—and this he feels so strongly that he thinks he can present his picture in strong and agreeable language to others. He sits down and tells his story because he has a story to tell; as you, my friend, when you have heard something which has at once tickled your fancy or moved your pathos, will hurry to tell it to the first person you meet. But when that first novel has been received graciously by the public and has made for itself a success, then the writer, naturally feeling that the writing of novels is within his grasp, looks about for something to tell in another. He cudgels his brains, not always successfully, and sits down to write, not because he has something which he burns to tell, but because he feels it to be incumbent on him to be telling something. As you, my friend, if you are very successful in the telling of that first story, will become ambitious of further story-telling, and will look out for anecdotes, in the narration of which you will not improbably sometimes distress your audience.

So it has been with many novelists, who, after some good work, perhaps after very much good work, have distressed their audience because they have gone on with their work till their work has become simply a trade with them. Need I make a list of such, seeing that it would contain the names of those who have been greatest in the art of British novel-writing. They have at last become weary of that portion of a novelist's work which is of all the most essential to success. That a man as he grows old should feel the labour of writing to be a fatigue is natural enough. But a man to whom writing has become a habit may write well though he be fatigued. But the weary novelist refuses any longer to give his mind to that work of observation and reception from which has come his power, without which work his power cannot be continued, —which work should be going on not only when he is at his desk, but in all his walks abroad, in all his movements through the world, in all his intercourse with his fellow-creatures. He has become a novelist, as another has become a poet, because he has in those walks abroad, unconsciously for the most part, been drawing in matter from all that he has seen and heard. But this has not been done without labour, even when the labour has been unconscious. Then there comes a time when he shuts his eyes and shuts his ears. When we talk of memory fading as age comes on, it is such shutting of eyes and ears that we mean. The things around cease to interest us, and we cannot exercise our minds upon them. To the novelist thus wearied there comes the demand for further novels. He does not know his own defect, and even if he did he does not wish to abandon his own profession. He still writes ; but he writes because he has to tell a story, not because he has a story to tell. What reader of novels has not felt the ' woodenness ' of this mode of telling ? The characters do not live and move, but are cut out of blocks and are propped against the wall. The incidents are arranged in certain lines—the arrangement being as palpable to the reader as it has been to the writer—but do not follow each other as results naturally demanded by previous action. The reader can never feel—as he ought to feel—that only for that flame of the eye, only for that angry word, only for that moment of weakness, all might have been different. The course of the tale is one piece of stiff mechanism, in which there is no room for a doubt.

These, it may be said, are reflections which I, being an old novelist, might make useful to myself for discontinuing my work, but can hardly be needed by those tyros of whom I have spoken. That they are applicable to myself I readily admit, but I also find that they apply to many beginners. Some of us who are old fail at last because we are old. It would be well that each of us should say to himself,

> ‘Solve senescentem mature sanus equum, ne
> Peccet ad extremum ridendus.’

But many young fail also, because they endeavour to tell stories when they have none to tell. And this comes from idleness rather than from innate incapacity. The mind has not been sufficiently at work, when the tale has been commenced, nor is it kept sufficiently at work as the tale is continued. I have never troubled myself much about the construction of plots, and am not now insisting specially on thoroughness in a branch of work in which I myself have not been very thorough. I am not sure that the construction of a perfected plot has been at any period within my power. But the novelist has other aims than the elucidation of his plot. He desires to make his readers so intimately acquainted with his characters that the creatures of his brain should be to them speaking, moving, living, human creatures. This he can never do unless he know those fictitious personages himself, and he can never know them unless he can live with them in the full reality of established intimacy. They must be with him as he lies down to sleep, and as he wakes from his dreams. He must learn to hate them and to love them. He must argue with them, quarrel with them, forgive them, and even submit to them. He must know of them whether they be cold-blooded or passionate, whether true or false, and how far true, and how far false. The depth and the breadth, and the narrowness and the shallowness of each should be clear to him. And, as here, in our outer world, we know that men and women change,—become worse or better as temptation or conscience may guide them,—so should these creations of his change, and every change should be noted by him. On the last day of each month recorded, every person in his novel should be a month older than on the first. If the would-be novelist have aptitudes that way, all this will come to him without much struggling ;— but if it do not come, I think he can only make novels of wood.

It is so that I have lived with my characters, and thence has come whatever success I have obtained. There is a gallery of them, and of all in that gallery I may say that I know the tone of the voice, and the colour of the hair, every flame of the eye, and the very clothes they wear. Of each man I could assert whether he would have said these or the other words ; of every woman, whether she would then have smiled or so have frowned. When I shall feel that this intimacy ceases, then I shall know that the old horse should be turned out to grass. That I shall feel it when

I ought to feel it, I will by no means say. I do
not know that I am at all wiser than Gil Blas'
canon; but I do know that the power indicated
is one without which the teller of tales cannot tell
them to any good effect.

The language in which the novelist is to put
forth his story, the colours with which he is to
paint his picture, must of course be to him matter
of much consideration. Let him have all other
possible gifts,—imagination, observation, erudition,
and industry,—they will avail him nothing for his
purpose, unless he can put forth his work in pleasant
words. If he be confused, tedious, harsh, or unhar-
monious, readers will certainly reject him. The
reading of a volume of history or on science may
represent itself as a duty; and though the duty
may by a bad style be made very disagreeable, the
conscientious reader will perhaps perform it. But
the novelist will be assisted by no such feeling.
Any reader may reject his work without the burden
of a sin. It is the first necessity of his position that
he make himself pleasant. To do this, much more
is necessary than to write correctly. He may
indeed be pleasant without being correct,—as I
think can be proved by the works of more than
one distinguished novelist. But he must be intelligible,—intelligible without trouble; and he must
be harmonious.

Any writer who has read even a little will know
what is meant by the word intelligible. It is not
sufficient that there be a meaning that may be
hammered out of the sentence, but that the language should be so pellucid that the meaning should
be rendered without an effort of the reader;—
and not only some proposition of meaning, but the

very sense, no more and no less, which the writer
has intended to put into his words. What Macaulay says should be remembered by all writers :
' How little the all-important art of making
meaning pellucid is studied now ! Hardly any
popular author except myself thinks of it.' The
language used should be as ready and as efficient
a conductor of the mind of the writer to the mind
of the reader as is the electric spark which passes
from one battery to another battery. In all
written matter the spark should carry everything ;
but in matters recondite the recipient will search
to see that he misses nothing, and that he takes
nothing away too much. The novelist cannot
expect that any such search will be made. A young
writer, who will acknowledge the truth of what I
am saying, will often feel himself tempted by the
difficulties of language to tell himself that some
one little doubtful passage, some single collocation
of words, which is not quite what it ought to be,
will not matter. I know well what a stumbling-
block such a passage may be. But he should leave
none such behind him as he goes on. The habit
of writing clearly soon comes to the writer who is
a severe critic to himself.

As to that harmonious expression which I think
is required, I shall find it more difficult to express
my meaning. It will be granted, I think, by readers
that a style may be rough, and yet both forcible
and intelligible ; but it will seldom come to pass
that a novel written in a rough style will be
popular,—and less often that a novelist who habitually uses such a style will become so. The harmony which is required must come from the
practice of the ear. There are few ears naturally

so dull that they cannot, if time be allowed to them, decide whether a sentence, when read, be or be not harmonious. And the sense of such harmony grows on the ear, when the intelligence has once informed itself as to what is, and what is not harmonious. The boy, for instance, who learns with accuracy the prosody of a Sapphic stanza, and has received through his intelligence a knowledge of its parts, will soon tell by his ear whether a Sapphic stanza be or be not correct. Take a girl, endowed with gifts of music, well instructed in her art, with perfect ear, and read to her such a stanza with two words transposed, as, for instance—

> Mercuri, nam te docilis magistro
> Movit Amphion *canendo lapides*,
> Tuque testudo resonare septem
> Callida nervis—

and she will find no halt in the rhythm. But a schoolboy with none of her musical acquirements or capacities, who has, however, become familiar with the metres of the poet, will at once discover the fault. And so will the writer become familiar with what is harmonious in prose. But in order that familiarity may serve him in his business, he must so train his ear that he shall be able to weigh the rhythm of every word as it falls from his pen. This, when it has been done for a time, even for a short time, will become so habitual to him that he will have appreciated the metrical duration of every syllable before it shall have dared to show itself upon paper. The art of the orator is the same. He knows beforehand how each sound which he is about to utter will affect the force of his climax. If a writer will do so he will charm his readers, though his readers will probably not know how they have been charmed.

In writing a novel the author soon becomes aware that a burden of many pages is before him. Circumstances require that he should cover a certain and generally not a very confined space. Short novels are not popular with readers generally. Critics often complain of the ordinary length of novels,—of the three volumes to which they are subjected; but few novels which have attained great success in England have been told in fewer pages. The novel-writer who sticks to novel-writing as his profession will certainly find that this burden of length is incumbent on him. How shall he carry his burden to the end ? How shall he cover his space ? Many great artists have by their practice opposed the doctrine which I now propose to preach ;—but they have succeeded I think in spite of their fault and by dint of their greatness. There should be no episodes in a novel. Every sentence, every word, through all those pages, should tend to the telling of the story. Such episodes distract the attention of the reader, and always do so disagreeably. Who has not felt this to be the case even with *The Curious Impertinent* and with the *History of the Man of the Hill*. And if it be so with Cervantes and Fielding, who can hope to succeed ? Though the novel which you have to write must be long, let it be all one. And this exclusion of episodes should be carried down into the smallest details. Every sentence and every word used should tend to the telling of the story. ' But,' the young novelist will say, ' with so many pages before me to be filled, how shall I succeed if I thus confine myself ;—

how am I to know beforehand what space this
story of mine will require ? There must be the
three volumes, or the certain number of magazine
pages which I have contracted to supply. If I may
not be discursive should occasion require, how
shall I complete my task ? The painter suits the
size of his canvas to his subject, and must I in my
art stretch my subject to my canvas ? ' This
undoubtedly must be done by the novelist; and if
he will learn his business, may be done without
injury to his effect. He may not paint different
pictures on the same canvas, which he will do if he
allow himself to wander away to matters outside
his own story ; but by studying proportion in his
work, he may teach himself so to tell his story that
it shall naturally fall into the required length.
Though his story should be all one, yet it may
have many parts. Though the plot itself may
require but few characters, it may be so enlarged
as to find its full development in many. There
may be subsidiary plots, which shall all tend to
the elucidation of the main story, and which will
take their places as part of one and the same work,
—as there may be many figures on a canvas which
shall not to the spectator seem to form themselves
into separate pictures.

There is no portion of a novelist's work in which
this fault of episodes is so common as in the
dialogue. It is so easy to make any two persons
talk on any casual subject with which the writer
presumes himself to be conversant ! Literature,
philosophy, politics, or sport, may thus be handled
in a loosely discursive style ; and the writer, while
indulging himself and filling his pages, is apt to
think that he is pleasing his reader. I think he

can make no greater mistake. The dialogue is generally the most agreeable part of a novel; but it is only so as long as it tends in some way to the telling of the main story. It need not seem to be confined to that, but it should always have a tendency in that direction. The unconscious critical acumen of a reader is both just and severe. When a long dialogue on extraneous matter reaches his mind, he at once feels that he is being cheated into taking something which he did not bargain to accept when he took up that novel. He does not at that moment require politics or philosophy, but he wants his story. He will not perhaps be able to say in so many words that at some certain point the dialogue has deviated from the story; but when it does so he will feel it, and the feeling will be unpleasant. Let the intending novel-writer, if he doubt this, read one of Bulwer's novels,—in which there is very much to charm,— and then ask himself whether he has not been offended by devious conversations.

And the dialogue, on which the modern novelist in consulting the taste of his probable readers must depend most, has to be constrained also by other rules. The writer may tell much of his story in conversations, but he may only do so by putting such words into the mouths of his personages as persons so situated would probably use. He is not allowed for the sake of his tale to make his characters give utterance to long speeches, such as are not customarily heard from men and women. The ordinary talk of ordinary people is carried on in short sharp expressive sentences, which very frequently are never completed,—the language of which even among educated people is often incorrect. The novel-writer in constructing his dialogue must so steer between absolute accuracy of language—which would give to his conversation an air of pedantry, and the slovenly inaccuracy of ordinary talkers, which if closely followed would offend by an appearance of grimace —as to produce upon the ear of his readers a sense of reality. If he be quite real he will seem to attempt to be funny. If he be quite correct he will seem to be unreal. And above all, let the speeches be short. No character should utter much above a dozen words at a breath,—unless the writer can justify to himself a longer flood of speech by the speciality of the occasion.

In all this human nature must be the novel-writer's guide. No doubt effective novels have been written in which human nature has been set at defiance. I might name *Caleb Williams* as one and *Adam Blair* as another. But the exceptions are not more than enough to prove the rule. But in following human nature he must remember that he does so with a pen in his hand, and that the reader who will appreciate human nature will also demand artistic ability and literary aptitude.

The young novelist will probably ask, or more probably bethink himself how he is to acquire that knowledge of human nature which will tell him with accuracy what men and women would say in this or that position. He must acquire it as the compositor, who is to print his words, has learned the art of distributing his type—by constant and intelligent practice. Unless it be given to him to listen and to observe,—so to carry away, as it were, the manners of people in his memory, as to be able to say to himself with

assurance that these words might have been said
in a given position, and that those other words
could not have been said,—I do not think that in
these days he can succeed as a novelist.

And then let him beware of creating tedium!
Who has not felt the charm of a spoken story up
to a certain point, and then suddenly become
aware that it has become too long and is the reverse
of charming? It is not only that the entire book
may have this fault, but that this fault may occur
in chapters, in passages, in pages, in paragraphs.
I know no guard against this so likely to be effective
as the feeling of the writer himself. When once
the sense that the thing is becoming long has
grown upon him, he may be sure that it will grow
upon his readers. I see the smile of some who will
declare to themselves that the words of a writer
will never be tedious to himself. Of the writer
of whom this may be truly said, it may be said
with equal truth that he will always be tedious to
his readers.

CHAPTER XIII

ON ENGLISH NOVELISTS OF THE PRESENT DAY

In this chapter I will venture to name a few successful novelists of my own time, with whose works I am acquainted; and will endeavour to point whence their success has come, and why they have failed when there has been failure.

I do not hesitate to name Thackeray the first. His knowledge of human nature was supreme, and his characters stand out as human beings, with a force and a truth which has not, I think, been within the reach of any other English novelist in any period. I know no character in fiction, unless it be Don Quixote, with whom the reader becomes so intimately acquainted as with Colonel Newcombe. How great a thing it is to be a gentleman at all parts! How we admire the man of whom so much may be said with truth! Is there any one of whom we feel more sure in this respect than of Colonel Newcombe? It is not because Colonel Newcombe is a perfect gentleman that we think Thackeray's work to have been so excellent, but because he has had the power to describe him as such, and to force us to love him, a weak and silly old man, on account of this grace of character.

It is evident from all Thackeray's best work
that he lived with the characters he was creating.
He had always a story to tell until quite late in
life; and he shows us that this was so, not by
the interest which he had in his own plots,—for
I doubt whether his plots did occupy much of his
mind,—but by convincing us that his characters
were alive to himself. With Becky Sharpe, with
Lady Castlewood and her daughter, and with
Esmond, with Warrington, Pendennis, and the
Major, with Colonel Newcombe, and with Barry
Lyndon, he must have lived in perpetual intercourse. Therefore he has made these personages
real to us.

Among all our novelists his style is the purest,
as to my ear it is also the most harmonious. Sometimes it is disfigured by a slight touch of affectation,
by little conceits which smell of the oil;—but the
language is always lucid. The reader, without
labour, knows what he means, and knows all that
he means. As well as I can remember, he deals
with no episodes. I think that any critic, examining his work minutely, would find that every scene,
and every part of every scene, adds something
to the clearness with which the story is told.
Among all his stories there is not one which does
not leave on the mind a feeling of distress that
women should ever be immodest or men dishonest,—and of joy that women should be so
devoted and men so honest. How we hate the
idle selfishness of Pendennis, the worldliness of
Beatrix, the craft of Becky Sharpe!—how we love
the honesty of Colonel Newcombe, the nobility of
Esmond, and the devoted affection of Mrs. Pendennis! The hatred of evil and love of good can

hardly have come upon so many readers without doing much good.

Late in Thackeray's life,—he never was an old man, but towards the end of his career,—he failed in his power of charming, because he allowed his mind to become idle. In the plots which he conceived, and in the language which he used, I do not know that there is any perceptible change; but in *The Virginians* and in *Philip* the reader is introduced to no character with which he makes a close and undying acquaintance. And this, I have no doubt, is so because Thackeray himself had no such intimacy. His mind had come to be weary of that fictitious life which is always demanding the labour of new creation, and he troubled himself with his two Virginians and his Philip only when he was seated at his desk.

At the present moment George Eliot is the first of English novelists, and I am disposed to place her second of those of my time. She is best known to the literary world as a writer of prose fiction, and not improbably whatever of permanent fame she may acquire will come from her novels. But the nature of her intellect is very far removed indeed from that which is common to the tellers of stories. Her imagination is no doubt strong, but it acts in analysing rather than in creating. Everything that comes before her is pulled to pieces so that the inside of it shall be seen, and be seen if possible by her readers as clearly as by herself. This searching analysis is carried so far that, in studying her latter writings, one feels oneself to be in company with some philosopher rather than with a novelist. I doubt whether any young person can read with pleasure

either *Felix Holt*, *Middlemarch*, or *Daniel Deronda*.
I know that they are very difficult to many that
are not young.

Her personifications of character have been
singularly terse and graphic, and from them has
come her great hold on the public,—though by no
means the greatest effect which she has produced.
The lessons which she teaches remain, though it
is not for the sake of the lessons that her pages are
read. Seth Bede, Adam Bede, Maggie and Tom
Tulliver, old Silas Marner, and, much above all,
Tito, in *Romola*, are characters which, when once
known, can never be forgotten. I cannot say
quite so much for any of those in her later works,
because in them the philosopher so greatly over-
tops the portrait painter, that, in the dissection
of the mind, the outward signs seem to have
been forgotten. In her, as yet, there is no symp-
tom whatever of that weariness of mind which,
when felt by the reader, induces him to declare
that the author has written himself out. It is
not from decadence that we do not have another
Mrs. Poyser, but because the author soars to things
which seem to her to be higher than Mrs. Poyser.

It is, I think, the defect of George Eliot that she
struggles too hard to do work that shall be excellent. She lacks ease. Latterly the signs of
this have been conspicuous in her style, which has
always been and is singularly correct, but which
has become occasionally obscure from her too
great desire to be pungent. It is impossible not
to feel the struggle, and that feeling begets a
flavour of affectation. In *Daniel Deronda*, of
which at this moment only a portion has been
published, there are sentences which I have found

myself compelled to read three times before I
have been able to take home to myself all that the
writer has intended. Perhaps I may be permitted
here to say, that this gifted woman was among
my dearest and most intimate friends. As I am
speaking here of novelists, I will not attempt to
speak of George Eliot's merit as a poet.

There can be no doubt that the most popular
novelist of my time—probably the most popular
English novelist of any time—has been Charles
Dickens. He has now been dead nearly six years,
and the sale of his books goes on as it did during
his life. The certainty with which his novels are
found in every house—the familiarity of his name
in all English-speaking countries—the popularity
of such characters as Mrs. Gamp, Micawber, and
Pecksniff, and many others whose names have
entered into the English language and become
well-known words—the grief of the country at his
death, and the honours paid to him at his funeral,—
all testify to his popularity. Since the last book
he wrote himself, I doubt whether any book has
been so popular as his biography by John Forster.
There is no withstanding such testimony as this.
Such evidence of popular appreciation should go
for very much, almost for everything, in criticism
on the work of a novelist. The primary object
of a novelist is to please ; and this man's novels
have been found more pleasant than those of any
other writer. It might of course be objected to
this, that though the books have pleased they
have been injurious, that their tendency has been
immoral and their teaching vicious ; but it is
almost needless to say that no such charge has
ever been made against Dickens. His teaching

has ever been good. From all which, there arises to
the critic a question whether, with such evidence
against him as to the excellence of this writer,
he should not subordinate his own opinion to the
collected opinion of the world of readers. To me
it almost seems that I must be wrong to place
Dickens after Thackeray and George Eliot, knowing as I do that so great a majority put him above
those authors.

My own peculiar idiosyncrasy in the matter
forbids me to do so. I do acknowledge that
Mrs. Gamp, Micawber, Pecksniff, and others have
become household words in every house, as though
they were human beings; but to my judgment
they are not human beings, nor are any of the
characters human which Dickens has portrayed.
It has been the peculiarity and the marvel of this
man's power, that he has invested his puppets with
a charm that has enabled him to dispense with
human nature. There is a drollery about them, in
my estimation, very much below the humour of
Thackeray, but which has reached the intellect of
all; while Thackeray's humour has escaped the
intellect of many. Nor is the pathos of Dickens
human. It is stagey and melodramatic. But it is
so expressed that it touches every heart a little.
There is no real life in Smike. His misery, his
idiotcy, his devotion for Nicholas, his love for Kate,
are all overdone and incompatible with each other.
But still the reader sheds a tear. Every reader can
find a tear for Smike. Dickens's novels are like
Boucicault's plays. He has known how to draw
his lines broadly, so that all should see the colour.

He, too, in his best days, always lived with
his characters;—and he, too, as he gradually

ceased to have the power of doing so, ceased to charm. Though they are not human beings, we all remember Mrs. Gamp and Pickwick. The Boffins and Veneerings do not, I think, dwell in the minds of so many.

Of Dickens's style it is impossible to speak in praise. It is jerky, ungrammatical, and created by himself in defiance of rules—almost as completely as that created by Carlyle. To readers who have taught themselves to regard language, it must therefore be unpleasant. But the critic is driven to feel the weakness of his criticism, when he acknowledges to himself—as he is compelled in all honesty to do—that with the language, such as it is, the writer has satisfied the great mass of the readers of his country. Both these great writers have satisfied the readers of their own pages; but both have done infinite harm by creating a school of imitators. No young novelist should ever dare to imitate the style of Dickens. If such a one wants a model for his language, let him take Thackeray.

Bulwer, or Lord Lytton,—but I think that he is still better known by his earlier name,—was a man of very great parts. Better educated than either of those I have named before him, he was always able to use his erudition, and he thus produced novels from which very much not only may be but must be learned by his readers. He thoroughly understood the political status of his own country, a subject on which, I think, Dickens was marvellously ignorant, and which Thackeray had never studied. He had read extensively, and was always apt to give his readers the benefit of what he knew. The result has been that very much more than amusement may be obtained from Bulwer's novels. There is also a brightness about them—the result rather of thought than of imagination, of study and of care, than of mere intellect—which has made many of them excellent in their way. It is perhaps improper to class all his novels together, as he wrote in varied manners, making in his earlier works, such as *Pelham* and *Ernest Maltravers*, pictures of a fictitious life, and afterwards pictures of life as he believed it to be, as in *My Novel* and *The Caxtons*. But from all of them there comes the same flavour of an effort to produce effect. The effects are produced, but it would have been better if the flavour had not been there.

I cannot say of Bulwer as I have of the other novelists whom I have named that he lived with his characters. He lived with his work, with the doctrines which at the time he wished to preach, thinking always of the effects which he wished to produce ; but I do not think he ever knew his own personages,—and therefore neither do we know them. Even Pelham and Eugene Aram are not human beings to us, as are Pickwick, and Colonel Newcombe, and Mrs. Poyser.

In his plots Bulwer has generally been simple, facile, and successful. The reader never feels with him, as he does with Wilkie Collins, that it is all plot, or, as with George Eliot, that there is no plot. The story comes naturally without calling for too much attention, and is thus proof of the completeness of the man's intellect. His language is clear, good, intelligible English, but it is defaced by mannerism. In all that he did, affectation was his fault.

How shall I speak of my dear old friend Charles Lever, and his rattling, jolly, joyous, swearing Irishmen. Surely never did a sense of vitality come so constantly from a man's pen, nor from man's voice, as from his! I knew him well for many years, and whether in sickness or in health, I have never come across him without finding him to be running over with wit and fun. Of all the men I have encountered, he was the surest fund of drollery. I have known many witty men, many who could say good things, many who would sometimes be ready to say them when wanted, though they would sometimes fail;—but he never failed. Rouse him in the middle of the night, and wit would come from him before he was half awake. And yet he never monopolised the talk, was never a bore. He would take no more than his own share of the words spoken, and would yet seem to brighten all that was said during the night. His earlier novels—the later I have not read—are just like his conversation. The fun never flags, and to me, when I read them, they were never tedious. As to character he can hardly be said to have produced it. Corney Delaney, the old man-servant, may perhaps be named as an exception.

Lever's novels will not live long,—even if they may be said to be alive now,—because it is so. What was his manner of working I do not know, but I should think it must have been very quick, and that he never troubled himself on the subject, except when he was seated with a pen in his hand.

Charlotte Brontë was surely a marvellous woman. If it could be right to judge the work of a novelist from one small portion of one novel, and

to say of an author that he is to be accounted as
strong as he shows himself to be in his strongest
morsel of work, I should be inclined to put
Miss Brontë very high indeed. I know no interest
more thrilling than that which she has been able
to throw into the characters of Rochester and the
governess, in the second volume of *Jane Eyre*. She
lived with those characters, and felt every fibre
of the heart, the longings of the one and the sufferings of the other. And therefore, though the end
of the book is weak, and the beginning not very
good, I venture to predict that *Jane Eyre* will be
read among English novels when many whose
names are now better known shall have been
forgotten. *Jane Eyre*, and *Esmond*, and *Adam
Bede* will be in the hands of our grandchildren,
when *Pickwick*, and *Pelham*, and *Harry Lorrequer*
are forgotten; because the men and women
depicted are human in their aspirations, human
in their sympathies, and human in their actions.

In *Villette*, too, and in *Shirley*, there is to
be found human life as natural and as real,
though in circumstances not so full of interest
as those told in *Jane Eyre*. The character of
Paul in the former of the two is a wonderful
study. She must herself have been in love with
some Paul when she wrote the book, and have
been determined to prove to herself that she was
capable of loving one whose exterior circumstances
were mean and in every way unprepossessing.

There is no writer of the present day who has
so much puzzled me by his eccentricities, imprac-
ticabilities, and capabilities as Charles Reade.
I look upon him as endowed almost with genius,
but as one who has not been gifted by nature with

ordinary powers of reasoning. He can see what
is grandly noble and admire it with all his heart.
He can see, too, what is foully vicious and hate
it with equal ardour. But in the common affairs
of life he cannot see what is right or wrong; and
as he is altogether unwilling to be guided by the
opinion of others, he is constantly making mistakes
in his literary career, and subjecting himself to
reproach which he hardly deserves. He means
to be honest. He means to be especially honest,—
more honest than other people. He has written
a book called *The Eighth Commandment* on behalf
of honesty in literary transactions,—a wonderful
work, which has I believe been read by a very few.
I never saw a copy except that in my own library,
or heard of any one who knew the book. Nevertheless it is a volume that must have taken very
great labour, and have been written,—as indeed
he declares that it was written,—without the hope
of pecuniary reward. He makes an appeal to the
British Parliament and British people on behalf of
literary honesty, declaring that should he fail—
' I shall have to go on blushing for the people
I was born among.' And yet of all the writers of
my day he has seemed to me to understand literary
honesty the least. On one occasion, as he tells
us in this book, he bought for a certain sum from
a French author the right of using a plot taken
from a play,—which he probably might have used
without such purchase, and also without infringing
any international copyright act. The French
author not unnaturally praises him for the transaction, telling him that he is ' un vrai gentleman '.
The plot was used by Reade in a novel; and a
critic discovering the adaptation, made known his

discovery to the public. Whereupon the novelist
became angry, called his critic a pseudonymuncle,
and defended himself by stating the fact of his
own purchase. In all this he seems to me to ignore
what we all mean when we talk of literary plagiarism and literary honesty. The sin of which the
author is accused is not that of taking another
man's property, but of passing off as his own
creation that which he does not himself create.
When an author puts his name to a book he
claims to have written all that there is therein,
unless he makes direct signification to the contrary.
Some years subsequently there arose another
similar question, in which Mr. Reade's opinion
was declared even more plainly, and certainly very
much more publicly. In a tale which he wrote
he inserted a dialogue which he took from Swift,
and took without any acknowledgment. As might
have been expected, one of the critics of the day
fell foul of him for this barefaced plagiarism. The
author, however, defended himself, with much
abuse of the critic, by asserting, that whereas
Swift had found the jewel he had supplied the
setting ;—an argument in which there was some
little wit, and would have been much excellent
truth, had he given the words as belonging to
Swift and not to himself.

The novels of a man possessed of so singular
a mind must themselves be very strange,—and
they are strange. It has generally been his object
to write down some abuse with which he has been
particularly struck,—the harshness, for instance,
with which paupers or lunatics are treated, or
the wickedness of certain classes,—and he always,
I think, leaves upon his readers an idea of great

earnestness of purpose. But he has always left
at the same time on my mind so strong a conviction that he has not really understood his
subject, that I have ever found myself taking the
part of those whom he has accused. So good a
heart, and so wrong a head, surely no novelist
ever before had combined! In story-telling he
has occasionally been almost great. Among his
novels I would especially recommend *The Cloister
and the Hearth*. I do not know that in this work,
or in any, that he has left a character that will
remain; but he has written some of his scenes
so brightly that to read them would always be
a pleasure.

Of Wilkie Collins it is impossible for a true critic
not to speak with admiration, because he has
excelled all his contemporaries in a certain most
difficult branch of his art; but as it is a branch
which I have not myself at all cultivated, it is not
unnatural that his work should be very much lost
upon me individually. When I sit down to write
a novel I do not at all know, and I do not very
much care, how it is to end. Wilkie Collins seems
so to construct his that he not only, before writing,
plans everything on, down to the minutest detail,
from the beginning to the end; but then plots it
all back again, to see that there is no piece of
necessary dove-tailing which does not dove-tail
with absolute accuracy. The construction is most
minute and most wonderful. But I can never
lose the taste of the construction. The author
seems always to be warning me to remember that
something happened at exactly half-past two
o'clock on Tuesday morning; or that a woman
disappeared from the road just fifteen yards beyond

the fourth milestone. One is constrained by mysteries and hemmed in by difficulties, knowing, however, that the mysteries will be made clear, and the difficulties overcome at the end of the third volume. Such work gives me no pleasure. I am, however, quite prepared to acknowledge that the want of pleasure comes from fault of my intellect.

There are two ladies of whom I would fain say a word, though I feel that I am making my list too long, in order that I may declare how much I have admired their work. They are Annie Thackeray and Rhoda Broughton. I have known them both, and have loved the former almost as though she belonged to me. No two writers were ever more dissimilar,—except in this that they are both feminine. Miss Thackeray's characters are sweet, charming, and quite true to human nature. In her writings she is always endeavouring to prove that good produces good, and evil evil. There is not a line of which she need be ashamed,— not a sentiment of which she should not be proud. But she writes like a lazy writer who dislikes her work, and who allows her own want of energy to show itself in her pages.

Miss Broughton, on the other hand, is full of energy,—though she too, I think, can become tired over her work. She, however, does take the trouble to make her personages stand upright on the ground. And she has the gift of making them speak as men and women do speak. ' You beast ! ' said Nancy, sitting on the wall, to the man who was to be her husband,—thinking that she was speaking to her brother. Now Nancy, whether right or wrong, was just the girl who would, as circum-

stances then were, have called her brother a beast.
There is nothing wooden about any of Miss Broughton's novels; and in these days so many novels
are wooden! But they are not sweet-savoured as
are those by Miss Thackeray, and are, therefore,
less true to nature. In Miss Broughton's determination not to be mawkish and missish, she has
made her ladies do and say things which ladies
would not do and say. They throw themselves at
men's heads, and when they are not accepted only
think how they may throw themselves again.
Miss Broughton is still so young that I hope she
may live to overcome her fault in this direction.

There is one other name, without which the
list of the best known English novelists of my
own time would certainly be incomplete, and that
is the name of the present Prime Minister of
England. Mr. Disraeli has written so many novels,
and has been so popular as a novelist that, whether
for good or for ill, I feel myself compelled to speak
of him. He began his career as an author early in
life, publishing *Vivian Grey* when he was twenty-
three years old. He was very young for such work,
though hardly young enough to justify the excuse
that he makes in his own preface, that it is a book
written by a boy. Dickens was, I think, younger
when he wrote his *Sketches by Boz*, and as young
when he was writing the *Pickwick Papers*. It was
hardly longer ago than the other day when
Mr. Disraeli brought out *Lothair*, and between the
two there were eight or ten others. To me they
have all had the same flavour of paint and un-
reality. In whatever he has written he has affected
something which has been intended to strike
his readers as uncommon and therefore grand.

Because he has been bright and a man of genius, he has carried his object as regards the young. He has struck them with astonishment and aroused in their imagination ideas of a world more glorious, more rich, more witty, more enterprising, than their own. But the glory has been the glory of pasteboard, and the wealth has been a wealth of tinsel. The wit has been the wit of hairdressers, and the enterprise has been the enterprise of mountebanks. An audacious conjurer has generally been his hero,—some youth who, by wonderful cleverness, can obtain success by every intrigue that comes to his hand. Through it all there is a feeling of stage properties, a smell of hair-oil, an aspect of buhl, a remembrance of tailors, and that pricking of the conscience which must be the general accompaniment of paste diamonds. I can understand that Mr. Disraeli should by his novels have instigated many a young man and many a young woman on their way in life, but I cannot understand that he should have instigated any one to good. Vivian Grey has had probably as many followers as Jack Sheppard, and has led his followers in the same direction.

Lothair, which is as yet Mr. Disraeli's last work, and, I think, undoubtedly his worst, has been defended on a plea somewhat similar to that by which he has defended *Vivian Grey*. As that was written when he was too young, so was the other when he was too old,—too old for work of that nature, though not too old to be Prime Minister. If his mind were so occupied with greater things as to allow him to write such a work, yet his judgment should have sufficed to induce him to destroy it when written. Here that flavour of hair-oil, that flavour of false jewels, that remembrance of tailors, comes out stronger than in all the others. Lothair is falser even than Vivian Grey, and Lady Corisande, the daughter of the Duchess, more inane and unwomanlike than Venetia or Henrietta Temple. It is the very bathos of story-telling. I have often lamented, and have as often excused to myself, that lack of public judgment which enables readers to put up with bad work because it comes from good or from lofty hands. I never felt the feeling so strongly, or was so little able to excuse it, as when a portion of the reading public received *Lothair* with satisfaction.

CHAPTER XIV

ON CRITICISM

LITERARY criticism in the present day has become a profession,—but it has ceased to be an art. Its object is no longer that of proving that certain literary work is good and other literary work is bad, in accordance with rules which the critic is able to define. English criticism at present rarely even pretends to go so far as this. It attempts, in the first place, to tell the public whether a book be or be not worth public attention; and, in the second place, so to describe the purport of the work as to enable those who have not time or inclination for reading it to feel that by a short cut they can become acquainted with its contents. Both these objects, if fairly well carried out, are salutary. Though the critic may not be a profound judge himself; though not unfrequently he be a young man making his first literary attempts, with tastes and judgment still unfixed, yet he probably has a conscience in the matter, and would not have been selected for that work had he not shown some aptitude for it. Though he may be not the best possible guide to the undiscerning, he will be better than no guide at all. Real substantial criticism must, from its nature, be costly, and that which the public wants should at any rate be cheap. Advice is given to many thousands, which, though it may not be the best advice possible, is better than no advice at all. Then that description of the work criticised, that compressing of the much into very little,—which is the work of many modern critics or reviewers,—does enable many to know something of what is being said, who without it would know nothing.

I do not think it is incumbent on me at present to name periodicals in which this work is well done, and to make complaints of others by which it is scamped. I should give offence, and might probably be unjust. But I think I may certainly say that as some of these periodicals are certainly entitled to great praise for the manner in which the work is done generally, so are others open to very severe censure,—and that the praise and that the censure are chiefly due on behalf of one virtue and its opposite vice. It is not critical ability that we have a right to demand, or its absence that we are bound to deplore. Critical ability for the price we pay is not attainable. It is a faculty not peculiar to Englishmen, and when displayed is very frequently not appreciated. But that critics should be honest we have a right to demand, and critical dishonesty we are bound to expose. If the writer will tell us what he thinks, though his thoughts be absolutely vague and useless, we can forgive him; but when he tells us what he does not think, actuated either by friendship or by animosity, then there should be no pardon for him. This is the sin in modern English criticism of which there is most reason to complain.

It is a lamentable fact that men and women lend themselves to this practice who are neither vindictive nor ordinarily dishonest. It has become 'the custom of the trade', under the veil of which excuse so many tradesmen justify their malpractices! When a struggling author learns that so much has been done for A by the *Barsetshire Gazette*, so much for B by the *Dillsborough Herald*, and, again, so much for C by that powerful metropolitan organ the *Evening Pulpit*, and is told also that A and B and C have been favoured through personal interest, he also goes to work among the editors, or the editors' wives,— or perhaps, if he cannot reach their wives, with their wives' first or second cousins. When once the feeling has come upon an editor or a critic that he may allow himself to be influenced by other considerations than the duty he owes to the public, all sense of critical or of editorial honesty falls from him at once. *Facilis descensus Averni*. In a very short time that editorial honesty becomes ridiculous to himself. It is for other purpose that he wields the power; and when he is told what is his duty, and what should be his conduct, the preacher of such doctrine seems to him to be quixotic. 'Where have you lived, my friend, for the last twenty years,' he says in spirit, if not in word, 'that you come out now with such stuff as old-fashioned as this?' And thus dishonesty begets dishonesty, till dishonesty seems to be beautiful. How nice to be good-natured! How glorious to assist struggling young authors, especially if the young author be also a pretty woman! How gracious to oblige a friend! Then the motive, though still pleasing, departs further from the border of what is good. In what way can the critic better repay the hospitality of his wealthy literary friend than by good-natured criticism,—

or more certainly ensure for himself a continuation of hospitable favours ?

Some years since a critic of the day, a gentleman well known then in literary circles, showed me the manuscript of a book recently published,—the work of a popular author. It was handsomely bound, and was a valuable and desirable possession. It had just been given to him by the author as an acknowledgment for a laudatory review in one of the leading journals of the day. As I was expressly asked whether I did not regard such a token as a sign of grace both in the giver and in the receiver, I said that I thought it should neither have been given nor have been taken. My theory was repudiated with scorn, and I was told that I was strait-laced, visionary, and impracticable ! In all that the damage did not lie in the fact of that one present, but in the feeling on the part of the critic that his office was not debased by the acceptance of presents from those whom he criticised. This man was a professional critic, bound by his contract with certain employers to review such books as were sent to him. How could he, when he had received a valuable present for praising one book, censure another by the same author ?

While I write this I well know that what I say, if it be ever noticed at all, will be taken as a straining at gnats, as a pretence of honesty, or at any rate as an exaggeration of scruples. I have said the same thing before, and have been ridiculed for saying it. But none the less am I sure that English literature generally is suffering much under this evil. All those who are struggling for success have forced upon them the idea that their strongest efforts should be made in touting for praise.

Those who are not familiar with the lives of authors will hardly believe how low will be the forms which their struggles will take :—how little presents will be sent to men who write little articles ; how much flattery may be expended even on the keeper of a circulating library ; with what profuse and distant genuflexions approaches are made to the outside railing of the temple which contains within it the great thunderer of some metropolitan periodical publication ! The evil here is not only that done to the public when interested counsel is given to them, but extends to the debasement of those who have at any rate considered themselves fit to provide literature for the public.

I am satisfied that the remedy for this evil must lie in the conscience and deportment of authors themselves. If once the feeling could be produced that it is disgraceful for an author to ask for praise, —and demands for praise are, I think, disgraceful in every walk of life,—the practice would gradually fall into the hands only of the lowest, and that which is done only by the lowest soon becomes despicable even to them. The sin, when perpetuated with unflagging labour, brings with it at best very poor reward. That work of running after critics, editors, publishers, the keepers of circulating libraries, and their clerks, is very hard, and must be very disagreeable. He who does it must feel himself to be dishonoured,—or she. It may perhaps help to sell an edition, but can never make an author successful.

I think it may be laid down as a golden rule in literature that there should be no intercourse at all between an author and his critic. The critic, as critic, should not know his author, nor the author,

as author, his critic. As censure should beget no
anger, so should praise beget no gratitude. The
young author should feel that criticisms fall upon
him as dew or hail from heaven,—which, as coming
from heaven, man accepts as fate. Praise let the
author try to obtain by wholesome effort ; censure
let him avoid, if possible, by care and industry.
But when they come, let him take them as coming
from some source which he cannot influence, and
with which he should not meddle.

I know no more disagreeable trouble into which
an author may plunge himself than of a quarrel
with his critics, or any more useless labour than
that of answering them. It is wise to presume, at
any rate, that the reviewer has simply done his
duty, and has spoken of the book according to the
dictates of his conscience. Nothing can be gained
by combating the reviewer's opinion. If the book
which he has disparaged be good, his judgment
will be condemned by the praise of others ; if bad,
his judgment will be confirmed by others. Or if,
unfortunately, the criticism of the day be in so
evil a condition generally that such ultimate truth
cannot be expected, the author may be sure that
his efforts made on behalf of his own book will
not set matters right. If injustice be done him,
let him bear it. To do so is consonant with the
dignity of the position which he ought to assume.
To shriek, and scream, and sputter, to threaten
actions, and to swear about the town that he has
been belied and defamed in that he has been accused
of bad grammar or a false metaphor, of a dull
chapter, or even of a borrowed heroine, will leave
on the minds of the public nothing but a sense of
irritated impotence.

If, indeed, there should spring from an author's work any assertion by a critic injurious to the author's honour, if the author be accused of falsehood or of personal motives which are discreditable to him, then, indeed, he may be bound to answer the charge. It is hoped, however, that he may be able to do so with clean hands, or he will so stir the mud in the pool as to come forth dirtier than he went into it.

I have lived much among men by whom the English criticism of the day has been vehemently abused. I have heard it said that to the public it is a false guide, and that to authors it is never a trustworthy Mentor. I do not concur in this wholesale censure. There is, of course, criticism and criticism. There are at this moment one or two periodicals to which both public and authors may safely look for guidance, though there are many others from which no spark of literary advantage may be obtained. But it is well that both public and authors should know what is the advantage which they have a right to expect. There have been critics,—and there probably will be again, though the circumstances of English literature do not tend to produce them,—with power sufficient to entitle them to speak with authority. These great men have declared, *tanquam ex cathedrâ*, that such a book has been so far good and so far bad, or that it has been altogether good or altogether bad;— and the world has believed them. When making such assertions they have given their reasons, explained their causes, and have carried conviction. Very great reputations have been achieved by such critics, but not without infinite study and the labour of many years.

Such are not the critics of the day, of whom we are now speaking. In the literary world as it lives at present some writer is selected for the place of critic to a newspaper, generally some young writer, who for so many shillings a column shall review whatever book is sent to him and express an opinion,—reading the book through for the purpose, if the amount of honorarium as measured with the amount of labour will enable him to do so. A labourer must measure his work by his pay or he cannot live. From criticism such as this must for the most part be, the general reader has no right to expect philosophical analysis, or literary judgment on which confidence may be placed. But he probably may believe that the books praised will be better than the books censured, and that those which are praised by periodicals which never censure are better worth his attention than those which are not noticed. And readers will also find that by devoting an hour or two on Saturday to the criticisms of the week, they will enable themselves to have an opinion about the books of the day. The knowledge so acquired will not be great, nor will that little be lasting; but it adds something to the pleasure of life to be able to talk on subjects of which others are speaking; and the man who has sedulously gone through the literary notices in the *Spectator* and the *Saturday* may perhaps be justified in thinking himself as well able to talk about the new book as his friend who has brought that new book on the *tapis*, and who, not improbably, obtained his information from the same source.

As an author, I have paid careful attention to the reviews which have been written on my

own work; and I think that now I well know
where I may look for a little instruction, where
I may expect only greasy adulation, where I shall
be cut up into mince-meat for the delight of those
who love sharp invective, and where I shall find
an equal mixture of praise and censure so adjusted,
without much judgment, as to exhibit the impar-
tiality of the newspaper and its staff. Among
it all there is much chaff, which I have learned
how to throw to the winds, with equal disregard
whether it praises or blames;—but I have also
found some corn, on which I have fed and nourished
myself, and for which I have been thankful.

CHAPTER XV

'THE LAST CHRONICLE OF BARSET'— LEAVING THE POST OFFICE— 'ST PAUL'S MAGAZINE'

I WILL now go back to the year 1867, in which I was still living at Waltham Cross. I had some time since bought the house there which I had at first hired, and added rooms to it, and made it for our purposes very comfortable. It was, however, a rickety old place, requiring much repair, and occasionally not as weather-tight as it should be. We had a domain there sufficient for the cows, and for the making of our butter and hay. For strawberries, asparagus, green peas, out-of-door peaches, for roses especially, and such every-day luxuries, no place was ever more excellent. It was only twelve miles from London, and admitted therefore of frequent intercourse with the metropolis. It was also near enough to the Roothing country for hunting purposes. No doubt the Shoreditch Station, by which it had to be reached, had its drawbacks. My average distance also to the Essex mèets was twenty miles. But the place combined as much or more than I had a right to expect. It was within my own postal district, and had, upon the whole, been well chosen.

The work I did during the twelve years that I remained there, from 1859 to 1871, was certainly

very great. I feel confident that in amount no
other writer contributed so much during that time
to English literature. Over and above my novels,
I wrote political articles, critical, social, and
sporting articles, for periodicals, without number.
I did the work of a surveyor of the General Post
Office, and so did it as to give the authorities of the
department no slightest pretext for fault-finding.
I hunted always at least twice a week. I was
frequent in the whist-room at the Garrick. I
lived much in society in London, and was made
happy by the presence of many friends at Waltham
Cross. In addition to this we always spent six
weeks at least out of England. Few men, I think,
ever lived a fuller life. And I attribute the power
of doing this altogether to the virtue of early
hours. It was my practice to be at my table every
morning at 5.30 A.M. ; and it was also my practice
to allow myself no mercy. An old groom, whose
business it was to call me, and to whom I paid £5
a year extra for the duty, allowed himself no
mercy. During all those years at Waltham Cross
he was never once late with the coffee which it was
his duty to bring me. I do not know that I ought
not to feel that I owe more to him than to any one
else for the success I have had. By beginning at
that hour I could complete my literary work before
I dressed for breakfast.

All those I think who have lived as literary men,
—working daily as literary labourers,—will agree
with me that three hours a day will produce as
much as a man ought to write. But then he
should so have trained himself that he shall be
able to work continuously during those three hours,
—so have tutored his mind that it shall not be

necessary for him to sit nibbling his pen, and gazing at the wall before him, till he shall have found the words with which he wants to express his ideas. It had at this time become my custom, —and it still is my custom, though of late I have become a little lenient to myself,—to write with my watch before me, and to require from myself 250 words every quarter of an hour. I have found that the 250 words have been forthcoming as regularly as my watch went. But my three hours were not devoted entirely to writing. I always began my task by reading the work of the day before, an operation which would take me half an hour, and which consisted chiefly in weighing with my ear the sound of the words and phrases. I would strongly recommend this practice to all tyros in writing. That their work should be read after it has been written is a matter of course,— that it should be read twice at least before it goes to the printers, I take to be a matter of course. But by reading what he has last written, just before he recommences his task, the writer will catch the tone and spirit of what he is then saying, and will avoid the fault of seeming to be unlike himself. This division of time allowed me to produce over ten pages of an ordinary novel volume a day, and if kept up through ten months, would have given as its results three novels of three volumes each in the year;—the precise amount which so greatly acerbated the publisher in Paternoster Row, and which must at any rate be felt to be quite as much as the novel-readers of the world can want from the hands of one man.

I have never written three novels in a year, but by following the plan above described I have written more than as much as three volumes ; and by adhering to it over a course of years, I have been enabled to have always on hand,—for some time back now,—one or two or even three unpublished novels in my desk beside me. Were I to die now there are three such besides *The Prime Minister*, half of which has only yet been issued. One of these has been six years finished, and has never seen the light since it was first tied up in the wrapper which now contains it. I look forward with some grim pleasantry to its publication after another period of six years, and to the declaration of the critics that it has been the work of a period of life at which the power of writing novels had passed from me. Not improbably, however, these pages may be printed first.

In 1866 and 1867 *The Last Chronicle of Barset* was brought out by George Smith in sixpenny monthly numbers. I do not know that this mode of publication had been tried before, or that it answered very well on this occasion. Indeed the shilling magazines had interfered greatly with the success of novels published in numbers without other accompanying matter. The public finding that so much might be had for a shilling, in which a portion of one or more novels was always included, were unwilling to spend their money on the novel alone. Feeling that this certainly had become the case in reference to novels published in shilling numbers, Mr. Smith and I determined to make the experiment with sixpenny parts. As he paid me £3000 for the use of my MS., the loss, if any, did not fall upon me. If I remember right, the enterprise was not altogether successful.

Taking it as a whole, I regard this as the best

novel I have written. I was never quite satisfied with the development of the plot, which consisted in the loss of a cheque, of a charge made against a clergyman for stealing it, and of absolute uncertainty on the part of the clergyman himself as to the manner in which the cheque had found its way into his hands. I cannot quite make myself believe that even such a man as Mr. Crawley could have forgotten how he got it; nor would the generous friend who was anxious to supply his wants have supplied them by tendering the cheque of a third person. Such fault I acknowledge,— acknowledging at the same time that I have never been capable of constructing with complete success the intricacies of a plot that required to be un- ravelled. But while confessing so much, I claim to have portrayed the mind of the unfortunate man with great accuracy and great delicacy. The pride, the humility, the manliness, the weakness, the conscientious rectitude and bitter prejudices of Mr. Crawley were, I feel, true to nature and well described. The surroundings too are good. Mrs. Proudie at the palace is a real woman ; and the poor old dean dying at the deanery is also real. The archdeacon in his victory is very real. There is a true savour of English country life all through the book. It was with many misgivings that I killed my old friend Mrs. Proudie. I could not, I think, have done it, but for a resolution taken and declared under circumstances of great momentary pressure.

It was thus that it came about. I was sitting one morning at work upon the novel at the end of the long drawing-room of the Athenæum Club,— as was then my wont when I had slept the previous night in London. As I was there, two clergymen, each with a magazine in his hand, seated themselves, one on one side of the fire and one on the other, close to me. They soon began to abuse what they were reading, and each was reading some part of some novel of mine. The gravamen of their complaint lay in the fact that I reintroduced the same characters so often ! 'Here,' said one, ' is that archdeacon whom we have had in every novel he has ever written.' 'And here,' said the other, ' is the old duke whom he has talked about till everybody is tired of him. If I could not invent new characters, I would not write novels at all.' Then one of them fell foul of Mrs. Proudie. It was impossible for me not to hear their words, and almost impossible to hear them and be quiet. I got up, and standing between them, I acknowledged myself to be the culprit. 'As to Mrs. Proudie,' I said, ' I will go home and kill her before the week is over.' And so I did. The two gentlemen were utterly confounded, and one of them begged me to forget his frivolous observations.

I have sometimes regretted the deed, so great was my delight in writing about Mrs. Proudie, so thorough was my knowledge of all the little shades of her character. It was not only that she was a tyrant, a bully, a would-be priestess, a very vulgar woman, and one who would send headlong to the nethermost pit all who disagreed with her ; but that at the same time she was conscientious, by no means a hypocrite, really believing in the brimstone which she threatened, and anxious to save the souls around her from its horrors. And as her tyranny increased so did the bitterness of the moments of her repentance increase, in that she knew herself to be a tyrant,—till that bitterness killed her. Since her time others have grown up equally dear to me,—Lady Glencora and her husband, for instance; but I have never dissevered myself from Mrs. Proudie, and still live much in company with her ghost.

I have in a previous chapter said how I wrote *Can You Forgive Her?* after the plot of a play which had been rejected,—which play had been called *The Noble Jilt*. Some year or two after the completion of *The Last Chronicle*, I was asked by the manager of a theatre to prepare a piece for his stage, and I did so, taking the plot of this novel. I called the comedy *Did He Steal It?* But my friend the manager did not approve of my attempt. My mind at this time was less attentive to such a matter than when dear old George Bartley nearly crushed me by his criticism,—so that I forget the reason given. I have little doubt but that the manager was right. That he intended to express a true opinion, and would have been glad to have taken the piece had he thought it suitable, I am quite sure.

I have sometimes wished to see during my lifetime a combined republication of those tales which are occupied with the fictitious county of Barsetshire. These would be *The Warden*, *Barchester Towers*, *Doctor Thorne*, *Framley Parsonage*, and *The Last Chronicle of Barset*. But I have hitherto failed. The copyrights are in the hands of four different persons, including myself, and with one of the four I have not been able to prevail to act in concert with the others.[1]

In 1867 I made up my mind to take a step in life

---

[1] Since this was written I have made arrangements for doing as I have wished, and the first volume of the series will now very shortly be published.

which was not unattended with peril, which many would call rash, and which, when taken, I should be sure at some period to regret. This step was the resignation of my place in the Post Office. I have described how it was that I contrived to combine the performance of its duties with my other avocations in life. I got up always very early; but even this did not suffice. I worked always on Sundays,—as to which no scruple of religion made me unhappy,—and not unfrequently I was driven to work at night. In the winter when hunting was going on, I had to keep myself very much on the alert. And during the London season, when I was generally two or three days of the week in town, I found the official work to be a burden. I had determined some years previously, after due consideration with my wife, to abandon the Post Office when I had put by an income equal to the pension to which I should be entitled if I remained in the department till I was sixty. That I had now done, and I sighed for liberty.

The exact time chosen, the autumn of 1867 was selected because I was then about to undertake other literary work in editing a new magazine, —of which I shall speak very shortly. But in addition to these reasons there was another, which was, I think, at last the actuating cause. When Sir Rowland Hill left the Post Office, and my brother-in-law, Mr. Tilley, became Secretary in his place, I applied for the vacant office of UnderSecretary. Had I obtained this I should have given up my hunting, have given up much of my literary work,—at any rate would have edited no magazine,—and would have returned to the habit of my youth in going daily to the General Post

Office. There was very much against such a change in life. The increase of salary would not have amounted to above £400 a year, and I should have lost much more than that in literary remuneration. I should have felt bitterly the slavery of attendance at an office, from which I had then been exempt for five-and-twenty years. I should, too, have greatly missed the sport which I loved. But I was attached to the department, had imbued myself with a thorough love of letters,—I mean the letters which are carried by the post,—and was anxious for their welfare as though they were all my own. In short, I wished to continue the connection. I did not wish, moreover, that any younger officer should again pass over my head. I believed that I had been a valuable public servant, and I will own to a feeling existing at that time that I had not altogether been well treated. I was probably wrong in this. I had been allowed to hunt,—and to do as I pleased, and to say what I liked, and had in that way received my reward. I applied for the office, but Mr. Scudamore was appointed to it. He no doubt was possessed of gifts which I did not possess. He understood the manipulation of money and the use of figures, and was a great accountant. I think that I might have been more useful in regard to the labours and wages of the immense body of men employed by the Post Office. However, Mr. Scudamore was appointed; and I made up my mind that I would fall back upon my old intention, and leave the department. I think I allowed two years to pass before I took the step; and the day on which I sent the letter was to me most melancholy.

The rule of the service in regard to pensions is very just. A man shall serve till he is sixty before he is entitled to a pension,—unless his health fail him. At that age he is entitled to one-sixtieth of his salary for every year he has served up to forty years. If his health do fail him so that he is unfit for further work before the age named, then he may go with a pension amounting to one-sixtieth for every year he has served. I could not say that my health had failed me, and therefore I went without any pension. I have since felt occasionally that it has been supposed that I left the Post Office under pressure,—because I attended to hunting and to my literary work rather than to postal matters. As it had for many years been my ambition to be a thoroughly good servant to the public, and to give to the public much more than I took in the shape of salary, this feeling has some-times annoyed me. And as I am still a little sore on the subject, and as I would not have it imagined after my death that I had slighted the public service to which I belonged, I will venture here to give the reply which was sent to the letter containing my resignation.

GENERAL POST OFFICE,
October 9th, 1867.

' SIR,—I have received your letter of the 3d inst., in which you tender your resignation as Surveyor in the Post Office service, and state as your reason for this step that you have adopted another profession, the exigencies of which are so great as to make you feel you cannot give to the duties of the Post Office that amount of attention which you consider the Postmaster-General has a right to expect.

' You have for many years ranked among the most conspicuous members of the Post Office, which, on several occasions when you have been employed on large and difficult matters, has reaped much benefit from the great abilities which you have been able to place at its disposal ; and in mentioning this, I have been especially glad to record that, notwithstanding the many calls upon your time, you have never permitted your other avocations to interfere with your Post Office work, which has been faithfully and indeed energetically performed.' (There was a touch of irony in this word ' energetically,' but still it did not displease me.)

' In accepting your resignation, which he does with much regret, the Duke of Montrose desires me to convey to you his own sense of the value of your services, and to state how alive he is to the loss which will be sustained by the department in which you have long been an ornament, and where your place will with difficulty be replaced.

(Signed)   J. TILLEY.'

Readers will no doubt think that this is official flummery ; and so in fact it is. I do not at all imagine that I was an ornament to the Post Office, and have no doubt that the secretaries and assistant-secretaries very often would have been glad to be rid of me ; but the letter may be taken as evidence that I did not allow my literary enterprises to interfere with my official work. A man who takes public money without earning it is to me so odious that I can find no pardon for him in my heart. I have known many such, and some who have craved the power to do so. Nothing would annoy me more than to think that I should even be supposed to have been among the number.

And so my connection was dissolved with the department to which I had applied the thirty-three best years of my life;—I must not say devoted, for devotion implies an entire surrender, and I certainly had found time for other occupations. It is however absolutely true that during all those years I had thought very much more about the Post Office than I had of my literary work, and had given to it a more unflagging attention. Up to this time I had never been angry, never felt myself injured or unappreciated in that my literary efforts were slighted. But I had suffered very much bitterness on that score in reference to the Post Office, and I had suffered not only on my own personal behalf, but also and more bitterly when I could not promise to be done the things which I thought ought to be done for the benefit of others. That the public in little villages should be enabled to buy postage stamps; that they should have their letters delivered free and at an early hour; that pillar letter-boxes should be put up for them (of which accommodation in the streets and ways of England I was the originator, having, however, got the authority for the erection of the first at St Heliers in Jersey); that the letter-carriers and sorters should not be over-worked; that they should be adequately paid, and have some hours to themselves, especially on Sundays; above all, that they should be made to earn their wages; and latterly that they should not be crushed by what I thought to be the damnable system of so-called merit;—these were the matters by which I was stirred to what the secretary was pleased to call energetic performance of my duties. How I loved, when I was contradicted,—as I was very often and no doubt very properly,—to do instantly as I was bid, and then to prove that what I was doing was fatuous, dishonest, expensive, and impracticable! And then there were feuds,—such delicious feuds! I was always an anti-Hillite, acknowledging, indeed, the great thing which Sir Rowland Hill had done for the country, but believing him to be entirely unfit to manage men or to arrange labour. It was a pleasure to me to differ from him on all occasions; —and looking back now, I think that in all such differences I was right.

Having so steeped myself, as it were, in postal waters, I could not go out from them without a regret. I wonder whether I did anything to improve the style of writing in official reports! I strove to do so gallantly, never being contented with the language of my own reports unless it seemed to have been so written as to be pleasant to be read. I took extreme delight in writing them, not allowing myself to re-copy them, never having them re-copied by others, but sending them up with their original blots and erasures,—if blots and erasures there were. It is hardly manly, I think, that a man should search after a fine neatness at the expense of so much waste labour; or that he should not be able to exact from himself the necessity of writing words in the form in which they should be read. If a copy be required, let it be taken afterwards,—by hand or by machine, as may be. But the writer of a letter, if he wish his words to prevail with the reader, should send them out as written by himself, by his own hand, with his own marks, his own punctuation, correct or incorrect, with the evidence upon them that they have come out from his own mind.

And so the cord was cut, and I was a free man to run about the world where I would.

A little before the date of my resignation, Mr. James Virtue, the printer and publisher, had asked me to edit a new magazine for him, and had offered me a salary of £1000 a year for the work, over and above what might be due to me for my own contributions. I had known something of magazines, and did not believe that they were generally very lucrative. They were, I thought, useful to some publishers as bringing grist to the mill; but as Mr Virtue's business was chiefly that of a printer, in which he was very successful, this consideration could hardly have had much weight with him. I very strongly advised him to abandon the project, pointing out to him that a large expenditure would be necessary to carry on the magazine in accordance with my views,—that I could not be concerned in it on any other understanding, and that the chances of an adequate return to him of his money were very small. He came down to Waltham, listened to my arguments with great patience, and then told me that if I would not do the work he would find some other editor.

Upon this I consented to undertake the duty. My terms as to salary were those which he had himself proposed. The special stipulations which I demanded were: firstly, that I should put whatever I pleased into the magazine, or keep whatever I pleased out of it, without interference; secondly, that I should from month to month give in to him a list of payments to be made to contributors, and that he should pay them, allowing me to fix the amounts; and thirdly, that the arrangement should remain in force at any rate for two years. To all this he made no objection; and during the time that he and I were thus bound together, he not only complied with these stipulations, but also with every suggestion respecting the magazine that I made to him. If the use of large capital, combined with wide liberality and absolute confidence on the part of the proprietor, and perpetual good humour, would have produced success, our magazine certainly would have succeeded.

In all such enterprises the name is the first great difficulty. There is the name which has a meaning and the name which has none,—of which two the name that has none is certainly the better, as it never belies itself. *The Liberal* may cease to be liberal, or *The Fortnightly*, alas! to come out once a fortnight. But *The Cornhill* and *The Argosy* are under any set of circumstances as well adapted to these names as under any other. Then there is the proprietary name, or possibly the editorial name, which is only amiss because the publication may change hands. *Blackwood's* has indeed always remained *Blackwood's*, and *Fraser's*, though it has been bought and sold, still does not sound amiss. Mr. Virtue, fearing the too attractive qualities of his own name, wished the magazine to be called *Anthony Trollope's*. But to this I objected eagerly. There were then about the town—still are about the town—two or three literary gentlemen, by whom to have had myself editored would have driven me an exile from my country. After much discussion, we settled on *St. Paul's* as the name for our bantling,—not as being in any way new, but as enabling it to fall easily into the ranks with many others. If we were to make ourselves in any way peculiar, it was not by our name that we were desirous of doing so.

I do not think that we did make ourselves in any way peculiar,—and yet there was a great struggle made. On the part of the proprietor, I may say that money was spent very freely. On my own part, I may declare that I omitted nothing which I thought might tend to success. I read all manuscripts sent to me, and endeavoured to judge impartially. I succeeded in obtaining the services of an excellent literary corps. During the three years and a half of my editorship I was assisted by Mr. Goschen, Captain Brackenbury, Edward Dicey, Percy Fitzgerald, H. A. Layard, Allingham, Leslie Stephen, Mrs. Lynn Linton, my brother, T. A. Trollope, and his wife, Charles Lever, E. Arnold, Austin Dobson, R. A. Proctor, Lady Pollock, G. H. Lewes, C. Mackay, Hardman (of the *Times*), George Macdonald, W. R. Greg, Mrs. Oliphant, Sir Charles Trevelyan, Leoni Levi, Dutton Cook,—and others, whose names would make the list too long. It might have been thought that with such aid the *St. Paul's* would have succeeded. I do not think that the failure—for it did fail—arose from bad editing. Perhaps too much editing might have been the fault. I was too anxious to be good, and did not enough think of what might be lucrative.

It did fail, for it never paid its way. It reached, if I remember right, a circulation of nearly 10,000 —perhaps on one or two occasions may have gone beyond that. But the enterprise had been set

on foot on a system too expensive to be made
lucrative by anything short of a very large circulation. Literary merit will hardly set a magazine
afloat, though when afloat it will sustain it. Time
is wanted,—or the hubbub, and flurry, and excitement created by ubiquitous sesquipedalian ad-
vertisement. Merit and time together may be
effective, but they must be backed by economy and
patience.

I think, upon the whole, that publishers themselves have been the best editors of magazines,
when they have been able to give time and intelligence to the work. Nothing certainly has ever
been done better than *Blackwood's*. The *Cornhill*,
too, after Thackeray had left it and before Leslie
Stephen had taken it, seemed to be in quite
efficient hands,—those hands being the hands of
proprietor and publisher. The proprietor, at any
rate, knows what he wants and what he can afford,
and is not so frequently tempted to fall into that
worst of literary quicksands, the publishing of
matter not for the sake of the readers, but for that
of the writer. I did not so sin very often, but often
enough to feel that I was a coward. ' My dear
friend, my dear friend, this is trash ! ' It is so
hard to speak thus,—but so necessary for an editor !
We all remember the thorn in his pillow of which
Thackeray complained. Occasionally I know
that I did give way on behalf of some literary
aspirant whose work did not represent itself to
me as being good ; and as often as I did so,
I broke my trust to those who employed me.
Now, I think that such editors as Thackeray
and myself—if I may for the moment be allowed to
couple men so unequal—will always be liable to

commit such faults, but that the natures of publishers and proprietors will be less soft.

Nor do I know why the pages of a magazine should be considered to be open to any aspirant who thinks that he can write an article, or why the manager of a magazine should be doomed to read all that may be sent to him. The object of the proprietor is to produce a periodical that shall satisfy the public, which he may probably best do by securing the services of writers of acknowledged ability.

CHAPTER XVI

BEVERLEY

VERY early in life, very soon after I had become a clerk in St. Martin's le Grand, when I was utterly impecunious and beginning to fall grievously into debt, I was asked by an uncle of mine, who was himself a clerk in the War Office, what destination I should like best for my future life. He probably meant to inquire whether I wished to live married or single, whether to remain in the Post Office or to leave it, whether I should prefer the town or the country. I replied that I should like to be a Member of Parliament. My uncle, who was given to sarcasm, rejoined that, as far as he knew, few clerks in the Post Office did become Members of Parliament. I think it was the remembrance of this jeer which stirred me up to look for a seat as soon as I had made myself capable of holding one by leaving the public service. My uncle was dead, but if I could get a seat, the knowledge that I had done so might travel to that bourne from whence he was not likely to return, and he might there feel that he had done me wrong.

Independently of this, I have always thought that to sit in the British Parliament should be the highest object of ambition to every educated Englishman. I do not by this mean to suggest that every educated Englishman should set before himself a seat in Parliament as a probable or even a possible career ; but that the man in Parliament has reached a higher position than the man out,— that to serve one's country without pay is the grandest work that a man can do,—that of all studies the study of politics is the one in which a man may make himself most useful to his fellow-creatures,—and that of all lives, public political lives are capable of the highest efforts. So thinking,—though I was aware that fifty-three was too late an age at which to commence a new career,—I resolved with much hesitation that I would make the attempt.

Writing now at an age beyond sixty, I can say that my political feelings and convictions have never undergone any change. They are now what they became when I first began to have political feelings and convictions. Nor do I find in myself any tendency to modify them as I have found generally in men as they grow old. I consider myself to be an advanced, but still a Conservative-Liberal, which I regard not only as a possible but as a rational and consistent phase of political existence. I can, I believe, in a very few words, make known my political theory ; and as I am anxious that any who know aught of me should know that, I will endeavour to do so.

It must, I think, be painful to all men to feel inferiority. It should, I think, be a matter of some pain to all men to feel superiority, unless when it has been won by their own efforts. We do not understand the operations of Almighty wisdom, and are therefore unable to tell the causes of the terrible inequalities that we see,— why some, why so many, should have so little to make life enjoyable, so much to make it painful, while a few others, not through their own merit, have had gifts poured out to them from a full hand. We acknowledge the hand of God and His wisdom, but still we are struck with awe and horror at the misery of many of our brethren. We who have been born to the superior condition,— for in this matter I consider myself to be standing on a platform with dukes and princes, and all others to whom plenty and education and liberty have been given,—cannot, I think, look upon the inane, unintellectual, and frost-bound life of those who cannot even feed themselves sufficiently by their sweat, without some feeling of injustice, some feeling of pain.

This consciousness of wrong has induced in many enthusiastic but unbalanced minds a desire to set all things right by a proclaimed equality. In their efforts such men have shown how powerless they are in opposing the ordinances of the Creator. For the mind of the thinker and the student is driven to admit, though it be awestruck by apparent injustice, that this inequality is the work of God. Make all men equal to-day, and God has so created them that they shall be all unequal to-morrow. The so-called Conservative, the conscientious philanthropic Conservative, seeing this, and being surely convinced that such inequalities are of divine origin, tells himself that it is his duty to preserve them. He thinks that the preservation of the welfare of the world depends on the maintenance of those distances between the prince and the peasant by which he finds himself to be surrounded;—and perhaps, I may add, that the duty is not unpleasant. as he feels himself to be one of the princes.

But this man, though he sees something, and sees that very clearly, sees only a little. The divine inequality is apparent to him, but not the equally divine diminution of that inequality. That such diminution is taking place on all sides is apparent enough ; but it is apparent to him as an evil, the consummation of which it is his duty to retard. He cannot prevent it ; and therefore the society to which he belongs is, in his eyes, retrograding. He will even, at times, assist it ; and will do so conscientiously, feeling that, under the gentle pressure supplied by him, and with the drags and holdfasts which he may add, the movement would be slower than it would become if subjected to his proclaimed and absolute opponents. Such, I think, are Conservatives ;—and I speak of men who, with the fear of God before their eyes and the love of their neighbours warm in their hearts, endeavour to do their duty to the best of their ability.

Using the term which is now common, and which will be best understood, I will endeavour to explain how the equally conscientious Liberal is opposed to the Conservative. He is equally aware that these distances are of divine origin, equally averse to any sudden disruption of society in quest of some Utopian blessedness ;—but he is alive to the fact that these distances are day by day becoming less, and he regards this continual diminution as a series of steps towards that human millennium of which he dreams. He is even willing to help the many to ascend the ladder a little, though he knows, as they come up towards him, he must go down to meet them. What is really in his mind is,—I will not say equality, for the word is offensive, and presents to the imaginations of men ideas of communism, of ruin, and insane democracy,—but a tendency towards equality. In following that, however, he knows that he must be hemmed in by safeguards, lest he be tempted to travel too quickly ; and therefore he is glad to be accompanied on his way by the repressive action of a Conservative opponent. Holding such views, I think I am guilty of no absurdity in calling myself an advanced Conservative-Liberal. A man who entertains in his mind any political doctrine, except as a means of improving the condition of his fellows, I regard as a political intriguer, a charlatan, and a conjurer, —as one who thinks that, by a certain amount of wary wire-pulling, he may raise himself in the estimation of the world.

I am aware that this theory of politics will seem to many to be stilted, overstrained, and, as the Americans would say, high-faluten. Many will declare that the majority even of those who call themselves politicians,—perhaps even of those who take an active part in politics,—are stirred by no such feelings as these, and acknowledge no such motives. Men become Tories or Whigs, Liberals or Conservatives, partly by education,—following their fathers,—partly by chance, partly as openings come, partly in accordance with the bent of their minds, but still without any far-fetched reasonings as to distances and the diminution of distances. No doubt it is so ;—and in the battle of politics, as it goes, men are led further and further away from first causes, till at last a measure is opposed by one simply because it is advocated by another, and members of Parliament swarm into lobbies, following the dictation of their leaders, and not their own individual judgments. But the principle is at work throughout. To many, though hardly acknowledged, it is still apparent. On almost all it has its effect; though there are the intriguers, the clever conjurers, to whom politics is simply such a game as is billiards or rackets, only played with greater results. To the minds that create and lead and sway political opinion, some such theory is, I think, ever present.

The truth of all this I had long since taken home to myself. I had now been thinking of it for thirty years, and had never doubted. But I had always been aware of a certain visionary weakness about myself in regard to politics. A man, to be useful in Parliament, must be able to confine himself and conform himself, to be satisfied with doing a little bit of a little thing at a time. He must patiently get up everything connected with the duty on mushrooms, and then be satisfied with himself when at last he has induced a Chancellor of the Exchequer to say that he will consider the impost at the first opportunity. He must be content to be beaten six times in order that, on a seventh, his work may be found to be of assistance to some one else. He must remember that he is one out of 650, and be content with 1-650th part of the attention of the nation. If he have grand ideas, he must keep them to himself, unless by chance he can work his way up to the top of the tree. In short, he must be a practical man. Now I knew that in politics I could never become a practical man. I should never be satisfied with a soft word from the Chancellor of the Exchequer, but would always be flinging my over-taxed ketchup in his face.

Nor did it seem to me to be possible that I should ever become a good speaker. I had no special gifts that way, and had not studied the art early enough in life to overcome natural difficulties. I had found that, with infinite labour, I could learn a few sentences by heart, and deliver them, monotonously indeed, but clearly. Or, again, if there were something special to be said, I could say it in a commonplace fashion,—but always as though I were in a hurry, and with the fear before me of being thought to be prolix. But I had no power of combining, as a public speaker should always do, that which I had studied with that which occurred to me at the moment. It must be all lesson,—which I found to be best; or else all impromptu,—which was very bad indeed, unless I had something special on my mind. I was thus aware that I could do no good by going into Parliament,—that the time for it, if there could have been a time, had gone by. But still I had an almost insane desire to sit there, and be able to assure myself that my uncle's scorn had not been deserved.

In 1867 it had been suggested to me that, in the event of a dissolution, I should stand for one division of the county of Essex; and I had promised that I would do so, though the promise at that time was as rash a one as a man could make. I was instigated to this by the late Charles Buxton, a man whom I greatly loved, and who was very anxious that the county for which his brother had sat, and with which the family were connected, should be relieved from what he

regarded as the thraldom of Toryism. But there
was no dissolution then. Mr. Disraeli passed his
Reform Bill, by the help of the Liberal member
for Newark, and the summoning of a new Parliament was postponed till the next year. By this
new Reform Bill Essex was portioned out into
three instead of two electoral divisions, one of
which—that adjacent to London—would, it was
thought, be altogether Liberal. After the promise
which I had given, the performance of which
would have cost me a large sum of money absolutely in vain, it was felt by some that I should
be selected as one of the candidates for the new
division,—and as such I was proposed by Mr.
Charles Buxton. But another gentleman, who
would have been bound by previous pledges to
support me, was put forward by what I believe
to have been the defeating interest, and I had to
give way. At the election this gentleman, with
another Liberal, who had often stood for the
county, were returned without a contest. Alas!
alas! They were both unseated at the next
election, when the great Conservative reaction
took place.

In the spring of 1868 I was sent to the United
States on a postal mission, of which I will speak
presently. While I was absent the dissolution
took place. On my return I was somewhat too
late to look out for a seat, but I had friends who
knew the weakness of my ambition; and it was
not likely, therefore, that I should escape the
peril of being put forward for some impossible
borough as to which the Liberal party would not
choose that it should go to the Conservatives
without a struggle. At last, after one or two

others, Beverley was proposed to me, and to
Beverley I went.

I must, however, exculpate the gentleman who
acted as my agent, from undue persuasion exercised towards me. He was a man who thoroughly
understood Parliament, having sat there himself,—
and he sits there now at this moment. He understood Yorkshire,—or at least the East Riding of
Yorkshire, in which Beverley is situated,—certainly
better than any one alive. He understood all the
mysteries of canvassing, and he knew well the
traditions, the condition, and the prospect of the
Liberal party. I will not give his name, but they
who knew Yorkshire in 1868 will not be at a loss
to find it. ' So,' said he, ' you are going to stand
for Beverley ? ' I replied gravely that I was
thinking of doing so. ' You don't expect to get
in ? ' he said. Again I was grave. I would not,
I said, be sanguine, but nevertheless I was disposed to hope for the best. ' Oh no ! ' continued
he, with good-humoured raillery, ' you won't get
in. I don't suppose you really expect it. But
there is a fine career open to you. You will spend
£1000, and lose the election. Then you will
petition, and spend another £1000. You will
throw out the elected members. There will be a
commission, and the borough will be disfranchised.
For a beginner such as you are, that will be
a great success.' And yet, in the teeth of this,
from a man who knew all about it, I persisted in
going to Beverley !

The borough, which returned two members,
had long been represented by Sir Henry Edwards,
of whom, I think, I am justified in saying that he
had contracted a close intimacy with it for the

sake of the seat. There had been many contests, many petitions, many void elections, many members, but, through it all, Sir Henry had kept his seat, if not with permanence, yet with a fixity of tenure next door to permanence. I fancy that with a little management between the parties the borough might at this time have returned a member of each colour quietly;—but there were spirits there who did not love political quietude, and it was at last decided that there should be two Liberal and two Conservative candidates. Sir Henry was joined by a young man of fortune in quest of a seat, and I was grouped with Mr. Maxwell, the eldest son of Lord Herries, a Scotch Roman Catholic peer who lives in the neighbourhood.

When the time came I went down to canvass, and spent, I think, the most wretched fortnight of my manhood. In the first place, I was subject to a bitter tyranny from grinding vulgar tyrants. They were doing what they could, or said that they were doing so, to secure me a seat in Parliament, and I was to be in their hands for at any rate the period of my candidature. On one day both of us, Mr. Maxwell and I, wanted to go out hunting. We proposed to ourselves but the one holiday during this period of intense labour; but I was assured, as was he also, by a publican who was working for us, that if we committed such a crime he and all Beverley would desert us. From morning to evening every day I was taken round the lanes and by-ways of that uninteresting town, canvassing every voter, exposed to the rain, up to my knees in slush, and utterly unable to assume that air of triumphant joy with which a jolly, successful candidate should be invested. At night, every night I had to speak somewhere,—which was bad; and to listen to the speaking of others,—which was much worse. When, on one Sunday, I proposed to go to the Minster Church, I was told that was quite useless, as the Church party were all certain to support Sir Henry! 'Indeed,' said the publican, my tyrant, 'he goes there in a kind of official profession, and you had better not allow yourself to be seen in the same place.' So I stayed away and omitted my prayers. No Church of England church in Beverley would on such an occasion have welcomed a Liberal candidate. I felt myself to be a kind of pariah in the borough, to whom was opposed all that was pretty, and all that was nice, and all that was— ostensibly—good.

But perhaps my strongest sense of discomfort arose from the conviction that my political ideas were all leather and prunella to the men whose votes I was soliciting. They cared nothing for my doctrines, and could not be made to understand that I should have any. I had been brought to Beverley either to beat Sir Henry Edwards,— which, however, no one probably thought to be feasible,—or to cause him the greatest possible amount of trouble, inconvenience, and expense. There were, indeed, two points on which a portion of my wished-for supporters seemed to have opinions, and on both these two points I was driven by my opinions to oppose them. Some were anxious for the Ballot,—which had not then become law,—and some desired the Permissive Bill. I hated, and do hate, both these measures, thinking it to be unworthy of a great people to

free itself from the evil results of vicious conduct
by unmanly restraints. Undue influence on voters
is a great evil from which this country had already
done much to emancipate itself by extended
electoral divisions and by an increase of inde-
pendent feeling. These, I thought, and not secret
voting, were the weapons by which electoral
intimidation should be overcome. And as for
drink, I believe in no Parliamentary restraint;
but I do believe in the gradual effect of moral
teaching and education. But a Liberal, to do
any good at Beverley, should have been able to
swallow such gnats as those. I would swallow
nothing, and was altogether the wrong man.

I knew, from the commencement of my candidature, how it would be. Of course that well-trained
gentleman who condescended to act as my agent,
had understood the case, and I ought to have
taken his thoroughly kind advice. He had seen
it all, and had told himself that it was wrong that
one so innocent in such ways as I, so utterly unable
to fight such a battle, should be carried down into
Yorkshire merely to spend money and to be
annoyed. He could not have said more than he
did say, and I suffered for my obstinacy. Of
course I was not elected. Sir Henry Edwards and
his comrade became members for Beverley, and
I was at the bottom of the poll. I paid £400
for my expenses, and then returned to London.

My friendly agent in his raillery had of course
exaggerated the cost. He had, when I arrived at
Beverley, asked me for a cheque for £400, and
told me that that sum would suffice. It did suffice.
How it came to pass that exactly that sum should
be required I never knew, but such was the case.

Then there came a petition,—not from me, but from the town. The inquiry was made, the two gentlemen were unseated, the borough was disfranchised, Sir Henry Edwards was put on his trial for some kind of Parliamentary offence and was acquitted. In this way Beverley's privilege as a borough and my Parliamentary ambition were brought to an end at the same time.

When I knew the result I did not altogether regret it. It may be that Beverley might have been brought to political confusion and Sir Henry Edwards relegated to private life without the expenditure of my hard-earned money, and without that fortnight of misery; but connecting the things together, as it was natural that I should do, I did flatter myself that I had done some good. It had seemed to me that nothing could be worse, nothing more unpatriotic, nothing more absolutely opposed to the system of representative government, than the time-honoured practices of the borough of Beverley. It had come to pass that political cleanliness was odious to the citizens. There was something grand in the scorn with which a leading Liberal there turned up his nose at me when I told him that there should be no bribery, no treating, not even a pot of beer on one side. It was a matter for study to see how at Beverley politics were appreciated because they might subserve electoral purposes, and how little it was understood that electoral purposes, which are in themselves a nuisance, should be endured in order that they may subserve politics. And then the time, the money, the mental energy, which had been expended in making the borough a secure seat for a gentleman who had realised the idea that it would become him to be a member of Parliament! This use of the borough seemed to be realised and approved in the borough generally. The inhabitants had taught themselves to think that it was for such purposes that boroughs were intended! To have assisted in putting an end to this, even in one town, was to a certain extent a satisfaction.

CHAPTER XVII

THE AMERICAN POSTAL TREATY—THE QUESTION OF COPYRIGHT WITH AMERICA—FOUR MORE NOVELS

In the spring of 1868,—before the affair of Beverley, which, as being the first direct result of my resignation of office, has been brought in a little out of its turn,—I was requested to go over to the United States and make a postal treaty at Washington. This, as I had left the service, I regarded as a compliment, and of course I went. It was my third visit to America, and I have made two since. As far as the Post Office work was concerned, it was very far from being agreeable. I found myself located at Washington, a place I do not love, and was harassed by delays, annoyed by incompetence, and opposed by what I felt to be personal and not national views. I had to deal with two men,—with one who was a working officer of the American Post Office, than whom I have never met a more zealous, or, as far as I could judge, a more honest public servant. He had his views and I had mine, each of us having at heart the welfare of the service in regard to his own country,—each of us also having certain orders which we were bound to obey. But the other gentleman, who was in rank the

superior,—whose executive position was dependent
on his official status, as is the case with our own
Ministers,—did not recommend himself to me
equally. He would make appointments with me
and then not keep them, which at last offended
me so grievously, that I declared at the Washington
Post Office that if this treatment were continued,
I would write home to say that any further action
on my part was impossible. I think I should
have done so had it not occurred to me that
I might in this way serve his purpose rather than
my own, or the purposes of those who had sent me.
The treaty, however, was at last made,—the
purport of which was, that everything possible
should be done, at a heavy expenditure on the
part of England, to expedite the mails from
England to America, and that nothing should be
done by America to expedite the mails from
thence to us. The expedition I believe to be now
equal both ways; but it could not be maintained
as it is without the payment of a heavy subsidy
from Great Britain, whereas no subsidy is paid by
the States.[1]

I had also a commission from the Foreign
Office, for which I had asked, to make an effort
on behalf of an international copyright between
the United States and Great Britain,—the want of
which is the one great impediment to pecuniary
success which still stands in the way of successful
English authors. I cannot say that I have never
had a shilling of American money on behalf of

[1] This was a state of things which may probably have
appeared to American politicians to be exactly that which
they should try to obtain. The whole arrangement has
again been altered since the time of which I have spoken.

reprints of my work; but I have been conscious of no such payment. Having found many years ago—in 1861, when I made a struggle on the subject, being then in the States, the details of which are sufficiently amusing [1]—that I could not myself succeed in dealing with American booksellers, I have sold all foreign right to the English publishers; and though I do not know that I have raised my price against them on that score, I may in this way have had some indirect advantage from the American market. But I do know that what the publishers have received here is very trifling. I doubt whether Messrs. Chapman & Hall, my present publishers, get for early sheets sent to the States as much as 5 per cent. on the price they pay me for my manuscript. But the American readers are more numerous than the English, and taking them all through, are probably more wealthy. If I can get £1000 for a book here (exclusive of their market), I ought to be able to get as much there. If a man supply 600 customers

---

[1] In answer to a question from myself, a certain American publisher—he who usually reprinted my works—promised me that *if any other American publisher republished my work on America before he had done so*, he would not bring out a competing edition, though there would be no law to hinder him. I then entered into an agreement with another American publisher, stipulating to supply him with early sheets; and he stipulating to supply me a certain royalty on his sales, and to supply me with accounts half-yearly. I sent the sheets with energetic punctuality, and the work was brought out with equal energy and precision—by my old American publishers. The gentleman who made the promise had not broken his word. No other American edition had come out before his. I never got any account, and, of course, never received a dollar.

with shoes in place of 300, there is no question as to such result. Why not, then, if I can supply 60,000 readers instead of 30,000 ?

I fancied that I knew that the opposition to an international copyright was by no means an American feeling, but was confined to the bosoms of a few interested Americans. All that I did and heard in reference to the subject on this further visit,—and having a certain authority from the British Secretary of State with me I could hear and do something,—altogether confirmed me in this view. I have no doubt that if I could poll American readers, or American senators,—or even American representatives, if the polling could be unbiassed,—or American booksellers,[1] that an assent to an international copyright would be the result. The state of things as it is is crushing to American authors, as the publishers will not pay them on a liberal scale, knowing that they can supply their customers with modern English literature without paying for it. The English amount of production so much exceeds the American, that the rate at which the former can be published rules the market. It is equally injurious to American booksellers,—except to two or three of the greatest houses. No small man can now acquire the exclusive right of printing and selling an English book. If such a one attempt it, the work is printed instantly by one of the leviathans,—who alone are the gainers. The argument of course is, that the American readers are the gainers,—that as they can get for

[1] I might also say American publishers, if I might count them by the number of heads, and not by the amount of work done by the firms.

nothing the use of certain property, they would be cutting their own throats were they to pass a law debarring themselves from the power of such appropriation. In this argument all idea of honesty is thrown to the winds. It is not that they do not approve of a system of copyright,— as many great men have disapproved,—for their own law of copyright is as stringent as is ours. A bold assertion is made that they like to appropriate the goods of other people; and that, as in this case, they can do so with impunity, they will continue to do so. But the argument, as far as I have been able to judge, comes not from the people, but from the book-selling leviathans, and from those politicians whom the leviathans are able to attach to their interests. The ordinary American purchaser is not much affected by slight variations in price. He is at any rate too high-hearted to be affected by the prospect of such variation. It is the man who wants to make money, not he who fears that he may be called upon to spend it, who controls such matters as this in the United States. It is the large speculator who becomes powerful in the lobbies of the House, and understands how wise it may be to incur a great expenditure either in the creation of a great business, or in protecting that which he has created from competition. Nothing was done in 1868,—and nothing has been done since (up to 1876). A Royal Commission on the law of copyright is now about to sit in this country, of which I have consented to be a member; and the question must then be handled, though nothing done by a Royal Commission here can affect American legislators. But I do believe that if the

measure be consistently and judiciously urged,
the enemies to it in the States will gradually be
overcome. Some years since we had some *quasi*
private meetings, under the presidency of Lord
Stanhope, in Mr. John Murray's dining-room, on
the subject of international copyright. At one of
these I discussed this matter of American international copyright with Charles Dickens, who
strongly declared his conviction that nothing
would induce an American to give up the power
he possesses of pirating British literature. But he
was a man who, seeing clearly what was before
him, would not realise the possibility of shifting
views. Because in this matter the American
decision had been, according to his thinking,
dishonest, therefore no other than dishonest
decision was to be expected from Americans.
Against that idea I protested, and now protest.
American dishonesty is rampant ; but it is
rampant only among a few. It is the great misfortune of the community that those few have
been able to dominate so large a portion of the
population among which all men can vote, but
so few can understand for what they are
voting.

Since this was written the Commission on the
law of copyright has sat and made its report.
With the great body of it I agree, and could serve
no reader by alluding here at length to matters
which are discussed there. But in regard to this
question of international copyright with the
United States, I think that we were incorrect in
the expression of an opinion that fair justice,—
or justice approaching to fairness,—is now done by
American publishers to English authors by pay-

ments made by them for early sheets. I have just found that £20 was paid to my publisher in England for the use of the early sheets of a novel for which I received £1600 in England. When asked why he accepted so little, he assured me that the firm with whom he dealt would not give more. ' Why not go to another firm ? ' I asked. No other firm would give a dollar, because no other firm would care to run counter to that great firm which had assumed to itself the right of publishing my books. I soon after received a copy of my own novel in the American form, and found that it was published for 7½d. That a great sale was expected can be argued from the fact that without a great sale the paper and printing necessary for the republication of a three-volume novel could not be supplied. Many thousand copies must have been sold. But from these the author received not one shilling. I need hardly point out that the sum of £20 would not do more than compensate the publisher for his trouble in making the bargain. The publisher here no doubt might have refused to supply the early sheets, but he had no means of exacting a higher price than that offered. I mention the circumstance here because it has been boasted, on behalf of the American publishers, that though there is no international copyright, they deal so liberally with English authors as to make it unnecessary that the English author should be so protected. With the fact of the £20 just brought to my knowledge, and with the copy of my book published at 7½d. now in my hands, I feel that an international copyright is very necessary for my protection.

They among Englishmen who best love and most admire the United States, have felt themselves tempted to use the strongest language in denouncing the sins of Americans. Who can but love their personal generosity, their active and far-seeking philanthropy, their love of education, their hatred of ignorance, the general convictions in the minds of all of them that a man should be enabled to walk upright, fearing no one and conscious that he is responsible for his own actions? In what country have grander efforts been made by private munificence to relieve the sufferings of humanity? Where can the English traveller find any more anxious to assist him than the normal American, when once the American shall have found the Englishman to be neither sullen nor fastidious? Who, lastly, is so much an object of heart-felt admiration of the American man and the American woman as the well-mannered and well-educated Englishwoman or Englishman? These are the ideas which I say spring uppermost in the minds of the unprejudiced English traveller as he makes acquaintance with these near relatives. Then he becomes cognisant of their official doings, of their politics, of their municipal scandals, of their great ring-robberies, of their lobbyings and briberies, and the infinite baseness of their public life. There at the top of everything he finds the very men who are the least fit to occupy high places. American public dishonesty is so glaring that the very friends he has made in the country are not slow to acknowledge it,—speaking of public life as a thing apart from their own existence, as a state of dirt in which it would be an insult to suppose that they are concerned ! In the midst of it all the stranger, who sees so much that he hates and so much that he loves, hardly knows how to express himself.

' It is not enough that you are personally clean,' he says, with what energy and courage he can command,—' not enough though the clean out-number the foul as greatly as those gifted with eyesight outnumber the blind, if you that can see allow the blind to lead you. It is not by the private lives of the millions that the outside world will judge you, but by the public career of those units whose venality is allowed to debase the name of your country. There never was plainer proof given than is given here, that it is the duty of every honest citizen to look after the honour of his State.'

Personally, I have to own that I have met Americans,—men, but more frequently women,—who have in all respects come up to my ideas of what men and women should be : energetic, having opinions of their own, quick in speech, with some dash of sarcasm at their command, always intelligent, sweet to look at (I speak of the women), fond of pleasure, and each with a per-sonality of his or her own which makes no effort necessary on my own part in remembering the difference between Mrs. Walker and Mrs. Green, or between Mr. Smith and Mr. Johnson. They have faults. They are self-conscious, and are too prone to prove by ill-concealed struggles that they are as good as you,—whereas you perhaps have been long acknowledging to yourself that they are much better. And there is sometimes a pretence at personal dignity among those who think them-selves to have risen high in the world which is deliciously ludicrous. I remember two old gentle-men,—the owners of names which stand deservedly high in public estimation,—whose deportment at a public funeral turned the occasion into one for irresistible comedy. They are suspicious at first, and fearful of themselves. They lack that sim-plicity of manners which with us has become a habit from our childhood. But they are never fools, and I think that they are seldom ill-natured.

There is a woman, of whom not to speak in a work purporting to be a memoir of my own life would be to omit all allusion to one of the chief pleasures which has graced my later years. In the last fifteen years she has been, out of my family, my most chosen friend. She is a ray of light to me, from which I can always strike a spark by thinking of her. I do not know that I should please her or do any good by naming her. But not to allude to her in these pages would amount almost to a falsehood. I could not write truly of myself without saying that such a friend had been vouchsafed to me. I trust she may live to read the words I have now written, and to wipe away a tear as she thinks of my feeling while I write them.

I was absent on this occasion something over three months, and on my return I went back with energy to my work at the *St. Paul's Magazine*. The first novel in it from my own pen was called *Phineas Finn*, in which I commenced a series of semi-political tales. As I was debarred from expressing my opinions in the House of Commons, I took this method of declaring myself. And as I could not take my seat on those benches where I might possibly have been shone upon by the

Speaker's eye, I had humbly to crave his permission for a seat in the gallery, so that I might thus become conversant with the ways and doings of the House in which some of my scenes were to be placed. The Speaker was very gracious, and gave me a running order for, I think, a couple of months. It was enough, at any rate, to enable me often to be very tired,—and, as I have been assured by members, to talk of the proceedings almost as well as though Fortune had enabled me to fall asleep within the House itself.

In writing *Phineas Finn*, and also some other novels which followed it, I was conscious that I could not make a tale pleasing chiefly, or perhaps in any part, by politics. If I write politics for my own sake, I must put in love and intrigue, social incidents, with perhaps a dash of sport, for the benefit of my readers. In this way I think I made my political hero interesting. It was certainly a blunder to take him from Ireland— into which I was led by the circumstance that I created the scheme of the book during a visit to Ireland. There was nothing to be gained by the peculiarity, and there was an added difficulty in obtaining sympathy and affection for a politician belonging to a nationality whose politics are not respected in England. But in spite of this Phineas succeeded. It was not a brilliant success,—because men and women not conversant with political matters could not care much for a hero who spent so much of his time either in the House of Commons or in a public office. But the men who would have lived with Phineas Finn read the book, and the women who would have lived with Lady Laura Standish read it also. As this was what I had intended, I was contented. It is all fairly good except the ending,—as to which till I got to it I made no provision. As I fully intended to bring my hero again into the world, I was wrong to marry him to a simple pretty Irish girl, who could only be felt as an encumbrance on such return. When he did return I had no alternative but to kill the simple pretty Irish girl, which was an unpleasant and awkward necessity.

In writing *Phineas Finn* I had constantly before me the necessity of progression in character,—of marking the changes in men and women which would naturally be produced by the lapse of years. In most novels the writer can have no such duty, as the period occupied is not long enough to allow of the change of which I speak. In *Ivanhoe*, all the incidents of which are included in less than a month, the characters should be, as they are, consistent throughout. Novelists who have undertaken to write the life of a hero or heroine have generally considered their work completed at the interesting period of marriage, and have contented themselves with the advance in taste and manners which are common to all boys and girls as they become men and women. Fielding, no doubt, did more than this in *Tom Jones*, which is one of the greatest novels in the English language, for there he has shown how a noble and sanguine nature may fall away under temptation and be again strengthened and made to stand upright. But I do not think that novelists have often set before themselves the state of progressive change,— nor should I have done it, had I not found myself so frequently allured back to my old friends. So much of my inner life was passed in their

company, that I was continually asking myself
how this woman would act when this or that
event had passed over her head, or how that man
would carry himself when his youth had become
manhood, or his manhood declined to old age.
It was in regard to the old Duke of Omnium, of
his nephew and heir, and of his heir's wife, Lady
Glencora, that I was anxious to carry out this
idea; but others added themselves to my mind
as I went on, and I got round me a circle of persons as to whom I knew not only their present
characters, but how those characters were to be
affected by years and circumstances. The happy
motherly life of Violet Effingham, which was due
to the girl's honest but long-restrained love; the
tragic misery of Lady Laura, which was equally
due to the sale she made of herself in her wretched
marriage; and the long suffering but final success
of the hero, of which he had deserved the first by
his vanity, and the last by his constant honesty,
had been foreshadowed to me from the first.
As to the incidents of the story, the circumstances
by which these personages were to be effected,
I knew nothing. They were created for the most
part as they were described. I never could
arrange a set of events before me. But the evil
and the good of my puppets, and how the evil
would always lead to evil, and the good produce
good,—that was clear to me as the stars on a
summer night.

Lady Laura Standish is the best character in
Phineas Finn and its sequel *Phineas Redux*,—of
which I will speak here together. They are, in
fact, but one novel, though they were brought
out at a considerable interval of time and in

different form.   The first was commenced in the *St. Paul's Magazine* in 1867, and the other was brought out in the *Graphic* in 1873.   In this there was much bad arrangement, as I had no right to expect that novel-readers would remember the characters of a story after an interval of six years, or that any little interest which might have been taken in the career of my hero could then have been renewed.   I do not know that such interest was renewed.   But I found that the sequel enjoyed the same popularity as the former part, and among the same class of readers.   Phineas, and Lady Laura, and Lady Chiltern—as Violet had become—and the old duke,—whom I killed gracefully, and the new duke, and the young duchess, either kept their old friends or made new friends for themselves.   *Phineas Finn*, I certainly think, was successful from first to last.   I am aware, however, that there was nothing in it to touch the heart like the abasement of Lady Mason when confessing her guilt to her old lover, or any approach in delicacy of delineation to the character of Mr. Crawley.

Phineas Finn, the first part of the story, was completed in May 1867.   In June and July I wrote *Linda Tressel* for *Blackwood's Magazine*, of which I have already spoken.   In September and October I wrote a short novel, called *The Golden Lion of Granpère*, which was intended also for *Blackwood*,—with a view of being published anonymously; but Mr. Blackwood did not find the arrangement to be profitable, and the story remained on my hands, unread and unthought of, for a few years.   It appeared subsequently in *Good Words*.   It was written on the model of

Nina Balatka and *Linda Tressel*, but is very inferior to either of them. In November of the same year, 1867, I began a very long novel, which I called *He Knew He Was Right*, and which was brought out by Mr. Virtue, the proprietor of the *St. Paul's Magazine*, in sixpenny numbers, every week. I do not know that in any literary effort I ever fell more completely short of my own intention than in this story. It was my purpose to create sympathy for the unfortunate man who, while endeavouring to do his duty to all around him, should be led constantly astray by his unwillingness to submit his own judgment to the opinion of others. The man is made to be unfortunate enough, and the evil which he does is apparent. So far I did not fail, but the sympathy has not been created yet. I look upon the story as being nearly altogether bad. It is in part redeemed by certain scenes in the house and vicinity of an old maid in Exeter. But a novel which in its main parts is bad cannot, in truth, be redeemed by the vitality of subordinate characters.

This work was finished while I was at Washington in the spring of 1868, and on the day after I finished it, I commenced *The Vicar of Bullhampton*, a novel which I wrote for Messrs. Bradbury & Evans. This I completed in November 1868, and at once began *Sir Harry Hotspur of Humblethwaite*, a story which I was still writing at the close of the year. I look upon these two years, 1867 and 1868, of which I have given a somewhat confused account in this and the two preceding chapters, as the busiest in my life. I had indeed left the Post Office, but though I had left it I had been employed by it during a considerable portion of the time. I had established the *St. Paul's Magazine,* in reference to which I had read an enormous amount of manuscript, and for which, independently of my novels, I had written articles almost monthly. I had stood for Beverley and had made many speeches. I had also written five novels, and had hunted three times a week during each of the winters. And how happy I was with it all! I had suffered at Beverley, but I had suffered as a part of the work which I was desirous of doing, and I had gained my experience. I had suffered at Washington with that wretched American Postmaster, and with the mosquitoes, not having been able to escape from that capital till July; but all that had added to the activity of my life. I had often groaned over those manuscripts; but I had read them, considering it—perhaps foolishly—to be a part of my duty as editor. And though in the quick production of my novels I had always ringing in my ears that terrible condemnation and scorn produced by the great man in Paternoster Row, I was nevertheless proud of having done so much. I always had a pen in my hand. Whether crossing the seas, or fighting with American officials, or tramping about the streets of Beverley, I could do a little, and generally more than a little. I had long since convinced myself that in such work as mine the great secret consisted in acknowledging myself to be bound to rules of labour similar to those which an artisan or a mechanic is forced to obey. A shoemaker when he has finished one pair of shoes does not sit down and contemplate his work in idle satisfaction. 'There is my

pair of shoes finished at last! What a pair of
shoes it is!' The shoemaker who so indulged
himself would be without wages half his time.
It is the same with a professional writer of books.
An author may of course want time to study
a new subject. He will at any rate assure himself
that there is some such good reason why he should
pause. He does pause, and will be idle for a
month or two while he tells himself how beautiful
is that last pair of shoes which he has finished!
Having thought much of all this, and having
made up my mind that I could be really happy
only when I was at work, I had now quite accus-
tomed myself to begin a second pair as soon as
the first was out of my hands.

CHAPTER XVIII

'THE VICAR OF BULLHAMPTON'—'SIR HARRY HOTSPUR'—'AN EDITOR'S TALES'—'CAESAR'

IN 1869 I was called on to decide, in council with my two boys and their mother, what should be their destination in life. In June of that year the elder, who was then twenty-three, was called to the Bar; and as he had gone through the regular courses of lecturing tuition and study, it might be supposed that his course was already decided. But, just as he was called, there seemed to be an opening for him in another direction; and this, joined to the terrible uncertainty of the Bar, the terror of which was not in his case lessened by any peculiar forensic aptitudes, induced us to sacrifice dignity in quest of success. Mr. Frederic Chapman, who was then the sole representative of the publishing house known as Messrs. Chapman & Hall, wanted a partner, and my son Henry went into the firm. He remained there three years and a half; but he did not like it, nor do I think he made a very good publisher. At any rate he left the business with perhaps more pecuniary success than might have been expected from the short period of his labours, and has since taken himself to literature as a profession. Whether he

will work at it so hard as his father, and write as
many books, may be doubted.

My second son, Frederic, had very early in life
gone out to Australia, having resolved on a colonial
career when he found that boys who did not grow
so fast as he did got above him at school. This
departure was a great pang to his mother and me ;
but it was permitted on the understanding that he
was to come back when he was twenty-one, and
then decide whether he would remain in England
or return to the Colonies. In the winter of 1868
he did come to England, and had a season's
hunting in the old country ; but there was no
doubt in his own mind as to his settling in Australia.
His purpose was fixed, and in the spring of 1869
he made his second journey out. As I have since
that date made two journeys to see him,—of one
of which at any rate I shall have to speak, as I
wrote a long book on the Australasian Colonies,—
I will have an opportunity of saying a word or
two further on of him and his doings.

The Vicar of Bullhampton was written in 1868
for publication in *Once a Week*, a periodical then
belonging to Messrs. Bradbury & Evans. It was
not to come out till 1869, and I, as was my wont,
had made my terms long previously to the proposed date. I had made my terms and written
my story and sent it to the publisher long before
it was wanted ; and so far my mind was at rest.
The date fixed was the first of July, which date
had been named in accordance with the exigencies
of the editor of the periodical. An author who
writes for these publications is bound to suit
himself to these exigencies, and can generally
do so without personal loss or inconvenience, if

he will only take time by the forelock. With all the pages that I have written for magazines I have never been a day late, nor have I ever caused inconvenience by sending less or more matter than I had stipulated to supply. But I have sometimes found myself compelled to suffer by the irregularity of others. I have endeavoured to console myself by reflecting that such must ever be the fate of virtue. The industrious must feed the idle. The honest and simple will always be the prey of the cunning and fraudulent. The punctual, who keep none waiting for them, are doomed to wait perpetually for the unpunctual. But these earthly sufferers know that they are making their way heavenwards,—and their oppressors their way elsewards. If the former reflection does not suffice for consolation, the deficiency is made up by the second. I was terribly aggrieved on the matter of the publication of my new Vicar, and had to think very much of the ultimate rewards of punctuality and its opposite. About the end of March 1869 I got a dolorous letter from the editor. All the *Once a Week* people were in a terrible trouble. They had bought the right of translating one of Victor Hugo's modern novels, *L'Homme Qui Rit*; they had fixed a date, relying on positive pledges from the French publishers; and now the great French author had postponed his work from week to week and from month to month, and it had so come to pass that the Frenchman's grinning hero would have to appear exactly at the same time as my clergyman. Was it not quite apparent to me, the editor asked, that *Once a Week* could not hold the two? Would I allow my clergyman to make his appearance in the *Gentleman's Magazine* instead?

My disgust at this proposition was, I think, chiefly due to Victor Hugo's latter novels, which I regard as pretentious and untrue to nature. To this perhaps was added some feeling of indignation that I should be asked to give way to a Frenchman. The Frenchman had broken his engagement. He had failed to have his work finished by the stipulated time. From week to week and from month to month he had put off the fulfilment of his duty. And because of these laches on his part,—on the part of this sententious French Radical,—I was to be thrown over! Virtue sometimes finds it difficult to console herself even with the double comfort. I would not come out in the *Gentleman's Magazine*, and as the Grinning Man could not be got out of the way, my novel was published in separate numbers.

The same thing has occurred to me more than once since. ' You no doubt are regular,' a publisher has said to me, ' but Mr. —— is irregular. He has thrown me out, and I cannot be ready for you till three months after the time named.' In these emergencies I have given perhaps half what was wanted, and have refused to give the other half. I have endeavoured to fight my own battle fairly, and at the same time not to make myself unnecessarily obstinate. But the circumstances have impressed on my mind the great need there is that men engaged in literature should feel themselves to be bound to their industry as men know that they are bound in other callings. There does exist, I fear, a feeling that authors, because they are authors, are relieved from the necessity of paying attention to everyday rules. A writer, if he be making £800 a year, does not think himself

bound to live modestly on £600, and put by the
remainder for his wife and children. He does not
understand that he should sit down at his desk at
a certain hour. He imagines that publishers and
booksellers should keep all their engagements with
him to the letter ;—but that he, as a brain-worker,
and conscious of the subtle nature of the brain,
should be able to exempt himself from bonds
when it suits him. He has his own theory about
inspiration which will not always come,—especially
will not come if wine-cups overnight have been too
deep. All this has ever been odious to me, as
being unmanly. A man may be frail in health,
and therefore unable to do as he has contracted in
whatever grade of life. He who has been blessed
with physical strength to work day by day, year
by year—as has been my case—should pardon
deficiencies caused by sickness or infirmity. I may
in this respect have been a little hard on others,
—and, if so, I here record my repentance. But
I think that no allowance should be given to claims
for exemption from punctuality, made if not
absolutely on the score still with the conviction
of intellectual superiority.

The *Vicar of Bullhampton* was written chiefly
with the object of exciting not only pity but
sympathy for a fallen woman, and of raising a
feeling of forgiveness for such in the minds of
other women. I could not venture to make this
female the heroine of my story. To have made her
a heroine at all would have been directly opposed
to my purpose. It was necessary therefore that
she should be a second-rate personage in the tale ;
—but it was with reference to her life that the tale
was written, and the hero and the heroine with

their belongings are all subordinate. To this novel I affixed a preface,—in doing which I was acting in defiance of my old-established principle. I do not know that any one read it; but as I wish to have it read, I will insert it here again :—

' I have introduced in the *Vicar of Bullhampton* the character of a girl whom I will call,—for want of a truer word that shall not in its truth be offensive,—a castaway. I have endeavoured to endow her with qualities that may create sympathy, and I have brought her back at last from degradation, at least to decency. I have not married her to a wealthy lover, and I have endeavoured to explain that though there was possible to her a way out of perdition, still things could not be with her as they would have been had she not fallen.

' There arises, of course, the question whether a novelist, who professes to write for the amusement of the young of both sexes, should allow himself to bring upon his stage a character such as that of Carry Brattle. It is not long since,—it is well within the memory of the author,—that the very existence of such a condition of life as was hers, was supposed to be unknown to our sisters and daughters, and was, in truth, unknown to many of them. Whether that ignorance was good may be questioned; but that it exists no longer is beyond question. Then arises the further question,—how far the conditions of such unfortunates should be made a matter of concern to the sweet young hearts of those whose delicacy and cleanliness of thought is a matter of pride to so many of us. Cannot women, who are good, pity the sufferings of the vicious, and do something perhaps to mitigate and shorten them without contamination from the vice? It will be admitted probably by most men who have thought upon the subject that no fault among us is punished so heavily as that fault, often so light in itself but so terrible in its consequences to the less faulty of the two offenders, by which a woman falls. All her own sex is against her, and all those of the other sex in whose veins runs the blood which she is thought to have contaminated, and who, of nature, would befriend her, were her trouble any other than it is.

'She is what she is, and she remains in her abject, pitiless, unutterable misery, because this sentence of the world has placed her beyond the helping hand of Love and Friendship. It may be said, no doubt, that the severity of this judgment acts as a protection to female virtue,—deterring, as all known punishments do deter, from vice. But this punishment, which is horrible beyond the conception of those who have not regarded it closely, is not known beforehand. Instead of the punishment, there is seen a false glitter of gaudy life,—a glitter which is damnably false,—and which, alas! has been more often portrayed in glowing colours, for the injury of young girls, than have those horrors which ought to deter, with the dark shadowings which belong to them.

'To write in fiction of one so fallen as the noblest of her sex, as one to be rewarded because of her weakness, as one whose life is happy, bright, and glorious, is certainly to allure to vice and misery. But it may perhaps be possible that if the matter be handled with truth to life, some girl, who would have been thoughtless, may be made thoughtful, or some parent's heart may be softened.'

Those were my ideas when I conceived the story, and with that feeling I described the characters of Carry Brattle and of her family. I have not introduced her lover on the scene, nor have I presented her to the reader in the temporary enjoyment of any of those fallacious luxuries, the longing for which is sometimes more seductive to evil than love itself. She is introduced as a poor abased creature, who hardly knows how false were her dreams, with very little of the Magdalene about her—because though there may be Magdalenes they are not often found—but with an intense horror of the sufferings of her position. Such being her condition, will they who naturally are her friends protect her? The vicar who has taken her by the hand endeavours to excite them to charity; but father, and brother, and sister are alike hard-hearted. It had been my purpose at first that the hand of every Brattle should be against her; but my own heart was too soft to enable me to make the mother cruel,—or the unmarried sister who had been the early companion of the forlorn one.

As regards all the Brattles, the story is, I think, well told. The characters are true, and the scenes at the mill are in keeping with human nature. For the rest of the book I have little to say. It is not very bad, and it certainly is not very good. As I have myself forgotten what the heroine does and says—except that she tumbles into a ditch— I cannot expect that any one else should remember her. But I have forgotten nothing that was done or said by any of the Brattles.

The question brought in argument is one of fearful importance. As to the view to be taken first, there can, I think, be no doubt. In regard to a sin common to the two sexes, almost all the punishment and all the disgrace is heaped upon the one who in nine cases out of ten has been the least sinful. And the punishment inflicted is of such a nature that it hardly allows room for repentance. How is the woman to return to decency to whom no decent door is opened? Then comes the answer: It is to the severity of the punishment alone that we can trust to keep women from falling. Such is the argument used in favour of the existing practice, and such the excuse given for their severity by women who will relax nothing of their harshness. But in truth the severity of the punishment is not known beforehand; it is not in the least understood by women in general, except by those who suffer it. The gaudy dirt, the squalid plenty, the contumely of familiarity, the absence of all good words and all good things, the banishment from honest labour, the being compassed round with lies, the flaunting glare of fictitious revelry, the weary pavement, the horrid slavery to some horrid tyrant,—and then the quick depreciation of that one ware of beauty, the substituted paint, garments bright without but foul within like painted sepulchres, hunger, thirst, and strong drink, life without a hope, without the certainty even of a morrow's breakfast, utterly friendless, disease, starvation, and a quivering fear of that coming hell which still can hardly be worse than all that is suffered here! This is the life to which we doom our erring daughters, when because of their error we close our door upon them! But for our erring sons we find pardon easily enough.

Of course there are houses of refuge, from which it has been thought expedient to banish everything pleasant, as though the only repentance to which we can afford to give a place must necessarily be one of sackcloth and ashes. It is hardly thus that we can hope to recall those to decency who, if they are to be recalled at all, must be induced to obey the summons before they have reached the last stage of that misery which I have attempted to describe. To me the mistake which we too often make seems to be this,—that the girl who has gone astray is put out of sight, out of mind if possible, at any rate out of speech, as though she had never existed, and that this ferocity comes not only from hatred of the sin, but in part also from a dread of the taint which the sin brings with it. Very low as is the degradation to which a girl is brought when she falls through love or vanity, or perhaps from a longing for luxurious ease, still much lower is that to which she must descend perforce when, through the hardness of the world around her, she converts that sin into a trade. Mothers and sisters, when the misfortune comes upon them of a fallen female from among their number, should remember this, and not fear contamination so strongly as did Carry Brattle's married sister and sister-in-law.

In 1870 I brought out three books,—or rather of the latter of the three I must say that it was brought out by others, for I had nothing to do with it except to write it. These were *Sir Harry Hotspur of Humblethwaite, An Editor's Tales*, and a little volume on Julius Cæsar. *Sir Harry*

Hotspur was written on the same plan as *Nina Balatka* and *Linda Tressel*, and had for its object the telling of some pathetic incident in life rather than the portraiture of a number of human beings. *Nina* and *Linda Tressel* and *The Golden Lion* had been placed in foreign countries, and this was an English story. In other respects it is of the same nature, and was not, I think, by any means a failure. There is much of pathos in the love of the girl, and of paternal dignity and affection in the father.

It was published first in *Macmillan's Magazine*, by the intelligent proprietor of which I have since been told that it did not make either his fortune or that of his magazine. I am sorry that it should have been so ; but I fear that the same thing may be said of a good many of my novels. When it had passed through the magazine, the subsequent use of it was sold to other publishers by Mr. Macmillan, and then I learned that it was to be brought out by them as a novel in two volumes. Now it had been sold by me as a novel in one volume, and hence there arose a correspondence.

I found it very hard to make the purchasers understand that I had reasonable ground for objection to the process. What was it to me ? How could it injure me if they stretched my pages by means of lead and margin into double the number I had intended. I have heard the same argument on other occasions. When I have pointed out that in this way the public would have to suffer, seeing that they would have to pay Mudie for the use of two volumes in reading that which ought to have been given to them in one, I have been assured that the public are pleased

with literary short measure, that it is the object
of novel-readers to get through novels as fast as
they can, and that the shorter each volume is the
better! Even this, however, did not overcome
me, and I stood to my guns. *Sir Harry* was
published in one volume, containing something
over the normal 300 pages, with an average of 220
words to a page,—which I had settled with my
conscience to be the proper length of a novel
volume. I may here mention that on one occasion,
and on one occasion only, a publisher got the
better of me in a matter of volumes. He had
a two-volume novel of mine running through a
certain magazine, and had it printed complete in
three volumes before I knew where I was,—before
I had seen a sheet of the letterpress. I stormed
for a while, but I had not the heart to make him
break up the type.

The *Editor's Tales* was a volume republished
from the *St. Paul's Magazine*, and professed to
give an editor's experience of his dealings with
contributors. I do not think that there is a single
incident in the book which could bring back to
any one concerned the memory of a past event.
And yet there is not an incident in it the outline
of which was not presented to my mind by the
remembrance of some fact :—how an ingenious
gentleman got into conversation with me, I not
knowing that he knew me to be an editor, and
pressed his little article on my notice ; how I was
addressed by a lady with a becoming pseudonym
and with much equally becoming audacity ; how
I was appealed to by the dearest of little women
whom here I have called Mary Gresley ; how in
my own early days there was a struggle over an

abortive periodical which was intended to be the
best thing ever done ; how terrible was the tragedy
of a poor drunkard, who with infinite learning at
his command made one sad final effort to reclaim
himself, and perished while he was making it ;
and lastly how a poor weak editor was driven
nearly to madness by threatened litigation from a
rejected contributor. Of these stories *The Spotted
Dog*, with the struggles of the drunkard scholar, is
the best. I know now, however, that when the
things were good they came out too quick one
upon another to gain much attention ;—and so
also, luckily, when they were bad.

The *Cæsar* was a thing of itself. My friend John
Blackwood had set on foot a series of small volumes
called *Ancient Classics for English Readers*, and
had placed the editing of them, and the compiling
of many of them, in the hands of William Lucas
Collins, a clergyman who, from my connection
with the series, became a most intimate friend.
The *Iliad* and the *Odyssey* had already come out
when I was at Edinburgh with John Blackwood,
and, on my expressing my very strong admiration
for those two little volumes,—which I here recommend to all young ladies as the most charming
tales they can read,—he asked me whether I would
not undertake one myself. *Herodotus* was in the
press, but, if I could get it ready, mine should be
next. Whereupon I offered to say what might be
said to the readers of English on *The Commentaries
of Julius Cæsar*.

I at once went to work, and in three months
from that day the little book had been written.
I began by reading through the Commentaries
twice, which I did without any assistance either

by translation or English notes. Latin was not so familiar to me then as it has since become,—for from that date I have almost daily spent an hour with some Latin author, and on many days many hours. After the reading what my author had left behind him, I fell into the reading of what others had written about him, in Latin, in English, and even in French,—for I went through much of that most futile book by the late Emperor of the French. I do not know that for a short period I ever worked harder. The amount I had to write was nothing. Three weeks would have done it easily. But I was most anxious, in this soaring out of my own peculiar line, not to disgrace myself. I do not think that I did disgrace myself. Perhaps I was anxious for something more. If so, I was disappointed.

The book I think to be a good little book. It is readable by all, old and young, and it gives, I believe accurately, both an account of Cæsar's Commentaries,—which of course was the primary intention,—and the chief circumstances of the great Roman's life. A well-educated girl who had read it and remembered it would perhaps know as much about Cæsar and his writings as she need know. Beyond the consolation of thinking as I do about it, I got very little gratification from the work. Nobody praised it. One very old and very learned friend to whom I sent it thanked me for my ' comic Cæsar,' but said no more. I do not suppose that he intended to run a dagger into me. Of any suffering from such wounds, I think, while living, I never showed a sign ; but still I have suffered occasionally. There was, however, probably present to my friend's mind, and to that of others, a feeling that a man who has spent his life in writing English novels could not be fit to write about Cæsar. It was as when an amateur gets a picture hung on the walls of the Academy. What business had I there? *Ne sutor ultra crepidam*. In the press it was most faintly damned by most faint praise. Nevertheless, having read the book again within the last month or two, I make bold to say that it is a good book. The series, I believe, has done very well. I am sure that it ought to do well in years to come, for, putting aside Cæsar, the work has been done with infinite scholarship, and very generally with a light hand. With the leave of my sententious and sonorous friend, who had not endured that subjects which had been grave to him should be treated irreverently, I will say that such a work, unless it be light, cannot answer the purpose for which it is intended. It was not exactly a school-book that was wanted, but something that would carry the purposes of the school-room even into the leisure hours of adult pupils. Nothing was ever better suited for such a purpose than the *Iliad* and the *Odyssey*, as done by Mr. Collins. The *Virgil*, also done by him, is very good; and so is the *Aristophanes* by the same hand.

CHAPTER XIX

'RALPH THE HEIR'—'THE EUSTACE DIA-MONDS'—'LADY ANNA'—'AUSTRALIA'

IN the spring of 1871 we,—I and my wife,—had decided that we would go to Australia to visit our shepherd son. Of course before doing so I made a contract with a publisher for a book about the Colonies. For such a work as this I had always been aware that I could not fairly demand more than half the price that would be given for the same amount of fiction; and as such books have an indomitable tendency to stretch themselves, so that more is given than what is sold, and as the cost of travelling is heavy, the writing of them is not remunerative. This tendency to stretch comes not, I think, generally from the ambition of the writer, but from his inability to comprise the different parts in their allotted spaces. If you have to deal with a country, a colony, a city, a trade, or a political opinion, it is so much easier to deal with it in twenty than in twelve pages! I also made an engagement with the editor of a London daily paper to supply him with a series of articles,—which were duly written, duly published, and duly paid for. But with all this, travelling with the object of writing is not a good trade. If the travelling author can pay his bills, he must be a good manager on the road.

Before starting there came upon us the terrible necessity of coming to some resolution about our house at Waltham. It had been first hired, and then bought, primarily because it suited my Post Office avocations. To this reason had been added other attractions,—in the shape of hunting, gardening, and suburban hospitalities. Altogether the house had been a success, and the scene of much happiness. But there arose questions as to expense. Would not a house in London be cheaper? There could be no doubt that my income would decrease, and was decreasing. I had thrown the Post Office, as it were, away, and the writing of novels could not go on for ever. Some of my friends told me already that at fifty-five I ought to give up the fabrication of love-stories. The hunting, I thought, must soon go, and I would not therefore allow that to keep me in the country. And then, why should I live at Waltham Cross now, seeing that I had fixed on that place in reference to the Post Office ? It was therefore determined that we would flit, and as we were to be away for eighteen months, we determined also to sell our furniture. So there was a packing up, with many tears, and consultations as to what should be saved out of the things we loved.

As must take place on such an occasion, there was some heart-felt grief. But the thing was done, and orders were given for the letting or sale of the house. I may as well say here that it never was let, and that it remained unoccupied for two years before it was sold. I lost by the transaction about £800. As I continually hear that other men make money by buying and selling houses, I presume I am not well adapted for transactions of that sort.

I have never made money by selling anything except a manuscript. In matters of horseflesh I am so inefficient that I have generally given away horses that I have not wanted.

When we started from Liverpool, in May 1871, *Ralph the Heir* was running through the *St. Paul's*. This was the novel of which Charles Reade afterwards took the plot and made on it a play. I have always thought it to be one of the worst novels I have written, and almost to have justified that dictum that a novelist after fifty should not write love-stories. It was in part a political novel; and that part which appertains to politics, and which recounts the electioneering experiences of the candidates at Percycross, is well enough. Percycross and Beverley were, of course, one and the same place. Neefit, the breeches-maker, and his daughter, are also good in their way,—and Moggs, the daughter's lover, who was not only lover, but also one of the candidates at Percycross as well. But the main thread of the story,—that which tells of the doings of the young gentlemen and young ladies,—the heroes and the heroines,— is not good. Ralph the heir has not much life about him; while Ralph who is not the heir, but is intended to be the real hero, has none. The same may be said of the young ladies,—of whom one, she who was meant to be the chief, has passed utterly out of my mind, without leaving a trace of remembrance behind.

I also left in the hands of the editor of *The Fortnightly*, ready for production on the 1st of July following, a story called *The Eustace Diamonds*. In that I think that my friend's dictum was disproved. There is not much love in it; but

what there is, is good. The character of Lucy
Morris is pretty ; and her love is as genuine and
as well told as that of Lucy Robarts or Lily Dale.

But *The Eustace Diamonds* achieved the success
which it certainly did attain, not as a love-story,
but as a record of a cunning little woman of
pseudo-fashion, to whom, in her cunning, there
came a series of adventures, unpleasant enough
in themselves, but pleasant to the reader. As
I wrote the book, the idea constantly presented
itself to me that Lizzie Eustace was but a second
Becky Sharpe ; but in planning the character I had
not thought of this, and I believe that Lizzie would
have been just as she is though Becky Sharpe
had never been described. The plot of the diamond
necklace is, I think, well arranged, though it
produced itself without any forethought. I had
no idea of setting thieves after the bauble till
I had got my heroine to bed in the inn at Carlisle ;
nor of the disappointment of the thieves, till
Lizzie had been wakened in the morning with the
news that her door had been broken open. All
these things, and many more, Wilkie Collins could
have arranged before with infinite labour, preparing things present so that they should fit in with
things to come. I have gone on the very much
easier plan of making everything as it comes fit
in with what has gone before. At any rate, the
book was a success, and did much to repair the
injury which I felt had come to my reputation in
the novel-market by the works of the last few
years. I doubt whether I had written anything
so successful as *The Eustace Diamonds* since *The
Small House at Allington*. I had written what
was much better,—as, for instance, *Phineas Finn*

and *Nina Balatka ;* but that is by no means the
same thing.

I also left behind, in a strong box, the manuscript of *Phineas Redux*, a novel of which I have
already spoken, and which I subsequently sold
to the proprietors of the *Graphic* newspaper.
The editor of that paper greatly disliked the title,
assuring me that the public would take Redux
for the gentleman's surname,—and was dissatisfied
with me when I replied that I had no objection
to them doing so. The introduction of a Latin
word, or of a word from any other language, into
the title of an English novel is undoubtedly in
bad taste ; but after turning the matter much
over in my own mind, I could find no other suitable
name.

I also left behind me, in the same strong box,
another novel, called *An Eye for an Eye*, which
then had been some time written, and of which
as it has not even yet been published, I will not
further speak. It will probably be published
some day, though, looking forward. I can see no
room for it, at any rate, for the next two years.

If therefore the Great Britain, in which we
sailed for Melbourne, had gone to the bottom,
I had so provided that there would be new
novels ready to come out under my name for
some years to come. This consideration, however,
did not keep me idle while I was at sea. When
making long journeys, I have always succeeded
in getting a desk put up in my cabin, and this
was done ready for me in the Great Britain, so
that I could go to work the day after we left
Liverpool. This I did ; and before I reached
Melbourne I had finished a story called *Lady*

Anna. Every word of this was written at sea, during the two months required for our voyage, and was done day by day—with the intermission of one day's illness—for eight weeks, at the rate of 66 pages of manuscript in each week, every page of manuscript containing 250 words. Every word was counted. I have seen work come back to an author from the press with terrible deficiencies as to the amount supplied. Thirty-two pages have perhaps been wanted for a number, and the printers with all their art could not stretch the matter to more than twenty-eight or -nine! The work of filling up must be very dreadful. I have sometimes been ridiculed for the methodical details of my business. But by these contrivances I have been preserved from many troubles ; and I have saved others with whom I have worked— editors, publishers, and printers—from much trouble also.

A month or two after my return home, *Lady Anna* appeared in *The Fortnightly*, following *The Eustace Diamonds*. In it a young girl, who is really a lady of high rank and great wealth, though in her youth she enjoyed none of the privileges of wealth or rank, marries a tailor who had been good to her, and whom she had loved when she was poor and neglected. A fine young noble lover is provided for her, and all the charms of sweet living with nice people are thrown in her way, in order that she may be made to give up the tailor. And the charms are very powerful with her. But the feeling that she is bound by her troth to the man who had always been true to her overcomes everything,—and she marries the tailor. It was my wish of course to justify her in doing so, and to carry my readers along with me in my sympathy with her. But everybody found fault with me for marrying her to the tailor. What would they have said if I had allowed her to jilt the tailor and marry the good-looking young lord ? How much louder, then, would have been the censure ! The book was read, and I was satisfied. If I had not told my story well, there would have been no feeling in favour of the young lord. The horror which was expressed to me at the evil thing I had done, in giving the girl to the tailor, was the strongest testimony I could receive of the merits of the story.

I went to Australia chiefly in order that I might see my son among his sheep. I did see him among his sheep, and remained with him for four or five very happy weeks. He was not making money, nor has he made money since. I grieve to say that several thousands of pounds which I had squeezed out of the pockets of perhaps too liberal publishers have been lost on the venture. But I rejoice to say that this has been in no way due to any fault of his. I never knew a man work with more persistent honesty at his trade than he has done.

I had, however, the further intentions of writing a book about the entire group of Australasian Colonies ; and in order that I might be enabled to do that with sufficient information, I visited them all. Making my head-quarters at Melbourne, I went to Queensland, New South Wales, Tasmania, then to the very little known territory of Western Australia, and then, last of all, to New Zealand. I was absent in all eighteen months, and think that I did succeed in learning much of the political, social, and material condition of these countries. I wrote my book as I was travelling, and brought it back with me to England all but completed in December 1872.

It was a better book than that which I had written eleven years before on the American States, but not so good as that on the West Indies in 1859. As regards the information given, there was much more to be said about Australia than the West Indies. Very much more is said, —and very much more may be learned from the latter than from the former book. I am sure that any one who will take the trouble to read the book on Australia, will learn much from it. But the West Indian volume was readable. I am not sure that either of the other works are, in the proper sense of that word. When I go back to them I find that the pages drag with me;—and if so with me, how must it be with others who have none of that love which a father feels even for his ill-favoured offspring. Of all the needs a book has the chief need is that it be readable.

Feeling that these volumes on Australia were dull and long, I was surprised to find that they had an extensive sale. There were, I think, 2000 copies circulated of the first expensive edition; and then the book was divided into four little volumes, which were published separately, and which again had a considerable circulation. That some facts were stated inaccurately, I do not doubt; that many opinions were crude, I am quite sure; that I had failed to understand much which I attempted to explain, is possible. But with all these faults the book was a thoroughly honest book, and was the result of unflagging labour for a period of fifteen months. I spared myself no trouble in inquiry, no trouble in seeing, and no trouble in listening. I thoroughly imbued my mind with the subject, and wrote with the simple intention of giving trustworthy information on the state of the Colonies. Though there be inaccuracies,—those inaccuracies to which work quickly done must always be subject,—I think I did give much valuable information.

I came home across America from San Francisco to New York, visiting Utah and Brigham Young on the way. I did not achieve great intimacy with the great polygamist of the Salt Lake City. I called upon him, sending to him my card, apologising for doing so without an introduction, and excusing myself by saying that I did not like to pass through the territory without seeing a man of whom I had heard so much. He received me in his doorway, not asking me to enter, and inquired whether I were not a miner. When I told him that I was not a miner, he asked me whether I earned my bread. I told him I did. ' I guess you're a miner,' said he. I again assured him that I was not. ' Then how do you earn your bread ? ' I told him that I did so by writing books. ' I'm sure you're a miner,' said he. Then he turned upon his heel, went back into the house, and closed the door. I was properly punished, as I was vain enough to conceive that he would have heard my name.

I got home in December 1872, and in spite of any resolution made to the contrary, my mind was full of hunting as I came back. No real resolutions had in truth been made, for out of a stud of four horses I kept three, two of which were absolutely idle through the two summers and winters of my absence. Immediately on my arrival I bought another, and settled myself down to hunting from London three days a week. At first I went back to Essex, my old country, but finding that to be inconvenient, I took my horses to Leighton Buzzard, and became one of that numerous herd of sportsmen who rode with the 'Baron' and Mr. Selby Lowndes. In those days Baron Meyer was alive, and the riding with his hounds was very good. I did not care so much for Mr. Lowndes. During the winters of 1873, 1874, and 1875, I had my horses back in Essex, and went on with my hunting, always trying to resolve that I would give it up. But still I bought fresh horses, and, as I did not give it up, I hunted more than ever. Three times a week the cab has been at my door in London very punctually, and not unfrequently before seven in the morning. In order to secure this attendance, the man has always been invited to have his breakfast in the hall. I have gone to the Great Eastern Railway,— ah! so often with the fear that frost would make all my exertions useless, and so often too with that result! And then, from one station or another station, have travelled on wheels at least a dozen miles. After the day's sport, the same toil has been necessary to bring me home to dinner at eight. This has been work for a young man and a rich man, but I have done it as an old man and comparatively a poor man. Now at last, in April 1876, I do think that my resolution has been taken. I am giving away my old horses, and anybody is welcome to my saddles and horse-furniture.

'Singula de nobis anni prædantur euntes;
  Eripuere jocos, venerem, convivia, ludum;
  Tendunt extorquere poëmata.'

' Our years keep taking toll as they move on;
  My feasts, my frolics, are already gone,
  And now, it seems, my verses must go too.'

This is Conington's translation, but it seems
to me to be a little flat.

' Years as they roll cut all our pleasures short;
  Our pleasant mirth, our loves, our wine, our sport.
  And then they stretch their power, and crush at last
  Even the power of singing of the past.'

I think that I may say with truth that I rode
hard to my end.

' Vixi puellis nuper idoneus,
    Et militavi non sine gloria;
      Nunc arma defunctumque bello
        Barbiton hic paries habebit.'

' I've lived about the covert side,
    I've ridden straight, and ridden fast;
  Now breeches, boots, and scarlet pride
    Are but mementoes of the past.'

CHAPTER XX

'THE WAY WE LIVE NOW' AND 'THE PRIME MINISTER'—CONCLUSION

In what I have said at the end of the last chapter about my hunting, I have been carried a little in advance of the date at which I had arrived. We returned from Australia in the winter of 1872, and early in 1873 I took a house in Montagu Square,— in which I hope to live and hope to die. Our first work in settling there was to place upon new shelves the books which I had collected round myself at Waltham. And this work, which was in itself great, entailed also the labour of a new catalogue. As all who use libraries know, a catalogue is nothing unless it show the spot on which every book is to be found,—information which every volume also ought to give as to itself. Only those who have done it know how great is the labour of moving and arranging a few thousand volumes. At the present moment I own about 5000 volumes, and they are dearer to me even than the horses which are going, or than the wine in the cellar, which is very apt to go, and upon which I also pride myself.

When this was done, and the new furniture had got into its place, and my little book-room was settled sufficiently for work, I began a novel,

to the writing of which I was instigated by what
I conceived to be the commercial profligacy of the
age. Whether the world does or does not become
more wicked as years go on, is a question which
probably has disturbed the minds of thinkers
since the world began to think. That men have
become less cruel, less violent, less selfish, less
brutal, there can be no doubt ;—but have they
become less honest ? If so, can a world, retrograding from day to day in honesty, be considered to
be in a state of progress. We know the opinion on
this subject of our philosopher Mr. Carlyle. If
he be right, we are all going straight away to
darkness and the dogs. But then we do not put
very much faith in Mr. Carlyle,—nor in Mr. Ruskin
and his other followers. The loudness and extravagance of their lamentations, the wailing and gnash-
ing of teeth which comes from them, over a world
which is supposed to have gone altogether shoddy-
wards, are so contrary to the convictions of men
who cannot but see how comfort has been increased,
how health has been improved, and education
extended,—that the general effect of their teaching
is the opposite of what they have intended. It
is regarded simply as Carlylism to say that the
English-speaking world is growing worse from day
to day. And it is Carlylism to opine that the
general grand result of increased intelligence is a
tendency to deterioration.

Nevertheless a certain class of dishonesty,
dishonesty magnificent in its proportions, and
climbing into high places, has become at the same
time so rampant and so splendid that there seems
to be reason for fearing that men and women will
be taught to feel that dishonesty, if it can become

splendid, will cease to be abominable. If dishonesty can live in a gorgeous palace with pictures on all its walls, and gems in all its cupboards, with marble and ivory in all its corners, and can give Apician dinners, and get into Parliament, and deal in millions, then dishonesty is not disgraceful, and the man dishonest after such a fashion is not a low scoundrel. Instigated, I say, by some such reflections as these, I sat down in my new house to write *The Way We Live Now*. And as I had ventured to take the whip of the satirist into my hand, I went beyond the iniquities of the great speculator who robs everybody, and made an onslaught also on other vices,—on the intrigues of girls who want to get married, on the luxury of young men who prefer to remain single, and on the puffing propensities of authors who desire to cheat the public into buying their volumes.

The book has the fault which is to be attributed to almost all satires, whether in prose or verse. The accusations are exaggerated. The vices are coloured, so as to make effect rather than to represent truth. Who, when the lash of objurgation is in his hands, can so moderate his arm as never to strike harder than justice would require? The spirit which produces the satire is honest enough, but the very desire which moves the satirist to do his work energetically makes him dishonest. In other respects *The Way We Live Now* was, as a satire, powerful and good. The character of Melmotte is well maintained. The Beargarden is amusing,—and not untrue. The Longestaffe girls and their friend, Lady Monogram, are amusing,—but exaggerated. Dolly Longestaffe, is, I think, very good. And Lady Carbury's literary efforts are, I am sorry to say, such as are too frequently made. But here again the young lady with her two lovers is weak and vapid. I almost doubt whether it be not impossible to have two absolutely distinct parts in a novel, and to imbue them both with interest. If they be distinct, the one will seem to be no more than padding to the other. And so it was in *The Way We Live Now*. The interest of the story lies among the wicked and foolish people,—with Melmotte and his daughter, with Dolly and his family, with the American woman, Mrs. Hurtle, and with John Crumb and the girl of his heart. But Roger Carbury, Paul Montague, and Henrietta Carbury are uninteresting. Upon the whole, I by no means look upon the book as one of my failures; nor was it taken as a failure by the public or the press.

While I was writing *The Way We Live Now*, I was called upon by the proprietors of the *Graphic* for a Christmas story. I feel, with regard to literature, somewhat as I suppose an upholsterer and undertaker feels when he is called upon to supply a funeral. He has to supply it, however distasteful it may be. It is his business, and he will starve if he neglect it. So have I felt that, when anything in the shape of a novel was required, I was bound to produce it. Nothing can be more distasteful to me than to have to give a relish of Christmas to what I write. I feel the humbug implied by the nature of the order. A Christmas story, in the proper sense, should be the ebullition of some mind anxious to instil others with a desire for Christmas religious thought, or Christmas festivities,—or, better still, with Christmas charity. Such

was the case with Dickens when he wrote his two
first Christmas stories. But since that the things
written annually—all of which have been fixed to
Christmas like children's toys to a Christmas tree—
have had no real savour of Christmas about them.
I had done two or three before. Alas! at this very
moment I have one to write, which I have promised
to supply within three weeks of this time,—the
picture-makers always require a long interval,—as
to which I have in vain been cudgelling my brain
for the last month. I can't send away the order
to another shop, but I do not know how I shall
ever get the coffin made.

For the *Graphic*, in 1873, I wrote a little story
about Australia. Christmas at the antipodes is of
course midsummer, and I was not loth to describe
the troubles to which my own son had been subjected, by the mingled accidents of heat and bad
neighbours, on his station in the bush. So I wrote
Harry Heathcote of Gangoil, and was well through my
labour on that occasion. I only wish I may have no
worse success in that which now hangs over my
head.

When *Harry Heathcote* was over, I returned with
a full heart to Lady Glencora and her husband.
I had never yet drawn the completed picture of
such a statesman as my imagination had conceived. The personages with whose names my
pages had been familiar, and perhaps even the minds
of some of my readers—the Brocks, De Terriers,
Monks, Greshams, and Daubeneys—had been more
or less portraits, not of living men, but of living
political characters. The strong-minded, thick-
skinned, useful, ordinary member, either of the
Government or of the Opposition, had been very

easy to describe, and had required no imagination to conceive. The character reproduces itself from generation to generation; and as it does so, becomes shorn in a wonderful way of those little touches of humanity which would be destructive of its purposes. Now and again there comes a burst of human nature, as in the quarrel between Burke and Fox; but, as a rule, the men submit themselves to be shaped and fashioned, and to be formed into tools, which are used either for building up or pulling down, and can generally bear to be changed from this box into the other, without, at any rate, the appearance of much personal suffering. Four-and-twenty gentlemen will amalgamate themselves into one whole, and work for one purpose, having each of them to set aside his own idiosyncrasy, and to endure the close personal contact of men who must often be personally disagreeable, having been thoroughly taught that in no other way can they serve either their country or their own ambition. These are the men who are publicly useful, and whom the necessities of the age supply,—as to whom I have never ceased to wonder that stones of such strong calibre should be so quickly worn down to the shape and smoothness of rounded pebbles.

Such have been to me the Brocks and the Mildmays, about whom I have written with great pleasure, having had my mind much exercised in watching them. But I had also conceived the character of a statesman of a different nature—of a man who should be in something perhaps superior, but in very much inferior, to these men—of one who could not become a pebble, having too strong an identity of his own. To rid one's self of fine scruples—to fall into the traditions of a party—to feel the need of subservience, not only in acting but also even in thinking—to be able to be a bit, and at first only a very little bit,—these are the necessities of the growing statesman. The time may come, the glorious time when some great self action shall be possible, and shall be even demanded, as when Peel gave up the Corn Laws; but the rising man, as he puts on his harness, should not allow himself to dream of this. To become a good, round, smooth, hard, useful pebble is his duty, and to achieve this he must harden his skin and swallow his scruples. But every now and again we see the attempt made by men who cannot get their skins to be hard who after a little while generally fall out of the ranks. The statesman of whom I was thinking—of whom I had long thought—was one who did not fall out of the ranks, even though his skin would not become hard. He should have rank, and intellect, and parliamentary habits, by which to bind him to the service of his country; and he should also have unblemished, unextinguishable, inexhaustible love of country. That virtue I attribute to our statesmen generally. They who are without it are, I think, mean indeed. This man should have it as the ruling principle of his life; and it should so rule him that all other things should be made to give way to it. But he should be scrupulous, and, being scrupulous, weak. When called to the highest place in the council of his Sovereign, he should feel with true modesty his own insufficiency; but not the less should the greed of power grow upon him when he had once allowed himself to taste and enjoy it. Such was the character I endeavoured to depict in describing the

triumph, the troubles, and the failure of my Prime
Minister. And I think that I have succeeded.
What the public may think, or what the press
may say, I do not yet know, the work having
as yet run but half its course.[1]

That the man's character should be understood as I understand it—or that of his wife's,
the delineation of which has also been a matter
of much happy care to me—I have no right to
expect, seeing that the operation of describing
has not been confined to one novel, which might
perhaps be read through by the majority of those
who commenced it. It has been carried on through
three or four, each of which will be forgotten even
by the most zealous reader almost as soon as read.
In *The Prime Minister*, my Prime Minister will not
allow his wife to take office among, or even over,
those ladies who are attached by office to the
Queen's court. ' I should not choose,' he says to
her, ' that my wife should have any duties uncon-
nected with our joint family and home.' Who
will remember in reading those words that, in a
former story, published some years before, he tells
his wife, when she has twitted him with his willing-
ness to clean the Premier's shoes, that he would
even allow her to clean them if it were for the good
of the country ? And yet it is by such details as
these that I have, for many years past, been manu-
facturing within my own mind the characters of
the man and his wife.

---

[1] Writing this note in 1878, after a lapse of nearly three
years, I am obliged to say that, as regards the public, *The
Prime Minister* was a failure. It was worse spoken of by
the press than any novel I had written. I was specially
hurt by a criticism on it in the *Spectator*. The critic who

I think that Plantagenet Palliser, Duke of Omnium, is a perfect gentleman. If he be not, then am I unable to describe a gentleman. She is by no means a perfect lady; but if she be not all over a woman, then am I not able to describe a woman. I do not think it probable that my name will remain among those who in the next century will be known as the writers of English prose fiction; —but if it does, that permanence of success will probably rest on the character of Plantagenet Palliser, Lady Glencora, and the Rev. Mr. Crawley.

I have now come to the end of that long series of books written by myself, with which the public is already acquainted. Of those which I may hereafter be able to add to them I cannot speak; though I have an idea that I shall even yet once more have recourse to my political hero as the mainstay of another story. When *The Prime Minister* was finished, I at once began another novel, which is now completed in three volumes, and which is called *Is He Popenjoy?* There are two Popenjoys in the book, one succeeding to the title held by the other; but as they are both babies, and do not in the course of the story progress beyond babyhood, the future readers, should the tale ever be published, will not be much interested in them. Nevertheless the story, as a story, is not, I think, amiss. Since that I have written still another three-volume novel, to which, very much in opposition to my publisher, I have

wrote the article I know to be a good critic, inclined to be more than fair to me; but in this case I could not agree with him, so much do I love the man whose character I had endeavoured to portray.

given the name of *The American Senator*.[1] It is
to appear in *Temple Bar*, and is to commence its
appearance on the first of next month. Such
being its circumstances, I do not know that I can
say anything else about it here.

And so I end the record of my literary per-
formances,—which I think are more in amount than
the works of any other living English author. If
any English authors not living have written more—
as may probably have been the case—I do not
know who they are. I find that, taking the books
which have appeared under our names, I have
published much more than twice as much as
Carlyle. I have also published considerably more
than Voltaire, even including his letters. We are
told that Varro, at the age of eighty, had written
480 volumes, and that he went on writing for eight
years longer. I wish I knew what was the length
of Varro's volumes ; I comfort myself by reflecting
that the amount of manuscript described as a book
in Varro's time was not much. Varro, too, is dead,
and Voltaire ; whereas I am still living, and may
add to the pile.

The following is a list of the books I have written,
with the dates of publication and the sums I have
received for them. The dates given are the years in
which the works were published as a whole, most
of them having appeared before in some serial
form.

---

[1] *The American Senator* and *Popenjoy* have appeared,
each with fair success. Neither of them has encountered
that reproach which, in regard to *The Prime Minister*,
seemed to tell me that my work as a novelist should be
brought to a close. And yet I feel assured that they are
very inferior to *The Prime Minister*.

Names of Works.	Date of Publication.	Total Sums Received.		
The Macdermots of Ballycloran, .	1847	£48	6	9
The Kellys and the O'Kellys, .	1848	123	19	5
La Vendée, ...	1850	20	0	0
The Warden, ...	1855 }	727	11	3
Barchester Towers, . . .	1857 }			
The Three Clerks, . . .	1858	250	0	0
Doctor Thorne, . . .	1858	400	0	0
The West Indies and the Spanish Main, ...	1859	250	0	0
The Bertrams, ...	1859	400	0	0
Castle Richmond, . . .	1860	600	0	0
Framley Parsonage, . . .	1861	1000	0	0
Tales of All Countries—1st Series	1861 }			
„ „ 2d „	1863 }	1830	0	0
„ „ 3d „	1870 }			
Orley Farm, ...	1862	3135	0	0
North America,	1862	1250	0	0
Rachel Ray, ...	1863	1645	0	0
The Small House at Allington, .	1864	3000	0	0
Can You Forgive Her ? . .	1864	3525	0	0
Miss Mackenzie, . . .	1865	1300	0	0
The Belton Estate, . . .	1866	1757	0	0
The Claverings, ...	1867	2800	0	0
The Last Chronicle of Barset, .	1867	3000	0	0
Nina Balatka, ...	1867	450	0	0
Linda Tressel, ...	1868	450	0	0
Phineas Finn, ...	1869	3200	0	0
He Knew He Was Right, . .	1869	3200	0	0
Brown, Jones, and Robinson, .	1870	600	0	0
The Vicar of Bullhampton, .	1870	2500	0	0
An Editor's Tales, . . .	1870	378	0	0
Cæsar (Ancient Classics), . .	1870[1]	0	0	0
Sir Harry Hotspur of Humblethwaite,	1871	750	0	0
Ralph the Heir, . . .	1871	2500	0	0
The Golden Lion of Granpère, .	1872	550	0	0
The Eustace Diamonds, . .	1873	2500	0	0
Australia and New Zealand, .	1873	1300	0	0
Carry forward,		£45,439	17	5

[1] This was given by me as a present to my friend John Blackwood.

Names of Works.	Date of Publication.	Total Sums Received.		
Brought forward,		£45,439	17	5
Phineas Redux, . . .	1874	2500	0	0
Harry Heathcote of Gangoil, .	1874	450	0	0
Lady Anna, ...	1874	1200	0	0
The Way We Live Now, . .	1875	3000	0	0
The Prime Minister, . .	1876	2500	0	0
The American Senator, . .	1877	1800	0	0
Is He Popenjoy ? . .	1878	1600	0	0
South Africa, ...	1878	850	0	0
John Caldigate, . . .	1879	1800	0	0
Sundries, ...		7800	0	0
		£68,939	17	5

It will not, I am sure, be thought that, in making my boast as to quantity, I have endeavoured to lay claim to any literary excellence. That, in the writing of books, quantity without quality is a vice and a misfortune, has been too manifestly settled to leave a doubt on such a matter. But I do lay claim to whatever merit should be accorded to me for persevering diligence in my profession. And I make the claim, not with a view to my own glory, but for the benefit of those who may read these pages, and when young may intend to follow the same career. *Nulla dies sine lineâ.* Let that be their motto. And let their work be to them as is his common work to the common labourer. No gigantic efforts will then be necessary. He need tie no wet towels round his brow, nor sit for thirty hours at his desk without moving,—as men have sat, or said that they have sat. More than nine-tenths of my literary work has been done in the last twenty years, and during twelve of those years I followed another profession. I have never been a slave to this work, giving due time, if not more than due time, to the amusements I have

loved. But I have been constant,—and constancy
in labour will conquer all difficulties. *Gutta cavat
lapidem non vi, sed sæpe cadendo.*

It may interest some if I state that during the
last twenty years I have made by literature something near £70,000. As I have said before in these
pages, I look upon the result as comfortable, but
not splendid.

It will not, I trust, be supposed by any reader
that I have intended in this so-called autobiography to give a record of my inner life. No man
ever did so truly,—and no man ever will. Rousseau
probably attempted it, but who doubts but that
Rousseau has confessed in much the thoughts and
convictions rather than the facts of his life?
If the rustle of a woman's petticoat has ever stirred
my blood ; if a cup of wine has been a joy to me ;
if I have thought tobacco at midnight in pleasant
company to be one of the elements of an earthly
paradise ; if now and again I have somewhat
recklessly fluttered a £5 note over a card-table ;—
of what matter is that to any reader ? I have
betrayed no woman. Wine has brought me to no
sorrow. It has been the companionship of smoking
that I have loved, rather than the habit. I have
never desired to win money, and I have lost none.
To enjoy the excitement of pleasure, but to be
free from its vices and ill effects,—to have the sweet,
and leave the bitter untasted,—that has been my
study. The preachers tell us that this is impossible.
It seems to me that hitherto I have succeeded
fairly well. I will not say that I have never
scorched a finger,—but I carry no ugly wounds.

For what remains to me of life I trust for my
happiness still chiefly to my work—hoping that

when the power of work be over with me, God may
be pleased to take me from a world in which,
according to my view, there can be no joy;
secondly, to the love of those who love me; and
then to my books. That I can read and be happy
while I am reading, is a great blessing. Could
I remember, as some men do, what I read, I should
have been able to call myself an educated man.
But that power I have never possessed. Something is always left,—something dim and inaccurate,—but still something sufficient to preserve
the taste for more. I am inclined to think that
it is so with most readers.

Of late years, putting aside the Latin classics,
I have found my greatest pleasure in our old
English dramatists,—not from any excessive love
of their work, which often irritates me by its want
of truth to nature, even while it shames me by its
language,—but from curiosity in searching their
plots and examining their character. If I live
a few years longer, I shall, I think, leave in my
copies of these dramatists, down to the close of
James I, written criticisms on every play. No
one who has not looked closely into it knows how
many there are.

Now I stretch out my hand, and from the
further shore I bid adieu to all who have cared to
read any among the many words that I have
written.

THE END

READ MORE IN PENGUIN

In every corner of the world, on every subject under the sun, Penguin represents quality and variety – the very best in publishing today.

For complete information about books available from Penguin – including Puffins, Penguin Classics and Arkana – and how to order them, write to us at the appropriate address below. Please note that for copyright reasons the selection of books varies from country to country.

In the United Kingdom: Please write to *Dept. JC, Penguin Books Ltd, FREEPOST, West Drayton, Middlesex UB7 0BR*

If you have any difficulty in obtaining a title, please send your order with the correct money, plus ten per cent for postage and packaging, to *PO Box No. 11, West Drayton, Middlesex UB7 0BR*

In the United States: Please write to *Penguin USA Inc., 375 Hudson Street, New York, NY 10014*

In Canada: Please write to *Penguin Books Canada Ltd, 10 Alcorn Avenue, Suite 300, Toronto, Ontario M4V 3B2*

In Australia: Please write to *Penguin Books Australia Ltd, 487 Maroondah Highway, Ringwood, Victoria 3134*

In New Zealand: Please write to *Penguin Books (NZ) Ltd,182–190 Wairau Road, Private Bag, Takapuna, Auckland 9*

In India: Please write to *Penguin Books India Pvt Ltd, 706 Eros Apartments, 56 Nehru Place, New Delhi 110 019*

In the Netherlands: Please write to *Penguin Books Netherlands B.V., Keizersgracht 231 NL–1016 DV Amsterdam*

In Germany: Please write to *Penguin Books Deutschland GmbH, Friedrichstrasse 10–12, W–6000 Frankfurt/Main 1*

In Spain: Please write to *Penguin Books S. A., C. San Bernardo 117–6° E–28015 Madrid*

In Italy: Please write to *Penguin Italia s.r.l., Via Felice Casati 20, I–20124 Milano*

In France: Please write to *Penguin France S. A., 17 rue Lejeune, F–31000 Toulouse*

In Japan: Please write to *Penguin Books Japan, Ishikiribashi Building, 2–5–4, Suido, Tokyo 112*

In Greece: Please write to *Penguin Hellas Ltd, Dimocritou 3, GR–106 71 Athens*

In South Africa: Please write to *Longman Penguin Southern Africa (Pty) Ltd, Private Bag X08, Bertsham 2013*

READ MORE IN PENGUIN

ELIZABETH GASKELL – A SELECTION

North and South
Edited by Dorothy Collin with an Introduction by Martin Dodsworth

Through the medium of its central characters, John Thornton and Margaret Hale, *North and South* becomes a profound comment on the need for reconciliation among the English classes, on the importance of suffering, and above all on the value of placing the dictates of personal conscience above social respectability.

Cranford/Cousin Phillis
Edited by Peter Keating

Its analysis of an early Victorian country town, captured at the crucial moment of transition in English society, besieged by forces it is incapable of understanding or, ultimately, withstanding, is sharply observed and acutely penetrating. Like *Cranford*, the nouvelle *Cousin Phillis* is concerned with 'phases of society' – the old values as against the new.

Wives and Daughters
Edited by Frank Glover Smith with an Introduction by Laurence Lerner

The story of Mr Gibson's new marriage and its influence on the lives of those closest to him is a work of rare charm, combining pathos with wit, intelligence, and a perceptiveness about people and their relationships equalled only by Jane Austen and George Eliot.

Mary Barton
Edited by Stephen Gill

Mary Barton depicts Manchester in the 'hungry forties' with appalling precision. Illustrated here is Elizabeth Gaskell's genius for making her characters so individually human in their responses to poverty and injustice that we are touched by an appeal that goes beyond government statistics and beyond time.

THE PENGUIN TROLLOPE

THE PENGUIN TROLLOPE

...ck

BY LAWRENCE BLOCK